Self and Meaning in the Lives of Older People

More than thirty-five years ago, a longitudinal study was established to research the health and well-being of older people living in an English city. *Self and Meaning in the Lives of Older People* provides a unique set of portraits of forty members of this group who were interviewed in depth from their later seventies onwards. Focusing on sense of self-esteem and, especially, of continued meaning in life following the loss of a spouse and onset of frailty, this book sensitively illustrates these persons' efforts to maintain independence, to continue to have a sense of belonging and to contribute to the lives of others. It examines both the psychological and the social resources needed to flourish in later life and draws attention to this generation's ability to benefit from strong family support and from belonging to a faith community. In conclusion, it questions whether future generations will be as resilient.

PETER G. COLEMAN is Emeritus Professor of Psychogerontology and an associate member of the Centre for Research on Ageing at the University of Southampton. His research relates to the mental health of older people, especially the functions of reminiscence and life review and sources of self-esteem and meaning in later life.

CHRISTINE IVANI-CHALIAN has specialized in the study of adult development and learning, with a master's thesis on the University of the Third Age and a PhD on disability and open learning. She has also worked for the Open University teaching on social care and social work courses.

MAUREEN ROBINSON obtained an MPhil in psychology while working on the initial stages of this project. She works as an independent advocate for older people and persons experiencing dementia and is a long-standing community activist, serving for more than twenty years as a local councillor and holding non-executive posts within the National Health Service and housing organizations.

Self and Meaning in the Lives of Older People

Case Studies over Twenty Years

Peter G. Coleman
Christine Ivani-Chalian
Maureen Robinson

CAMBRIDGE
UNIVERSITY PRESS

CAMBRIDGE
UNIVERSITY PRESS

University Printing House, Cambridge CB2 8BS, United Kingdom

Cambridge University Press is part of the University of Cambridge.

It furthers the University's mission by disseminating knowledge in the pursuit of education, learning and research at the highest international levels of excellence.

www.cambridge.org
Information on this title: www.cambridge.org/9781107617230

© Peter G. Coleman, Christine Ivani-Chalian and Maureen Robinson 2015

First published 2015

Printed in the United Kingdom by Clays, St Ives plc

A catalogue record for this publication is available from the British Library

ISBN 978-1-107-04255-1 Hardback
ISBN 978-1-107-61723-0 Paperback

To Michael Hall and Roger Briggs, Professors Emeriti
of Geriatric Medicine, University of Southampton,
and to colleagues past and present in the
Southampton Medical School

Contents

Preface and acknowledgements

This book was composed much later than we originally expected. There are many reasons for the delay, not least the increasingly competing pressures of academic life. But as a result we have found ourselves writing what is essentially an historical account of a previous generation's experience of later life. However, most studies of human development, and certainly longitudinal studies such as this, eventually become works of history. Particularly in a fast-changing society, each generation's experience of the life course is clearly different from the previous one, and what constitutes an age cohort of similar social experiences increasingly narrows. Even a five-year age difference can have substantial implications in terms of a person's social attitudes and expectations.

Nevertheless, there is still much to learn from the experience of those who have lived before because fundamental human needs do not change that quickly. This applies especially to the existential challenges and dilemmas posed by ageing, how, for example, to respond to the loss of one's life partner, the onset of physical and mental frailty, and the steady approach of one's own death. Considering how previous generations faced the kind of issues that we will all one day probably encounter is of perennial interest.

There are many people to thank for the possibility of producing what we consider to be a rather unique study of ageing based as it is on detailed case studies of forty people interviewed regularly over the last twenty and more years of their lives. First, there are those who devised the original Southampton Ageing Project, especially Michael Hall, holder of the founding chair in Geriatric Medicine at the University of Southampton, and Don Marcer in the Psychology Department; we also thank Schwarzhaupt of Cologne, the generous first sponsor of the initial data collection and analysis over the years 1977–80. Many contributed to this first exercise in conducting a longitudinal study of ageing in Southampton including Roger Briggs, Peter Coleman, Fiona Everett, Ros Gray, John Harris, Terry McEvoy, Bill MacLennan, Joan Punnett, Maureen Robinson, Mary Scarborough and John Timothy. Particular thanks are due to the various general medical practitioner practices in Southampton who supported the research and especially of course their patients who agreed to be participants in the study.

With the encouragement of Roger Briggs, Michael Hall's successor as Professor of Geriatric Medicine, the second phase of the project on the later stages of ageing began ten years after the first. In 1988, the Medical School funded a ten-year follow-up of all the surviving Southampton Ageing Project participants, and a special mention must be made of the contribution of Anne Aubin, a mature medical student who collected and analyzed in depth the data on the younger members of this sample as part of her fourth-year medicine study in 1987–8. These data formed the basis for a subsequent research application to the Economic and Social Research Council (ESRC). In 1990, the ESRC funded what would be the first of four grants (R000232182, R000234404, R000221633 and R000222535) given to the University Department of Geriatric Medicine through the 1990s to conduct detailed studies on surviving members of the sample. Accounts of the aims of these particular projects are given in Chapter 3. These studies were conducted principally by the three authors of this book, but we would like to thank Hazel Killham, who provided administrative help throughout the latter part of the Southampton Ageing Project and Mark Mullee for support with computing and statistical analyses.

Acknowledgements to the authors of theoretical ideas, measures and methods of research employed in the work reported in this book are given in Chapters 2 and 3. Particular thanks, however, should be expressed here to Freya Dittmann-Kohli and Helen Kivnick, whose methods for investigating perception of self and meaning in later life feature strongly in our accounts of the case studies.

All three authors have had a long association with the Southampton Ageing Project. Peter Coleman designed some and selected others of the psychosocial measures used in the study from 1977 onwards and took a leading part in their subsequent analysis. From 1987, he took over the direction of the second phase of the project. Maureen Robinson was also a member of the original research team and, remarkably, has been an interviewer at all eight data collection points from 1977 to 1999. Christine Ivani-Chalian joined us for the second phase of the study beginning in 1990. Like Maureen, she continued to interview her portion of the sample until 1999. Further details on the structure and character of the forty case studies on individual participants that they composed throughout the 1990s are given in Chapter 2.

Of course, these forty people deserve the major thanks for their generosity of spirit in opening up their lives for investigation through good and bad times and being prepared to engage with us, their interviewers, over such a long period. They did this in the hope that our accounts of their experiences of ageing would be of value to others. We in our turn hope that in the necessarily abridged versions of the interviews produced for this book, we have done justice to the information with which they entrusted us.

1   Living a long life – why survive?

The ageing of the world's population has become one of the major concerns of the twenty-first century, yet it is sad that attitudes of 'concern' seem to outweigh the satisfaction that should arise from present civilization's achievement in enabling more and more people to live to the advanced ages that previously were reserved for a small minority of the population. The concerns are understandable in that they relate primarily to the frailties, physical and mental, that increase in the ninth and tenth decades of human life. Despite the advance warnings of demographers over the past fifty years, society has begun to adapt only slowly to the implications of an ageing population. In particular, it has failed to make the huge quantitative and qualitative changes to social care provision that the situation requires. As a result, individual ageing is beginning to seem almost an unwanted burden even after a life of considerable economic contribution. Contemporary culture seems more youth focused than ever in the innovations it encourages, the media representations of different age groups and the values and goals it prescribes. Ageism and ageist language remain firmly embedded in Western culture despite some recent advances in legislation to combat discrimination, and are even influencing other world cultures that were previously more respectful of age.

Robert Butler, a physician, psychiatrist and founding director of the US National Institute on Aging, addressed these issues forty years ago in his book *Why Survive? Being Old in America* (Butler, 1975). Since then the question of the meaning of living a long life has become more acute, as conditions for the oldest among us appear to be deteriorating rather than improving. If contemporary people were to choose the age at which they would die, would they decide to live to an advanced age with the likely implications of increasing frailty and sense of burden? Certainly many younger people appear not to want to survive to this state of being. Yet the paradox is that older frail people themselves do succeed, much more than younger people might imagine, in finding meaning in living the more circumscribed life that advanced ageing requires. How do they manage it?

The underlying argument of this book is that the ability to live well in later life depends on the older person's access to a variety of resources: physical,

1

economic, social, psychological and spiritual. These resources allow people to experience their everyday activities as meaningful, limited though these activities may appear to be compared with their previous achievements. The importance of each type of resource varies for each individual, but there is a minimum requirement. The way a person uses the different personal strengths and values, social relationships and environmental supports in maintaining his or her personal identity can be observed. Therefore, the outcomes of ageing are, to some extent, predictable. Coping resources are built up over a lifetime – not always under the person's own control, but they are the consequence of individual and societal development. We can predict when it is likely that resources will fail a person, and we can do much more than we currently do to help shore up older people in difficult times. We can prevent buildings from collapsing. We can also provide the necessary prosthetics to support human beings at the end of their lives.

This has also been the argument of Paul Baltes (1997), one of the most distinguished life span psychologists of the twentieth century. Our adaptation to the ageing of societies has been too slow, and we need to use our imaginations and ingenuity along with our basic human empathy to support those among us on a path we too expect to follow. We can also learn from them directly. As Plato has Socrates say at the beginning of *The Republic,* 'I enjoy talking to very old men, for they have gone before us, as it were, on a road that we too must probably tread, and it seems to me that we can find out from them what it is like and whether it is rough and difficult or broad and easy.... Is it a difficult time of life, or not?'

In the succeeding chapters, we describe the later lives of a group of older people who reached their eighties and nineties in the last decades of the twentieth century and who are all now deceased. There is a greater awareness in the social sciences at present of the importance of historical change in attitudes (Lazarus and Lazarus, 2006). We cannot assume that subsequent generations will have the same perspectives as those who have gone before them. Differences in political, moral and spiritual attitudes can be quite marked even in generations born only a few years apart, such as that between the pre–World War II birth generation and the 'baby boomers' born after that war who were formed during the huge social changes that began in the later 1950s and 1960s. The so-called millennial generation of youngsters growing to maturity in the first decades of the twenty-first century also seem to differ from their immediate predecessors not only in their more ready use of new technology but also in the greater scope such fluid access to different sources of information gives them.

The experience of ageing is also being affected by changing social attitudes and expectations. Social care practices, for example, have changed considerably since the 1990s. This does not mean we cannot learn from the experience of previous generations, however. The type of available resources to support ageing, for example, may change in character and intensity, but the need of ready and usable resources remains. In earlier periods, the presence of children acted as a type of promised guarantee for older people ageing with adequate support. That may be less possible in the present society in which families are smaller and people are much more mobile in search of work. Therefore, other resources may need to be more readily available to aid the family and substitute for it when necessary in its task of supporting ageing. What remains the same is the ability to have access to activities and social contacts that will support one's sense of self and meaning.

This book is based on a detailed study of forty members of the generation of older people born in the twenty years before the outbreak of the World War I who were thus growing old in the latter part of the twentieth century. At the time of the study's initiation, they were all living in Southampton, a long-established port city in the south of England, from which the *Titanic* sailed in 1912 on its fateful voyage to New York and which is now a major centre for the leisure cruise industry. Southampton is of moderately large size in the context of English cities, with more than a quarter of a million inhabitants. Together with Portsmouth, also a major maritime city with strong links to the Royal Navy, and surrounding areas, it forms the South Hampshire conurbation of nearly one million persons.

The British pre-WWI birth cohorts lived significantly longer than their predecessors. They mainly avoided service during the Great War, although they suffered from shortages of food during the conflict, then benefitted from improvements in social provision after the war and again as a result of the institution of the British National Health Service after WWII when they were in their thirties and forties. The social circumstances and history they lived through, including the employment difficulties of their early adulthood and wartime service and their experience of hardship and civilian bombing in WWII, are illustrated by the memories of the participants themselves. Their attitudes towards the more recent social changes they have experienced are also reflected in the accounts of their interviews.

The focus of our book, however, is the personal experience of our study participants in their later years. It concentrates on their lives between their later seventies and their deaths – in some cases beyond age 100 years. In particular, it examines their self-understanding, what is often referred to as 'identity' – the way people see themselves, their characteristics, values, needs and ways of fulfilling these needs, which they perceive as essential to their sense of self and which they could not easily or painlessly imagine themselves without. Often this core self is expressed in narrative terms that describe how these essential characteristics were formed, were expressed in the past and continue to be represented in the present (McAdams, 1993).

Identity as a key term in psychosocial development owes much to Erik Erikson's pioneering work with young people (Erikson, 1968). His key insight was that in modern societies, identity formation can take a long time. A person's sense of self and roles in life are no longer ascribed by the society within which they grow to adulthood but must arise from within themselves through processes of education, experience and reflection. Eventually they make choices about how they want to live within the society in which they find themselves, what beliefs and values they would feel justified in committing to and what particular contributions they might make to that society. Importantly for the study of ageing, Erikson was interested in the notion of development continuing throughout life and viewed the different stages of life as being interconnected. Healthy development at later stages had positive influences on the subsequent generations' development, and younger people's success contributed to older persons' sense of fulfilment. Because these ideas were formative to our research, we expand on them in the next chapter alongside other, more recent perspectives that influenced the study as it developed into the second phase.

Ageing inevitably involves the experience of loss – loss of close persons, previous important roles and eventually of independent functioning – but at each crisis point, adaptations do occur. We have already referred to the so-called ageing well-being paradox – that older people tend to be much happier than might be expected given their physical and social circumstances – and this idea has been a consistent observation of gerontological research over the past fifty years. The capacity for continued psychological development remains strong even as the body fades. Gene Cohen, for example, has expanded on Erikson's view of life span development – Erikson's formulation of life stages was first made in the 1950s when life expectancy was much shorter – to incorporate the possibility of developments throughout the seventies, eighties and nineties (Cohen, 2005).

The study reported in this book is based principally on individual case analysis. This method of research is still underappreciated in social scientific and especially psychological studies. It employs reasoning on a case-by-case basis to propose explanations at the level of the individual case before drawing any conclusions about a sample or group of people as a whole. Such a method relies on multiple sources of evidence for corroborating evidence, as in legal judgements, and also includes, where possible, the person's own understanding of his or her situation. Therefore, most of our case analyses also include material collected separately by two interviewers and comments by the participants themselves on the draft conclusions we initially drew about their sources of identity. We believe this method of research is particularly appropriate to the study of ageing (Coleman, 2002). Our approach to studying older persons is presented in Chapter 3, together with a description of the cases selected for analysis and their characteristics.

Chapters 4 through 9 present in abbreviated form the evidence and conclusions we have drawn about our cases. The chapters follow our participants through the different stages of their later years. We have structured them to reflect the two major transitions that typically occur in later life, from living together to living alone following bereavement of a spouse (partner) and from living independently to needing care and support. Both are experienced as major losses because a person's identity is largely based on a sense of relatedness to others and competence in handling matters of personal and shared interest. The onset of significant frailty and bereavement present a major challenge for adaptation, particularly if they occur in close conjunction to one another. Although most older people survive these transitions, we need more understanding of the processes involved to better help those who struggle to survive such threats to their identity. We also include a chapter focusing on some of those cases who succeeded in living well into their nineties and beyond, which considers the quality of life they experienced at this advanced stage. In the final chapter, we draw some general conclusions from our study and especially emphasize those we consider relevant for ageing in the first part of the twenty-first century.

We as authors, who are well aware of our own ageing, believe that these accounts of people in the later stages of ageing do provide lessons for us as we look to the years to come. We hope our readers do too. For the most part, we conclude that our participants aged well despite the many trials they encountered. Will we be as resilient? Will we have the same access to the needed resources that they had? Let us reflect on the answers this group of people from a previous generation found to the question, 'Why survive?'

2　From self-esteem to meaning – studying psychological well-being in later life

In this chapter, we present the rationale for collecting the material reported in this book and describe the actual processes involved in the study on which it is based. As in all research projects, the data we sought reflected the particular interests of the investigators and the key theoretical concepts and health and welfare concerns that were influential at the time the research was being planned. Our project originated in a multidisciplinary longitudinal study of ageing initiated by the Departments of Geriatric Medicine and of Psychology at the University of Southampton in the later 1970s. There were two distinct stages of data collection. The interviews conducted in the first ten years included clinical assessment as well as questionnaires, whereas a more focused investigation of psychological well-being involving in-depth interviewing was undertaken in the latter ten and more years. After a brief description of the history of the main study, we continue with a reflection on the main theoretical ideas and observations that inspired our investigation into identity and well-being in later life. We close with a consideration of our reasons for conducting detailed case studies on our surviving participants in the second part of the project.

Southampton Ageing Project

The original Southampton Ageing Project sample comprised 340 persons aged over sixty-five years (born before 1914) recruited in 1977–8 from two general medical practices in Southampton. The participants were originally recruited as part of a two-year double-blind trial of an early 'anti-ageing' pharmaceutical product, Gerovital (KH3; comprising principally procaine/haematoporphyrin) on the processes of ageing – in particular, on cognitive functioning and mood (Hall et al., 1983). Some small beneficial effects were found in regard to grip strength, as well as avoidance of incontinence and decline in cognitive performance, but there was no observable impact on depressive symptoms. However, the generous nature of the funding allowed for substantial clinical, social and psychological data to be collected on each occasion, and thus the possibility of longitudinal as well as cross-sectional analysis. Two interviews, one clinical and one social-psychological, were conducted in each of the three years 1977–8, 1978–9 and 1979–80. A first report on the data analysis carried out was issued in 1982 (Hall et al., 1982). Ethics approval was obtained from the local health authority for this initial study and all subsequent data collection with this sample of older persons.

A proportion of the original sample was followed up in subsequent years by the university's Department of Geriatric Medicine as part of studies on topics in elderly care including nutrition, and ten years later, in 1987, a decision was made to attempt to re-interview the surviving members of the original sample. In the following year, 101 participants, all then aged over seventy-five years, were interviewed using a shortened version of the original questionnaires. Funding was then sought from the UK Economic and Social Research Council to continue the longitudinal study with more in-depth investigation into psychological well-being in later life. Four successive applications were successful and interviews conducted in 1990–1, 1993, 1995–6 and 1998–9. Each of these studies concentrated on different issues of primarily psychological and social scientific interest but also allowed a repeat of the shortened version of the original questionnaires. Finally, a number of the few surviving participants were interviewed for the last time in the years 2000–2.

Like other multidisciplinary and longitudinal studies of ageing conducted in the post-war years, the Southampton project in its origin reflected an interest in the factors that promoted ageing well, defined principally in terms of relative freedom from physical and mental illness as well as from cognitive deterioration. Ageing was conceptualized as an intrinsically difficult process because of the increase in associated losses and stresses and therefore as requiring adjustment. We thus gave particular attention to assessment of clinical depression.

The focus of much interest in research of ageing in those years was on avoiding unnecessary negative life events, especially those associated with preventable disease. The efficacy of new pharmaceutical products was being actively researched. However, evidence on older people's resilience and relatively high levels of well-being was also beginning to emerge. For example, a UK national survey, The Elderly at Home (Hunt, 1978), pointed out that the over-sixties age group in Britain, compared with younger age groups, had a greater degree of expressed satisfaction with all aspects of life apart from health. These observations were reflected in our study in the inclusion in the questionnaire of items on social and psychological factors that might independently promote well-being, such as activities and social contacts, continuing roles, satisfaction with past and present life, attitudes to ageing and concerns and hopes for the future. However, a major interest from the outset of the study was in maintenance of self-esteem and especially sources of self-esteem.

Self-esteem, meaning and identity

Studying self-esteem and its sources

Maintaining a high level of self-esteem had emerged from the post-war gerontological literature as a key factor in adjustment to ageing, described by one US
author as the "linchpin of quality of life for elderly people" (Schwartz, 1975).
The importance of self-esteem to human flourishing was also stressed in other
fields, such as education and childrearing, and thus its emphasis within studies
on ageing was not exceptional. However, self-esteem had a particular resonance
there because of the recent findings from studies on adaptation to institutional-
ization, a major topic in research on ageing at the time. North American, British
and other Western societies were beginning to question whether residential care
should remain so dominant a part of welfare provision for later life. Quality of
provision was often poor, and research findings showed that entering an institution for older persons was associated with unacceptably high mortality and
morbidity rates. However, it was also noted that if a person's self-esteem could
be maintained after the move, this augured well for both length and quality of
life within the new setting (Carp, 1974).

That physical and mental deterioration was not an inevitable consequence of
institutional care but rather the result of the demeaning qualities of much US
and UK residential care provision was shown by a major longitudinal study in
the Netherlands on later-life relocation in which the first author participated.
At that time, Dutch residential care provision for older people was among
the highest in Europe both in quantity and quality, and the study showed that
residents' self-esteem, rather than declining, actually strengthened as a result
of the move (Remmerswaal, 1980; Wimmers, Buijssen and Mertens, 1989).

This investigation adopted a new approach to studying older people's self-
perception, which subsequently was also applied to the study in Southampton.
Although self-esteem was seen to be central to maintenance of well-being, there
had been relatively little interest in investigating how self-concept itself was
regulated. To maintain a stable view of oneself during the processes of ageing
requires the ability to call on sources that confirm this view, ideally in the
present-life situation but also in the past from which remembered achievements
continue to provide definitions for the self and in the future in which new
possibilities are envisaged. However, the dynamics of the changing basis of
support for the self with ageing had not been the subject of a significant amount
of research.

A source of insight into the processes of change in the ageing self was
provided by a major set of US studies on older people's relocation to institu-
tions conducted through the 1960s and 1970s, the results of which were later
assembled together in one publication by Lieberman and Tobin (1983). These

researchers asked participants to provide an illustration of current interpersonal behaviour for self-descriptive statements, before and after moving to an institution. They noticed that after the move, although there might be no overall change in the statements themselves, there was an overall increase in the proportion of illogical illustrations and non-examples given. The interpretation they gave to these findings was that these changes reflected the breakdown of customary sources of self-esteem and, unless new sources were found, were the likely precursor of a decline in the capacity to provide positive self-ascriptions. Indeed, subsequent observations confirmed that those who could not provide adequate evidence to support their self-image were more likely to show psychological deterioration in the longer term, both cognitive decline and depression.

This observation provided the inspiration for our approach to studying the self, which explicitly aimed to assess perceived sources as well as strength of self-esteem. Through pilot studies, we developed bipolar self-descriptive items, presented to the participant also visually on cards (e.g. 'I feel useful – I feel useless'), which both produced a valid and internally consistent assessment of self-esteem and were conducive to follow-through questioning for illustration. Thus, if the participants chose the positive or negative ascription (or could not make up their mind), we asked them to give an example from their current life that helped explain why they felt or thought that way about themselves. Eventually we developed an instrument that, in addition to showing a high level of coherence as a measure of self-esteem, also elicited illustrations that could be validly coded under a discrete number of categories. These were reference to family, to other interpersonal contacts, to interests and leisure activities, to maintenance of independence and personal care abilities, to paid or unpaid work or other organizational role, to inner convictions about themselves and their lives and to the external circumstances both physical and social in which they lived.

This way of approaching self-descriptions proved helpful in investigating both the advantages and the drawbacks of innovative services, whether new forms of residential care or community care services. The Dutch study of relocation to residential homes suggested that the improvement in self-esteem was a response to the high quality of the accommodation and care provided as well as of increased feelings of personal security. In an English study, by contrast, among older people who had come to live in a pilot sheltered housing scheme with extra domiciliary support provided, there were in fact more references to independence and personal care abilities and less to interests and leisure activities than in those who entered residential homes (Coleman, 1984). The instrument has also proved useful in studies of the most effective forms of service intervention with housebound older people (Baldock and Hadlow, 2002). Further details of our method for assessing self-esteem and its sources are provided in the following chapter, along with a brief account of the results obtained using it in the Southampton Ageing Project.

The study of meaning

By the later 1980s when the second phase of the project began, other explorative and multifaceted approaches to assessing adult well-being had been developed. The overriding importance previously attributed to self-esteem was beginning to be questioned. Lars Freden (1982) made a helpful distinction between 'self-evaluation', which constituted self-esteem in the sense of measuring up to some external standards of beauty, intelligence and capability, and 'self-worth', which was more concerned with perception of value rather than comparison of self with others. For example, individuals could still be said to have self-worth if they continued to express commitments to people and causes outside of themselves even though their abilities to make practical contributions might be declining.

A major influence on developing new forms of thinking about well-being in human adult development was provided by the work of Carol Ryff at the University of Wisconsin at Madison (Ryff, 1995). Her studies were rooted in a thorough consideration of the various strands in the existing theoretical literature on healthy psychological functioning in adulthood, from some of the early psychoanalytic thinkers such as Carl Jung and Erik Erikson to more recent gerontological theorists as Bernice Neugarten and James Birren. Ryff argued convincingly for a multidimensional view of psychological well-being in which self-acceptance was but one of six dimensions, comprising also positive relationships, autonomy, environmental mastery, personal growth and purpose in life.

Ryff's subsequent empirical studies showed that although self-acceptance tended to increase during middle adulthood and the first stages of ageing, the experience of personal growth and purpose in life diminished. The experience of ageing therefore appeared to present a challenge to meaning, at least in Western societies such as the United States. Other studies have also emphasized the significance of maintaining a sense of meaning in later life. The conclusion of one of the early US longitudinal studies of ageing conducted at Duke University in North Carolina is still worth citing:

> This longitudinal analysis of data demonstrates rather clearly that very few, even well functioning elderly escape depression. The legacy of a long life appears to be a confrontation and struggle with the value of living. The issue for older people may well be not just survival but meaningful and purposeful existence. (Busse, 1985, p. 220)

Meaning was understood to become more problematic in later life because of the loss of roles associated with social ageing in modern societies. For most of working life, the meaning of much everyday activity can be taken for granted, but with retirement, the need to 'get up in the morning' often disappears. Paul Thompson for example noted the same point, citing other authors, in his study of the different ways the older people he interviewed in the United Kingdom found meaning in their lives: "the elderly are distinctive . . . because they *must* choose; responsibility for structuring their lives is uniquely their own" (Thompson, 1992, p. 25). Finding and holding on to more deeply grounded sources of meaning in later life becomes increasingly important as previous support structures disappear. In particular, a continued or enhanced perception of meaning would compensate for the inevitable threats to self-esteem that accompany declining abilities.

Alfred Adler, a collaborator and then rival psychoanalytic thinker to Sigmund Freud in 1930s Vienna, emphasized this point in the therapy he developed for both older and younger persons having problems with low self-esteem (Brink, 1979). The most effective cure was found in engagement with others, absence of self-concern and development of *Gemeinschaftsgefühl*, usually translated as 'social interest' but probably best represented in English by the concept of 'team spirit'. Just as the difficulty of achieving perceived competence in adult roles might produce severe psychological malfunctioning in youth, so the loss of roles in later life could lead to pathological consequences in older people, even in those with previously high self-esteem. The solution he argued lay in taking the focus off the self and seeing value in group belonging and community goals. The sting would be taken away from perception of one's own growing weaknesses with age by a closer identification with the achievements of the larger group, whether of one's family, the local community in which one lives or wider fields of belonging, whether religious, spiritual or political.

Through the 1980s and 1990s, psychological measures began to be developed to assess the degree to which persons possessed a sense of meaning in their lives. Particularly influential was Viktor Frankl's early work on the means of psychological survival in desperate situations encountered by prisoners of the Nazi extermination camps (Frankl, 1964). Gary Reker and Paul Wong's operationalization of Frankl's concept in terms of dimensions of life purpose, existential vacuum, life control, death acceptance, will to meaning, goal seeking and future meaning, which could be assessed by questionnaire, was given early recognition in gerontological studies (Reker and Wong, 1988).

Another notable contribution from the field of adult development was Freya Dittmann-Kohli's research on the 'personal meaning system' (Dittmann-Kohli, 1990; Dittmann-Kohli and Westerhof, 2000). Particularly innovative was her approach to assessment via a sentence-completion procedure, which she described as follows:

Sentence stems were used to stimulate statements about positively and negatively valued characteristics and observations about the self and one's life; for example, abilities, weaknesses, feelings, and evaluations of self and life. Furthermore, a series of sentence stems asks for aspects that give direction to one's life, like plans, goals, desires, future expectations, fears and anxieties. Subjects were asked to finish the sentence stems so as to describe what they consider as true and important about themselves. (Dittmann-Kohli and Westerhof, 2000, p. 111)

We decided to apply this method to provide a more person-based assessment of self-perception in the interviews with Southampton Ageing Project participants in 1990–1, and our first results with its use are explained further in Chapter 3.

Identity processes in later life

Another significant shift in personality studies in the 1980s was the growth of narrative psychology, a rediscovery of the importance of motive and story in understanding human behaviour. Jerome Bruner likened this breakthrough to the cognitive revolution of the 1960s, in which he had also played a key role. This had moved experimental psychology beyond a focus solely on environmental stimuli and behavioural responses and opened the subject to investigation of models of the internal processes in the mind that mediate action. In his book *Actual Minds, Possible Worlds* (Bruner, 1986), he claimed that explanation of actions in terms of motives, and by extension stories that represented the operation of motives over time in individual lives, was as fundamental a form of explanation as the standard scientific paradigm of logical deduction from general premises.

The impact of narrative psychology was felt strongly in studies of identity. Dan McAdams reinterpreted Erik Erikson's concept of identity in narrative terms as a further stage of personality development in which individuals gradually come to create coherent stories of their lives. In so doing, they represent in narrative terms the key goals and values that have motivated and continue to energize them (McAdams 1990, 1993). Formulation of goals provided the building blocks of a person's life story, indicating what he or she was trying to obtain or become. They arose directly from experience and from what the person had come to value in his or her experience of life so far. McAdams also followed Bakan (1966) in drawing a sharp distinction between 'agency' and 'communion' values, between the traditional 'masculine' strengths of achievement, power and control and the 'feminine' virtues of intimacy, love and co-operation.

As Erikson had already stressed, initial identity formation could be seen as a particularly critical psychosocial task in the transition from adolescence to adulthood in the modern world as young people sought worthwhile values among a number of competing choices. But 're-storying' of the self was also a lifelong work, as new experience led to changes in the way commitments were understood and expressed. Only in later life could a final reckoning be made. It was then that the task of being a witness to ultimate meanings and beliefs came into special prominence. Erikson himself contributed to this theory of lifelong development of the self in the late conceptual work he conducted together with his wife Joan and with Helen Kivnick on what he described as 'vital involvement' in old age (Erikson, Erikson and Kivnick, 1986).

In the assessment of Southampton Ageing Project participants in 1993, we decided to develop a schedule based on Kivnick's subsequent translation of Erikson's key psychosocial tasks into an inventory of 'life strengths', which as a professor of social work she had used in improving assessment methods in long-term care settings (Kivnick, 1991). She encouraged staff to explore the dominant concerns, enjoyments, hopes and beliefs of the persons they cared for. Rather than focusing on older people's failings and weaknesses in such settings, it was necessary, she argued, to recognize, support and cultivate the qualities that they had nurtured throughout life. We describe our schedule further in Chapter 3.

At the same study point, we also developed a guided interview schedule, based on McAdams's concepts, to explore the participants' sense of their life as a story, its key events including its principal turning points, and particularly to what extent they had a sense of connection with their earlier life. We drew on Malcolm Johnson's concept of the biographical interview (Johnson, 1976) and its subsequent use in social work research to provide a more thorough assessment of older people's needs for support services (Gearing and Dant, 1990; Gearing and Coleman, 1996). We asked about the aspects of their past lives that they valued most and considered features of their present situation, both those that helped connect their life together and those that instead disconnected past from present. Our case study analyses had already started to be composed, and they were intended to provide justified accounts of each person's primary sources of self-esteem and meaning as they aged, as well as the stories they told of their lives.

We have brought a number of other theoretical interests to the writing of this book, perhaps the most significant being Deci and Ryan's conceptualization of human motivation in terms of three primary psychological needs for autonomy, competence and relatedness (Deci and Ryan, 2000). Despite the absence of research on ageing using this model, a little consideration makes it obvious that old age is a major arena of struggle for the satisfaction of each of these three needs, which often come into conflict with one another in later life (Coleman and O'Hanlon, 2004). Strong needs for autonomy, for example, often lead older people to isolate themselves and to reject offers of help, thus making satisfactory levels of both relatedness and competence more difficult to achieve.

Studying identity and well-being at the level of the individual person

Although it was one of the central concerns of the early founders of personality psychology, such as Gordon Allport and Henry Murray, the study of lives diminished in the 1950s and 1960s as far greater attention was given to psychometric personality measurement with large samples and experimental study of human behaviour in monitored laboratory situations. The 1980s did, however, see a renewed interest in the study of the individual case with some notable publications on methods both in case study analysis of particular episodes in individual lives as well as in large-scale psychobiographies (Runyan, 1982; Bromley, 1986; McAdams and Ochberg, 1988). The interest continues today (Schultz, 2005), although case study analysis remains unjustifiably neglected in departments of academic psychology.

Because of the changed academic context, 'personologists' have had to defend their subject. The most telling argument is simply to point out that understanding individual persons and lives is one of the major tasks of personality psychology, as important as developing general theories of personality, studying individual and group differences, and analyzing specific processes and classes of behaviours (Runyan, 1990). If not carried out by psychologists, analysis of the individual case will be conducted by others with likely less expertise or knowledge of psychological theory or scientific method. It is also important to note that the study of persons also provides ideas for, and validating illustrations to, principles that may be applicable to wider groups of individuals. However, this is not its primary purpose. Analysis of the individual case, including the development of theory at the level of the single person, should be a primary objective of personality study.

The methodological advances made in the 1980s provided answers to previous criticism of the way psychological case studies had been conducted. The seemingly arbitrary or subjective nature of some analysis had been countered by the development of methods for evaluating alternative explanations (Runyan, 1982; Bromley, 1986). Nevertheless, a common objection is still that the study of individuals is the rightful domain of biographers and historians but it is not science because the latter must be concerned with laws applicable to all individuals. Yet the criticism that it is impossible to apply systematic, reliable, quantitative or experimental methods has been refuted by the quality of more recent case studies that use precisely such methods. It is also clearly untenable to suggest that science as a whole is not concerned with the study of particulars, as is evidenced by those sciences concerned with unique processes as cosmology, geology and evolutionary biology.

One problem with recent psychobiography is the proliferation of studies on famous or infamous individuals. Although the popularity of such writing is understandable given the public interest and the financial benefits to be gained by publication, they often lack attention to scientific principles such as corroboration of evidence and testing of the validity of conclusions. A greater investment in studying ordinary living persons who would be prepared to be investigated in depth provides a wider and more representative range of cases and would also be of use in developing and validating personality theory. This would have the additional benefit of affirming that all persons are worthy of study and could provide paradigmatic examples to inspire high standards of practice by those professions concerned with making decisions at the level of the individual patient or client.

The study of ongoing lives over a long period of time is a major commitment and has rarely been attempted (an early example was Robert White's [1975] three-volume *'Lives in Progress'*). Case studies of particular episodes in people's lives, set against evidence on previous life history, are more feasible objectives of study, and most recent work using psychological theory and scientific methods has been of this kind. But particularly within a field such as the study of ageing, there is a strong case for carrying out longitudinal case studies on processes with a medium time duration. An ideal context is provided by a large-scale longitudinal study. Studies of individuals managing changes incurred in the ageing process – changes both in physical and social circumstances – provide obvious examples.

Therefore, when in 1989 we first drew up a proposal for external funding for a continuation of our study of the surviving members of the Southampton Ageing Project, we decided to include an element of case study research. It was also a time of changing attitudes to the role of participants in social psychological studies. They were no longer simply 'subjects', and their ability and right to comment on the conclusions drawn about them was increasingly respected. So from the outset, we intended to construct accounts of people's lives on which they could also comment and thus provide an additional element of validation. Psychologists have often been too wary of asking people directly for their own 'theory' about themselves. Obviously there are biases at play, but why neglect an obvious source of information? To slightly amend George Kelly's (1955) dictum: 'If you don't know what is right or wrong with someone, ask them; they may tell you'. Older people in particular often have less to hide.

3   Investigating older people's lives at the end of the twentieth century

In this chapter, we explain our selection of forty cases for individual study from members of the Southampton Ageing Project (1977–8 to 2002–3) and briefly comment on their general characteristics. We then survey the self-descriptions that were provided over the first ten and more years of the study. This is followed by an account of the methods we followed in the final ten years in assembling and analyzing material to produce detailed individual case studies. Finally, we provide an introduction to our present accounts of the cases in the subsequent chapters.

Participants included in the case analysis

Although we only received concentrated funding for case study analysis in 1995, we began to identify and interview in depth selected members of our sample from 1990 onwards, when the sample was all aged over seventy-seven years. In 1995–6, we were able to complete case study accounts on each of the twenty-eight remaining participants. Together with those cases that we had begun beforehand and who had died in the intervening years, we succeeded in composing a total of forty case analyses (twenty-three women and seventeen men). In most cases, we conducted a further interview in which we checked our written conclusions with the participants and invited their comments. Later interviews were also conducted with surviving members of the sample by the first author as well as by the second or third author who had interviewed them regularly over the preceding years.

Brief descriptive details on each case, including year of birth, principal occupation, age at leaving full-time education and age at death, are provided in the Appendix. Pseudonyms replace the original names in the Appendix and throughout the text. The majority of the sample (twenty-seven of forty) were still married when we first interviewed them in 1977–8, and all had been married at one time in their lives. Three persons were divorced or separated. The lack of never-married people reflected the low number in the original sample (3.5 percent) and the fact that the proportion of ever-married people was peaking in the UK population. The immediately preceding cohorts had experienced high rates of early widowhood and of women who never married because of the premature deaths of young men in World War I. The generation we studied, however, had shown a trend towards increasing life expectancy. Marriages were lasting longer because deaths were occurring, on average, at a more advanced age.

However, there were large gender differences in age of bereavement. By the time they were aged seventy-five years, as many as thirteen of the women but only two of the men were living alone. Beyond eighty years, only three of the women still had their spouses alive, whereas eleven of the men did. Six of the women, but none of the men, had been bereaved or left alone already in younger or middle adulthood (before age sixty). In Chapter 6, we consider those of the sample who lived a large part of their later years alone. These were predominantly women. This of course reflects the differential life expectation of men and women in marriage in the United Kingdom over the past century, with men tending to live on average six years less than women and to marry women younger than themselves in the first place. Widows as a result greatly outnumber widowers.

The original Southampton Ageing Project sample was of mixed background, with 57 percent from skilled occupations (social class III both manual and non-manual), 27 percent from professional and intermediate groups and 16 percent from partly skilled and unskilled occupations, reflecting the locality of the general medical practitioner (GP) practices in which we conducted the study. At least nine of our forty cases had their own or husbands' principal occupations related to the sea, ship building and the docks. Nearly two-thirds of the sample (63 percent) left school before age 15 years. Although the original sample was almost exclusively of Christian background, only 66 percent regarded themselves as members of Christian churches, and only 33 percent attended religious services. The occupational and educational background as well as religious character of our case study sample was not noticeably different from these figures.

The majority of the original sample when first interviewed had a high quality of life judged on the criteria of health and physical functioning, environmental and financial stability, as well as expressed sense of well-being. However, there was, as expected, a large difference between the 'younger' group aged between sixty-five and seventy-four years and those seventy-five years and older, particularly on the health indicators we used. Thus, whereas 4 percent of the 'older' group were not mobile and 17 percent needed help with bathing, all of the 'younger' group were mobile, and only 3 percent needed help with bathing. Falling was the most significant health risk, especially among the women in the sample. As many as 54 percent of the 'older' women and 35 percent of the 'older' men had fallen in the previous year. The corresponding figures for the 'older' group were 32 percent and 16 percent.

There was also an expected gender difference in the prevalence of depressive symptoms with 19 percent of the women and 7 percent of the men scoring above the criterion for indicating the presence of depression on the Wakefield Depression Scale (Snaith, Ahmed and Mehta, 1971). An entrance bias might have been expected of volunteers into a longitudinal study of ageing especially when the focus of interest was on monitoring health and well-being. It might be anticipated, for example, that those with acute or chronic major illness, and those who had recently suffered a major bereavement, would not want to join a research investigation of this nature. Nevertheless, there were examples of both these categories in our sample. Five of our eventual forty cases were already limited by chronic disease at the time of entry into our study in 1977–8.

Self-descriptions in the first part of the study

In this book, we focus on the inner resources our participants brought to the challenges of ageing – in particular, the attitudes they expressed to their own experiences of growing older, the life meanings they perceived, and the values and commitments they continued to nurture. In the first part of the study, our main perspective into the participants' thoughts and feelings about their lives were provided by their self-descriptions. These were obtained in answer to choices they made between evaluative statements about the self as well as the examples they gave from their daily life to illustrate these views of themselves. This material forms a significant part of the case studies presented in the following chapters because it was obtained at all eight interview points over the initial twenty years of the study.

The origins of the self-esteem and sources of self-esteem instrument we employed were referred to in Chapter 2. It was initially developed specifically for elderly people who were becoming frailer and in potential need of residential care. It was also designed to give as much weight to assessing the person's perceived sources of self-esteem as estimating the strength of their positive feelings about themselves. In line with the assumptions about ageing and self-esteem current at the time of its development, it was intended to gauge falling away from the optimal level of self-esteem reached in late middle age rather than any growth or development in self-evaluation that might occur with ageing. Choices for positive self-evaluations were therefore to be expected, and the first signs of likely decline in self-esteem shown in the failure to provide or the weakness of supportive statements.

As expected most choices for evaluative statements in the original sample were positive at the starting point of the study in 1977–8 when the average age of the sample was seventy-four years. The highest percentage was for those affirming that they were 'of importance to others' (91 percent), followed by 'capable of doing quite a lot' (88 percent). Most negative choices were for 'no aim left in life' (18 percent), 'being unsure of oneself' (16 percent) and 'feeling useless' (12 percent). In the cross-sectional comparisons within the original sample, there was no significant difference in positive and negative choices between those aged sixty-five to sixty-nine and seventy to seventy-four years, but for each of the succeeding five-year age groups, seventy-five to seventy-nine, eighty to eighty-four and eighty-five to eighty-nine, there was a small but statistically significant stepwise decline in amount of positive ascriptions made.

The different sources of self-esteem assessed by this same instrument varied in frequency of occurrence. Illustration of own self-care abilities was the most frequent, being referred to in as many as 28 percent of all responses, followed by mention of family relationships (22 percent), personal interests and activities (15 percent), inner characteristics and convictions (15 percent), other interpersonal relationships (13 percent), paid or voluntary work (5 percent) and external and environmental factors (3 percent). Further details on the initial part of this study are given in a previous account of this instrument's early use in both the Netherlands and England (Coleman, 1984).

At the ten-year follow-up, although the surviving members of the sixty-five to sixty-nine-year group did not make significantly fewer positive self-ascriptions at age seventy-five to seventy-nine, those of the seventy to seventy-four and seventy-five to seventy-nine age groups were both significantly more negative at the ages of eighty to eighty-four and eighty-five to eighty-nine, respectively. Five years later in 1993, the age groups showed further significant decline as they all passed into their eighties and beyond. Notably, the balance of positive and negative ascriptions for those aged eighty-five to eighty-nine in 1993 was almost identical to that of the earlier cohort aged eighty-five to eighty-nine fifteen years earlier. However, the youngest cohort of those aged sixty-five to sixty-nine in 1977–8 showed a less steep decline over time than their predecessors had (Coleman, 1997). Taken together, these findings support the view that our participants' self-esteem, at least as assessed in this form, did not decline significantly until they reached their ninth decade. This observation has guided the choice of age focus for the present case study analyses. Why does self-esteem tend to decline at this stage of life, and why is it that some remain resilient into their nineties and beyond?

The longitudinal study also highlighted how loss of self-esteem was not uniform as our participants aged but was composed of different elements for each of which precursors could be identified that significantly predicted change over a ten-year period (Coleman, Ivani-Chalian and Robinson, 1993). For example, statements about memory problems predicted loss of attributions of being 'bright and alert' ten years later. Perceiving religious belief as meaningful made it more likely that persons would maintain feelings of usefulness.

Our sample of forty cases showed a similar pattern of response at the outset of the study in 1977–8. All displayed a high self-esteem and provided plentiful illustrations of it in their daily life. As a relatively young sample of older people at the time, they showed some difference from the total sample in expressing more positive self-ascriptions overall. Nevertheless, there were also examples among our cases of persons with particularly low self-esteem scores and those who increased as well as decreased in self-esteem throughout the study.

Both the measure of strength of self-esteem and the frequency of mention and profile of sources of self-esteem remained relatively stable over the first ten and more years of the Southampton Ageing Project (Coleman, Ivani-Chalian and Robinson, 1993). However, as already mentioned, some overall decline in expressed self-esteem did occur with increased age. Significant declines occurred in mention of family as a source of self-esteem, typically as a result of bereavement and consequent fall in self-esteem, and also in mention of work, as the few participants still working retired. Mention of personal activities and interests by contrast increased.

An initial positive attitude to ageing emerged as the best predictor, among the characteristics we assessed, of a maintained high self-esteem over the first part of the study. Also significant was the association of mention both of other relationships in addition to family and of inner convictions about the self with a maintained high level of positive self-ascriptions over time. Likely explanations are that the presence of other relationships protected against the damaging effects of close family bereavements and that a strong sense of the inner person buffered the self against declining physical (and mental) capabilities with age. High self-esteem and greater mention of significant others (as distinct from family members) and of inner convictions about the self as a source of self-esteem, together with positive attitudes to ageing, number of hobbies and interests and outside activities were also predictive of resilience against depression in the succeeding ten years (Coleman et al., 1993).

Methods and materials for case analysis

As explained in Chapter 2, we decided for the second phase of the Southampton Ageing Project to include detailed individual case analysis of processes of identity development as well as statistical investigation of group changes over time among the surviving members. Underlying this decision was our view that it is insufficient to pursue explanations only at the level of the population or subgroup. We also need to improve our methods of enquiry for understanding the individual person's attitudes and behaviour. The individual or 'idiographic' (as opposed to 'nomothetic') perspective has a long history in psychology (Runyan, 1982; Schultz, 2005) but is relatively poorly represented in the discipline today. The result is a neglect of the study of unusual and exceptional cases that can be the most revealing in theoretical terms. Particularly in a field such as the study of ageing, which is dominated by deterministic and pessimistic scenarios that emphasize only decline, investigating different types of trajectories in later life, including developmental ones, can inspire a needed change of perspective. It can also provide the incentive to encourage what might seem to be an exceptional outcome or pattern of behaviour today to become more common tomorrow.

The first author has argued (Coleman, 2002) that the study of ageing, and particularly adaptation to the losses that come with age, are especially suited to the methods of longitudinal case study analysis. Systematically carrying out a series of case study analyses can lead inductively to the development of 'case law' (Bromley, 1977, 1986). This way of proceeding is especially appropriate to the practice of applied psychology in which one is not trying to develop universal theory but investigating ways of finding solutions to practical questions affecting human well-being in specific social contexts (Fishman, 1999).

We decided to limit the focus of our case analyses to the lives of our participants from their later seventies onwards. The recent gerontological literature as well as our earlier observations in this study suggested that the physical problems of ageing in the contemporary Western world do not usually become very troublesome until the ninth decade. Moreover, when we began the second phase of the Southampton Ageing Project, all of our participants had already reached at least their later seventies, and we wanted to focus on how they were dealing with their present situations rather than recalling more distant events. However, we have, where relevant to the argument on a particular case, incorporated data from earlier in the study and also included retrospective comments. From 1990 to 1996, we recorded all our interviews with the permission of the participants.

Because it was administered consistently throughout the study, the measure of self-esteem and its sources provided the bedrock of our analysis, but from 1990, we were able to incorporate additional perspectives on the participants' perception of themselves and the principal sources of meaning in their lives by using more recently developed instruments. How much new material we could incorporate in the interview on each occasion depended also, of course, on other aims of the investigation. In 1990–1 and 1993, our Economic and Social Research Council–funded projects were focused on the subjects, respectively, of coping with recent health problems and of perceived continuity across participants' past and present lives. Only from 1995 were we able to focus solely on the task of composing individual case analyses. However, in both 1990–1 and 1993, we asked all our participants to post back written responses on questionnaires chosen for their particular relevance to issues of identity and meaning in later life and began composing case studies on particular members of the sample.

In 1990–1, fifty-four of the seventy persons interviewed completed the questionnaire we left with them. This comprised thirty incomplete sentences (e.g. 'I am best at . . .'), an English version of an instrument developed at the Max Planck Institute of Human Development in Berlin by Freya Dittmann-Kohli to obtain data on self-perceptions and outlook on life (see also Chapter 2). The same questionnaire was completed by a group of young adults (university students aged eighteen to twenty-four years), and the comparison between the two sets of answers support the results reported by Dittmann-Kohli (1990). Our older participants had a more positive self-perception. The most striking differences were found in attitudes towards one's own appearance and perception of how others viewed oneself. Negative feelings were denied significantly more often by the older than younger people, for example, in response to sentence stems on the subjects of loneliness, unhappiness and fear. The university students expressed much anxiety about not fulfilling their goal and ambitions. In contrast, the older persons seemed more concerned with keeping their life situation stable and appeared relatively optimistic about their prospects for achieving this. Their criteria for reference were different from those of the young. They compared themselves with people of their own age and were less concerned with change and self-realization. Nevertheless, our older participants' written answers described, often eloquently as we shall see in the following chapters, personal worries about their own and other family members' health, as well as their own future needs of care.

From 1990–1 onwards, because of the importance of depression to our research interests, we introduced a new method of assessment, the Montgomery-Åsberg Depression Rating Scale (MADRS) (Montgomery and Asberg, 1979), which relied more on interviewers' ratings of observable symptoms of depression than on self-descriptive statements. (In 1988, we employed both the previous measure, the Wakefield Self-Report Questionnaire [Snaith, Ahmed and Mehta, 1971], and the MADRS and found a high correlation between the two scales, $r = 0.81$.)

In 1993, the structured interview on participants' perception of continuity across their life course that was the focus of the data collection in that year contained important material that we could use subsequently in the case analyses (Coleman, Ivani-Chalian and Robinson, 1998). Most of our sample did perceive firm connections between their past and present lives. Stability in family life was the principal source of continuity. It was represented in ongoing concern for children and grandchildren. It was often constituted by a lasting happy marriage but could also mean living according to the perceived wishes of a deceased partner. Strong friendships provided continuity for some members of the sample, and a different type of lasting connection was provided by continuing work, whether paid or voluntary. Less prevalent but significant sources of connection for those who mentioned them were continuity of place and surroundings and of religious faith and practice.

Nevertheless, a large minority, 30 percent of the participants (thirteen of the forty-three remaining in the sample at this time), expressed a feeling of 'disconnection' between their past and present lives. This was associated with a perception of reduced value in their lives as older persons. A smaller but still noticeable group of people, 16 percent of the sample, predominantly women, could not see their lives as a 'story' but more as a 'series of events'. All three attitudes tended to be related to low self-esteem and depressive symptoms. Some of the sample had experienced difficult early lives, but there appeared to be little association between a negative evaluation of early life and overall rating of past life satisfaction or contentment with later life. Some were proud of how they had transcended the difficulties of their childhood and young adult days through a happy marriage, working career and other contributions to family and social life. For a few individuals, old age had become the peak of life. Indeed, perception of lack of connection between past and present lives was not necessarily a negative perception. It could mean a transition from a difficult and unhappy life to a secure and contented old age.

Particularly for some men, however, the loss of a productive working life had resulted in an unsatisfying feeling of disconnection. Women referred more to loss of relationships. Thus, the gendered duality of 'agentic' (power, status, assertiveness, dominance) and 'communal' (intimacy, solidarity, social support) motivation was clearly reflected in the accounts of this generation of older people. However, other sources of disconnection and reduced value were provided by society itself and were cited as much by both men and women. The rapid social changes in the twentieth century, and the resulting intergenerational differences with the young, were often mentioned. Much influence was attributed to the two world wars, and the 'materialist society' that was thought to have developed since World War II.

In the same assessment, we also employed another semi-structured schedule that we left with the participants to complete after the interview. This was based on an inventory of 'life strengths' developed for use with elders in need of long-term care by Helen Kivnick at the University of Minnesota (Kivnick, 1991; see Chapter 2). She had collaborated with Erik Erikson in one of his last publications on 'vital involvement' in late life (Erikson, Erikson and Kivnick, 1986) and had subsequently taken it further in care practice with elders. The inventory was a conscious reinterpretation of each of Erik Erikson's eight psychosocial stages: hope and faith; wilfulness, independence and control; purposefulness, pleasure and imagination; competence and hard work; values and sense of self; love and friendship; care and productivity; wisdom and perspective.

Although Erikson presented his psychosocial tasks in stage terms, he did not view them as ever completed but as ongoing work and as needing to be addressed again at the end of life. Our open questions were designed to allow our participants to write as much or as little as they wanted (e.g. What is it about your life that makes you feel most alive?). The concept of identifying life strengths in older people's lives is a valuable one, and this particular assessment instrument has been evaluated in UK rehabilitation settings (Pomeroy, Conroy and Coleman, 1997). Its use is helpful in counteracting the tendency in care work with older people to emphasize problems and weaknesses and to neglect strengths, to be both mobilized and reinforced.

We began to compose individual case studies in 1990–1 and succeeded in completing thirteen of them in that period. We chose six persons whose self-esteem had declined in the course of our study and an additional seven whose self-esteem appeared to have remained high relative to the physical and/or social losses they had incurred. Each case study sought to develop a theory of that particular individual's identity, the principal elements in their life that sustained their sense of self. An effort was made to include predictions about what might happen to their sense of self in the future if changes occurred in their living circumstances.

In 1993, the case studies that had been composed two years earlier were reopened and examined afresh. We learned from previous predictions that had been made, especially where they were not borne out in subsequent observations. We also took the opportunity to encourage a final year psychology student to re-interview two of the persons and to write her own case accounts using the principles set out by Bromley (1986). We were thus able to compare the results with those of our own case studies. Particularly interesting was the possibility this provided to examine the influence of the investigator on the evidence collected for case study analysis. In 1993, we also had the resources to carry out an additional six new case studies bringing our total number up to nineteen, choosing three persons whose self-esteem had recently declined and another three who continued to show a resilient sense of self.

Two years later in 1995, we received specific funding to complete our case study analyses with the remaining participants as well as to discuss our observations with the participants themselves. Our reasons for including the latter were both scientific and ethical. We considered that the inclusion of the participants' perspective would help increase the validity of our conclusions. But we also thought it necessary to allow persons the opportunity to comment on conclusions drawn about their lives where this was both feasible and relevant to establishing the truth value of the published account. Because the Southampton Ageing Project had always been a study in which the participants had regularly been kept informed of progress, it also seemed only appropriate to present them with an account of the final product at the idiographic as well as nomothetic level. The director of the study also made a final visit at this stage, partly to thank participants for their contributions over so many years but also to provide further corroborative material.

By the time of the 1995–6 interviews only twenty-eight of our participants were still alive and willing to be interviewed, and we succeeded in updating or composing anew case studies on every person. As a result, the final number of completed case studies reached a total of forty persons, twelve of whom had already died or were unable to be interviewed in 1995–6. Further interviews of all survivors were conducted as part of the final phase of the Southampton Ageing Project in 1998–9 and again in 2000–2, including the collection of data from more than one interviewer. However, reanalysis of case studies did not occur during this period. That task has had to wait for the writing of the present book.

The forty case studies written between 1990 and 1996 were composed with an invariant structure. The introductory section provided relevant background information on the participants' personal histories before the beginning of the Southampton Ageing Project. This was followed by a chronological account of the data collected on social circumstances, health status and self-esteem and its sources during the initial three years of the project 1977–8 to 1979–80, and then successively for each of the subsequent data collection points at 1988, 1990–1, 1993 and 1995–6. A major analytic section then sought to explain, as far as the evidence allowed, the basis of the person's self-presentation over time and the trajectory it had followed. A final section provided the person's own comments on the explanations offered in the previous section.

When it came to revising and editing these case accounts for the present book, we have been able to draw on an even wider range of material, interviews and letters from the last years of the project, obtained from the participants as well as from their relatives and GPs. However, we have continued to respect our participants' own opinions as the experts on themselves, and in this book, although we present material from all forty cases, we give priority to those with whom we were able to check our conclusions.

Structure of the following chapters

The results of our combined efforts are displayed in the next six chapters. As well as focusing on the later stages of ageing, we have also concentrated on the two most common crises of late life in modern Western societies, bereavement of spouse or partner and increasing personal frailty. Although we do present material from earlier in the study where it is highly relevant to our account of the person in question, we do not except in a few cases provide detailed descriptive passages or quotations from the participants when they themselves were in their sixties and early or middle seventies.

We follow our participants individually through the succeeding chapters as their lives change, most directly as a result of the ill health and eventual loss of their spouses and their own increasing frailty and difficulty in managing the tasks of daily life. When we do group together our cases, we typically do so according to age, gender or to the primary commitments or 'life themes' that they described to us from their later seventies. The experiences, motivations and personal needs of men and women of this generation of British people had diverged already earlier in life, and the later stages brought further noticeable differences, especially women's longer period growing old alone and their resulting greater need of external support.

Many of both our female and male participants could count on help from their children as they became frailer. This was often a reflection of the strong mutual attachment bonds that the children had shown to them throughout their lives. Those who could count on such consistent and reliable support from their spouses and children as they aged were able to a large extent to override anxieties about losing independence. But for those who for various reasons, whether through absence of or distance from children, were left to cope alone, the later years of becoming frailer were more difficult. Some needed eventually to seek placement in residential care. Others succeeded in coping in their own home until or almost until the time of death.

In Chapter 4, we begin with a description of the married members of our sample in their later seventies and eighties. Because of the greater longevity of women and their younger age at marriage, a higher proportion of the men lived together with their wives until their own deaths. Marriage therefore in this sample was much more a man's story and generally a positive one that illustrated well the benefits of long-lasting marriages (partnerships). This was also true of the women participants, although they carried in consequence of their younger ages a greater load of caregiving responsibilities for their older husbands.

Chapter 5 describes our initially married participants' experience of bereavement of spouse from their later seventies onwards. For virtually all of them, this was a severe blow, and the recovery period was often long and painful. The impact of bereavement in later life is generally underestimated, and the comparison of cases that our study allowed helped in elucidating some of the key factors involved in prolonged grief reactions. However, there were some surprises in our sample, for example, persons who showed a stronger and earlier recovery than might have been expected from their situation before their spouse's death.

In Chapter 6, we consider those who had been living alone from before the second phase of our study began. In our sample, these were almost entirely women. Those who had lost their spouses later in adulthood had typically maintained close and sustaining relationships with surviving children and their families. Some of them, however, had had to learn to cope without a partner much earlier in adulthood and had even been obliged to bring up their children alone. Maintaining an independent household and their own activities had become core values for them. Those without children had typically sought major and lasting sources of meaning in friendship and other types of social roles and relationships in which they invested a great deal of their energies.

We consider the substantial evidence we obtained on how our participants, the women in Chapter 7 and the men in Chapter 8, adapted to what was usually a gradual process of becoming frailer and dependent on others. For some, however, this was a sudden change, usually as a result of a fall or other accident. We were able to interview most of them once they had reached this stage of life, and these chapters provide the expected main focus of this book. They illustrate the resilience of the vast majority of our sample in facing declining health and the need to make adjustments to their ways of life. The ready presence of a supportive spouse and children was often crucial to their success. Participants who lacked such close support as they became frailer often experienced a marked decline in quality of life, and some eventually had to enter residential care. Typically, however, these persons did not give in without a struggle, and a number of them were successful in maintaining some at least of their previous goals and aspirations.

In Chapter 9, we investigate the last period of the lives of six members of our sample who lived well into their nineties and were interviewed during that time. They illustrate that a high quality of life is possible in the nineties. We also ask the question of whether they had earlier shown qualities that might have marked them out as survivors. Some had had long histories of relatively poor health that made their longevity surprising. But what they all had in common was a strong sense of their lives as continuing to be meaningful, diverse though the sources of meaning were that they perceived and pursued.

In Chapter 10, we bring together some of the main conclusions from our study and also draw out implications for those growing old in the first part of the twenty-first century. Some of the major resources many of our participants were able to rely on as they grew older, such as belonging to a large extended family and adherence to a religious tradition, are likely to be less available to new generations of older people in the United Kingdom. Will alternative sources of meaning emerge sufficient to sustain people as they become frailer at the end of life? We examine in particular what can be learned from those of our cases that we studied in the greatest depth and with whom we reflected together on the value of living to an advanced age. What do they tell us about the personal qualities as well as social supports needed for persons to grow old well?

One final point should be made here about the use of quotations from our participants. Because many of our later interviews were tape-recorded, and earlier interviews often annotated, we had a rich range of material to draw on to illustrate important points and to give voice to the persons themselves by making liberal use of their own words. In editing this book, we have had to make careful selections through this material in order that the book should not become too long. All quotations in separate paragraphs (provided in italics) and within the rest of the text, in double inverted commas, are verbatim quotations from the participants themselves. Quotations in single inverted commas are either paraphrases of participants' comments or citations from the schedule of questions presented to the participant.

4   Ageing together

With few exceptions, our sample of older persons still living with spouses in their later seventies and older appeared happily married. This might also suggest difficulties in differentiating among our sample. As the famous first sentence from Tolstoy's *Anna Karenina* proposes: 'All happy families are more or less like one another; every unhappy family is unhappy in its own particular way'. Certainly at first analysis, there were many similarities in our participants' accounts of their married life. Nearly all the married women, for example, described their husbands as providing sources of enjoyment and comfort but also of a sense of importance and of a meaningful role in life, most obviously in caring for them.

However, it is possible to look beyond the obvious similarities to see ways in which the sources of self and meaning that older married people referred to in describing their lives differed from one another. A self-description exclusively based on family interactions and commitments might predict a different future from one that also included external involvements.

We start our account by providing a brief portrait of the one male and female married couple who were both participants at the outset of the Southampton Ageing Project and who survived to be part of the second phase of the project. Both enjoyed a high quality of life up to eighty-five years, and we were able to interview them in depth in their later years.

We then consider married men and married women separately, beginning with the larger group of men who were still married at age seventy-five years when our case analyses began. We describe their lives through their later seventies and into their eighties until either their spouse died or they became significantly frail and dependent on help from their spouse or others. The subsequent story of their lives is continued in the following chapters.

Ageing contentedly together: one couple's experience of a long and happy marriage

Marion and Henry Goodall were aged sixty-six and sixty-seven years, respectively, when first interviewed. They had known each other since school days and had two sons of whom they were "very proud." Their living circumstances were both comfortable and financially secure. Since Henry's retirement from the Gas Board at age sixty-five years, they had maintained good health, living active lives, travelling a lot, attending social clubs and even playing golf together. In their early seventies, Henry described these years as the "best years" of their lives so far and that they had "never been so happy." Their positive self-ascriptions were illustrated both by reference to their children's families who lived more than one hundred miles away and their very active lifestyles. Marion had worked in the WVS (Women's Voluntary Service) when she was younger, but her focus was now firmly on her family, friends and neighbours.

Their lives remained stable through the greater part of their seventies, but by seventy-eight years both had encountered some chronic health problems. At the time of the 1990 interview, Marion was affected by a hiatus hernia, a tendency to experience tremors, high blood pressure and some depressive symptoms. (The last could have been because Marion was still recovering from a chest infection, a virus that she had caught on holiday abroad, as she admitted 'not being her normal self'.) At the same interview, Henry spoke of problems with his joints that resulted in some pain when walking. Nevertheless, they both remained active and continued to base their self-ascriptions on their various activities and their involvement with their families.

One striking difference to emerge by their later seventies was a stronger involvement in religious activities than had been apparent in previous interviews. In her later sixties, Marion reported rarely going to a place of worship. At seventy-eight years, she emphasized how she had now become "keen on church", attended services weekly, and believed in "God and everlasting life." At eighty-three years, she indicated that her self-confidence was related to the strength that she derived from her faith: "I'm a Christian and that makes a difference"; "I don't say I live a good life because no one does . . . [but] I like church and I believe and I'm sure that helps."

Marion's future perspective was focused on her family, particularly interest in her grandsons "continuing with their careers." At eighty-three years, she repeated this theme when illustrating what gave her hope in life: "watching our family get on in life and seeing them do so much that is worthwhile." Henry also stressed family values in his self-ascriptions: "I feel really good when with my family"; "most important to me is the health and well-being of my wife and my family." Visiting their sons' families was an important part of their year, also the planning of new holidays. They were even considering visiting the United States for the first time.

Despite additional health difficulties as they grew older – Marion with arthritis and an episode of shingles, Henry with angina and thyroid problems – their morale remained at a relatively high level. Throughout their early eighties, they continued to emphasize the positives in their lives, the ability to take frequent holidays, enjoyment of their children's families and pleasures of "normal daily life." Henry repeated at eighty-five years that these had been their "best years" and hoped that they would continue so for as long as possible. They presented as an extremely contented couple, married for more than sixty years. At eighty-three years, Marion confirmed the centrality of marriage in her life: "my husband's first... but then the family." Henry also described their "very good marriage" as the most 'meaningful' aspect of his life, alongside his health.

It was noticeable that their activities increasingly coincided. Henry took up knitting in his later seventies: "the wife started it and seeing her doing it I wanted to try. It passes the time away." He also became closer to his wife in religious attitudes as he entered his eighties. He began attending church with her regularly and at eighty-five years agreed that his faith was now an important feature of his life: "it's not so strong as the wife's but I am a believer definitely – and try to live accordingly."

Henry died the following year at age eighty-six years, and Marion thereafter moved to live with one of her son's family in another part of the country. We were therefore unable to interview her again.

Marion and Henry had many reasons to be satisfied with their lives. Particularly striking was the consistency of their active lifestyle over so many years, as well as their unqualified expressions of satisfaction with their style of life. The religious element that became more prominent in their later years was another important feature of their lives that brought them even closer together in later life and may well have aided their adjustment to ageing.

Meaning in the lives of our ageing married men

Henry could be considered particularly fortunate in that he suffered neither the loss of his wife nor a major decline in functioning abilities. More important, perhaps, he lived a life in his later years that was full of interest and meaning, much of which he could also share with his wife.

Many of our other married men shared similar benefits of a relatively long mutually supportive relationship with their wife without suffering eventual bereavement. Only five of the thirteen initially married men described in this chapter had to come to terms with loss of spouse. An additional benefit for them is that they could often be cared for by their wives, sometimes with assistance from their children, if and when they became frail or disabled. Husbands' greater seniority and therefore earlier morbidity and mortality made this outcome much more likely than the reverse. Women's later lives often involved coping with their husbands' increasing frailty. It was rarer for this to be a fully reciprocal relationship, as in the cases of Henry and Marion Goodall, in which they supported one another as they became older.

Most of our married men had lived a 'traditional' marriage in which the husband had been the 'breadwinner' and the wife remained at home for the most part, looking after the household and bringing up the children. Some of the families had been large, and the men had also played important roles in nurturing their children. It is important to note that nearly all of these men indicated a strong investment in their families and that this investment generally increased the older they became. Of course, the character of their subsequent family life depended in the first place on whether they had children, how many, whether they were sons or daughters, whether they lived near or far away and their previous histories of relating to their children.

In seeking the most important distinctions between these married men we have examined closely the sources of self and meaning that they described in their later seventies. All referred to their wives as significant sources for personal feelings of usefulness and purpose. Those who had children generally also indicated an abiding and often increasing involvement in their lives. But there was significant variation among them in mention of social relationships beyond the immediate family, in personal interests and activities, and in wider values, beliefs and principles.

Six family men

The largest group comprised those who could be described as 'family men'. In describing their commitments and interests, they gave overriding importance to their family, including both their wives and their children.

Edward (Ted) Jackson was perhaps the best example of a 'family man' in our sample, much loved and respected by his children. His early experiences both of family responsibilities and family breakdown seemed to lie behind the strong value he gave to creating a happy family. Born into poor circumstances in the north of England, he had entered the army as a young man. At that early stage of life he already appreciated the importance of family solidarity.

I joined the army because I was hungry. It was a relief for the family to get a little donation of your pay each week to help them because we were a big family.

He rose to the rank of regimental sergeant major, serving in India and later in Egypt.

However, his first marriage collapsed while he was in India during the Second World War. His wife left him for another man (Ted said he was the "last to know") and with four children to care for. His superiors "shipped" him and his children back to England, where the children were cared for by his mother, while Ted continued his war service on the home front, including the D-day preparations. At the end of the war, he met his current wife who was also obtaining a divorce and already had two children of her own. They married in Gibraltar and joined their families together before his posting to Egypt. When his wife became ill there with tuberculosis, he decided to retire – he had completed thirty years of service – and joined the Post Office where he worked until his retirement at sixty-five years. In total, he and his wife had seven children, five daughters and two sons, to care for.

When first interviewed in his later sixties, Ted was living with his wife, who was four years younger, in a council house and sharing household tasks with her on an equal basis. He already had noticeable health problems. He was troubled by a slight tremor and shortness of breath and was also limited in his reading by his weak eyesight. His activity levels had declined as a result. His self-esteem was limited by his lack of self-confidence but was nevertheless strongly rooted in his family life, caring for his wife and enjoying his children. When asked whether he got much enjoyment out of life, he responded: "I can't help it with a family like mine!"

During the following ten years, Ted and his wife became noticeably more disabled. His hearing deteriorated, and he needed a stick to walk. His wife's arthritis was so severe that she needed his regular help. At the time of our interview soon after his eightieth birthday Ted had been suffering from a 'frozen shoulder' in his right arm and needing his wife's help with dressing for a long period of time. He described how their lifestyle had become more limited. For instance, they were no longer able to take the foreign holidays by coach that they had once enjoyed so much.

We didn't realize it was so bad until we got off the coach on a day tour to Salzburg. . . . Everybody went rushing up to these places where Mozart used to play. . . . We just walked to the nearest bench in the nearest park and we sat there until they came back.

The frozen shoulder in particular had made Ted start thinking about the extra help they might need at home.

But it was at this interview that Ted also provided us with considerable evidence on how highly he viewed the value of his family life. He said he looked to the future with confidence "especially with a wife as good as mine" and his aim was "to be able to look after my wife and enjoy the rest of our lives together." He acknowledged his importance to the wider family and said that his great-grandchildren gave him much enjoyment.

On the handwritten self-ascriptions he posted back to us at this time, his fears centred on his likely future disability, in particular his inability to manage his garden. This was clearly important to him because he wrote he felt really good "when the family visits or when someone remarks 'your garden looks lovely'." To the sentence stem about loneliness, he commented that "I did not know what loneliness was until the wife and I were separated for some reason or other, then I concentrated on my work or my garden." His principal goals concerned "the health and well-being of my wife and my family." His inner satisfaction came out most clearly in his answer to other sentence stems.

'When I compare myself to others'... "they with their cars, yachts, mansions etc, I wonder are they as happy as I am."

'My life up to now'... "maybe with a bit of thought I could have bettered my position in life, but I could not have been happier."

Ted's health continued to decline. In the following year, he was diagnosed as having rheumatoid arthritis and was admitted to hospital because he was unable to get out of bed or sit up. We take up his story again in Chapter 8.

Five of our other married men also demonstrated in their later seventies a sense of self strongly based within their families. *Robert Gardiner* had first been interviewed at age sixty-eight and lived to eighty-six years, remaining with his wife in the same house, which they owned. Their only financial support was Robert's state pension. Throughout this period of almost twenty years, he had a low depression rating and a high self-esteem rooted in family relationships. At the outset of the study, he commented that he "missed work" as a ship mender but was already identifying strongly with the life of his wider family. He had three children and numerous grandchildren. At the time, he and his wife had their seventeen-year-old grandson living with them. Robert also gained satisfaction from performing indoor and outdoor tasks, especially repairs in the home and gardening.

During the course of our study Robert encountered various health problems (including deterioration of hearing and vision, pain on walking, shortness of breath walking up hills, and high blood pressure) but regarded them all as "trivial." Towards the end of his life, he acknowledged that he had become marginally 'less active' but was still walking 'more than a mile a week' and remained relatively unconcerned about his health. When interviewed at eighty-four, he had recently had a tumour removed from his bowel and was experiencing mobility problems due to increased pain in his legs, but he was still continuing to enjoy his gardening and the occasional day trips, as well as "being out and active and mixing with people." He also felt he was maintaining his home well. Contacts with his children's families remained constant over the years. To the end of his life, his family remained of utmost importance to him. On the questionnaires he sent back to us, he indicated his principal goals as "helping others – especially the family" and "wanting to carry on due to my family." Robert died suddenly at age eighty-six years, shortly after he had agreed to be interviewed again, but before we could see him. His GP had indicated to us that he was suffering from ischaemic heart disease and also had a large bowel obstruction due to adenocarcinoma.

Leonard Johns provided a somewhat contrasting example to the previous two 'family men' because Leonard's wife was evidently "more the driving force." These were his wife's words but ones that her husband also seemed to accept. Throughout the study, she took an active, often dominant part in the interviews. Nevertheless, it was clear from his own comments that Leonard's identity was solidly based around his family.

He and his wife had moved around England during their lives. Leonard had been brought up in a poor but stable family in County Durham. After gaining some qualifications in bookkeeping, he had worked for many years in the administrative offices of the Consett steel works in County Durham while his wife was employed as a community nurse. After the war, during which Leonard had spent some years as a prisoner of war, the couple worked together in care homes for young people in various parts of the country, finally arriving in Southampton in the early 1950s. In his latter working years, Leonard took on part-time employment in the Post Office. As a result, his wife's pension provision from the NHS was the major contributor to their income. Nevertheless, they both prided themselves on the way they had managed their monies to enable them to have a fairly comfortable retirement. They had one son who lived at a distance and one daughter who worked as a schoolteacher.

When first interviewed in his early seventies Leonard was enjoying his retirement, engaging in various activities including rambling. He was also child-minding for his daughter while she was at work. His self-esteem was high and his ascriptions illustrated by his various interests, but especially by his contributions to the family. He enjoyed 'helping with' his grandchildren of whom he was very proud.

Leonard's health continued to be good throughout his seventies, although he showed a tendency towards depressive symptoms (sleep problems and restlessness), but an awareness of the likelihood of approaching problems led him and his wife to move when he was eighty-one years from their bungalow into a new ground-floor maisonette. They exercised great care in choosing their new home, looking for maximum convenience and comfort, while minimizing the chores such as gardening and maintenance that they envisaged would be become more difficult as they grew older. Leonard gave up driving because of cataracts, and even after an operation improved his sight, he decided that they could live better without a car.

However, their hopes for a peaceful retirement were dashed by unexpected factors. When interviewed two years later at age eighty-three years, Leonard displayed significant depressive symptoms, including pervasive feelings of sadness and edginess, difficulties starting activities, and reduced ability to enjoy his usual interests. A combination of circumstances seemed to have led to a decline in his mental health. These included distress at his son's recent divorce and symptoms of heart disease, especially breathlessness when walking. He had been diagnosed with atrial fibrillation (for which he was taking digoxin). But the most disturbing factor appeared to be an ongoing acrimonious dispute with their next-door neighbours, a divorced woman and her two teenage sons. Leonard and his wife recited a list of problems including offensive behaviour by the boys, bad language, loud music and antisocial hours, which had badly affected their peace and resulted in complaints to the council. Both of them had also developed an obsessive interest in their neighbours' comings and goings, which they described in great detail. As they commented to us, the anxiety of waiting for noise was "as bad as the actual noise."

Leonard's self-esteem was negatively affected in these years. Initially he was unable to affirm any positive self-ascription, and even by the time the most severe depressive symptoms had eased two years later, his self-ascriptions were tentative and uncertain. However, he remained buttressed by his secure place in the affections of his wife and children. We continue the story of his life as he became frailer in Chapter 8.

Dennis Wilcox, like Ted Jackson, had experienced a tough life as a young boy and man, having to work hard for everything.

Sometimes I used to take two goats on the way to school, tether them and pick them up after school and take them back and put them in their hut. I got a shilling a week for that. I worked for a chemist, taking films to be developed. . . . I used to take the films about twice a week to be developed, take some down and bring some back, they used to give me the tram fare. . . . I didn't go on the tram, I went on an old ladies' bike to save the tram fare. . . . But that's how my life was, nobody ever gave me anything. I had to earn it . . . and I think if you've been like that and you . . . it makes you be careful.

After leaving school, he tried several jobs, working first as a van boy on a horse-drawn bread round for a local baker before being transferred to the post of uniformed porter at a city centre café. He then became a trainee butcher, and for about six and a half years, he worked as a van driver. When he needed more pay to be able to get married, he dared not ask for more money from that employer who had already given him two raises, so he was advised to try the Automobile Association (AA). War provided him with new opportunities. Because the AA had an arrangement with the War Office that enabled their riders to join the supplementary reserve of the Military Police, Dennis could be employed as an outrider on security duties, providing escort and protection to key figures such as King George, Churchill and Montgomery. The war, he believed, had an important effect on his personal development, making him more broad-minded and tolerant.

At the time of our first interview, Dennis was sixty-five and recently retired. His mother-in-law, who lived next door and whom they had been looking after for the past eight years, had recently died. His self-esteem was high based on his importance to his wife, as well as his contacts with his three children and new granddaughter, and his activities around the house and garden. He and his wife were financially comfortable, and he was looking forward to new opportunities for travel.

However, before his retirement, he had been experiencing pain in his legs and had recently been diagnosed with pernicious anaemia. His wife was also suffering from cardiac problems for which she received major surgery in the following years. They encountered further health difficulties in their seventies, and when we interviewed Dennis at age seventy-six he was experiencing problems with both his eyesight and his hearing, which had led him to give up driving. Two years later, he had cut down further on activities and was only active in the garden.

Well, I'm seventy-eight you see and at the moment I can do the garden. Up to now I can do the garden quite alright. . . . I've got two or three places with seats and that, that I can sit down in the garden.

A greater blow was that two years previously, their eldest daughter had died with leukaemia, and in successive interviews over the next ten years, both he and his wife indicated that they were still mourning their loss. Nevertheless, they remained proud of their daughter's achievements. She had gained a good degree and a prestigious job in education management at county level. Indeed, they were proud of all their four children, whom they had encouraged to stay on in further education. Dennis said that he had been determined to give his children a good life, having learned from his own parents' failings in this regard.

Dennis's relationship with his wife was not without stress. Quarrels occurred over the management of the house. The fact that he concentrated on the garden and left his wife to do all the household chores caused her evident irritation. They had considered moving house, but the fall in the property prices in the early 1990s and the problem of shedding years of acquisition (Dennis admitted to being a 'hoarder') discouraged them.

Dennis's self-esteem had lowered in the preceding years with uncertainly supported ascriptions. The same was true of his answers to the sentence completion task he returned by post when he was seventy-eight years old.

'In the next few years' . . . "In view of my age I do not think very much about the next few years."

Indeed, he clearly had a lot of difficulty in completing the task, simply inserting a question mark for thirteen of the sentences. However, his pride in his children's success emerged strongly. By comparison, he felt himself to have been disadvantaged.

'I am very proud of' . . . "Our children, their academic achievements, one BA, one BA (hons), one RICS (a surveyor)."

'When I think about myself' . . . "I am sure that had I had the same educational opportunities as our children I would have had a better life."

A growing emphasis on his family was also evident in his self-ascriptions. His concern for the future and his dependence on his wife was also apparent.

'Later when I'm older' . . . *"I hope not to have to be dependent on other people."*
'I am afraid of' . . . *"surviving my wife (being left alone)."*

Despite the continuing friction between them, the marriage remained strong. Interviewed three years later at the age of eighty-one, Dennis reckoned that marrying his wife was "one thing I've done right", and a further three years on his wife herself commented:

. . . we irritate each other because we're under each other's nose. No, I wouldn't be without him and he wouldn't be without me.

After a married life of sixty years in which they had been through much together, they could not imagine themselves apart. However, they were both becoming significantly frailer. We continue our account of the following years of Dennis's life in Chapter 8.

Two of our other married men with strong family attachments lost their wives relatively early in our study, and thus their situation was more similar to that of the few older married women to be described later in this chapter. Although considerably more will be written about them in subsequent chapters, the character of their married lives when we first interviewed them should be briefly noted here.

Harold Rank had been married twice. His first wife had died of meningitis during World War II, leaving him alone with two children. He had subsequently married a widow eleven years younger than himself with two children of her own. She bore him another child. When we first interviewed Harold at age sixty-nine years, he was proud of the family life that he and his wife had developed together. His life was strongly family centred, and he spoke with particular pride of what his various children had achieved. A painter and decorator before and after the war, he was proud of their home, which they owned. He presented as fit and healthy, with many interests and hobbies and with a strong sense of self-esteem. He was still on the committee of the social club of the Southampton shipbuilding firm Thornycroft for which he had worked. He enjoyed his family and said he was looking forward to enjoying retirement.

But by the next year, his life had changed dramatically. His wife had been diagnosed with early-onset dementia. Harold would not accept the diagnosis and struggled to cope effectively with the situation. Unfortunately, his own physical health declined at the same time, and four years later, his wife had to be taken into care. She lived another five years in care before her death. Thus, his experience of bereavement was drawn out over a long period; his adaptation to it and his own increasing frailty are considered in Chapters 5 and 8.

Fred Hobson's health was already relatively poor at the time of our first interview when he was aged sixty-seven years. He had a heart condition that limited his outdoor activities. Nevertheless, he was not depressed and seemed to have found positive ways of coping. He kept up interests within his home environment, especially watching football on TV, and despite admitting to feelings of uselessness, he stressed his importance to his wife. He appeared to draw a lot on his experience working as a military nurse, a mental health nurse and social worker. He and his wife owned their own home and were attached to their son and daughter, both of whom lived nearby.

Fred's heart condition continued to be a source of concern over the succeeding ten years. But then when he was aged seventy-seven years, his wife died, and he was required to learn to cope living on his own and in a weakened health condition. As with Harold Rank, we continue his story of adaptation in the following chapters.

Two more close couples

Three of our married men were in marriages where the focus of attention was very much on one another either because their children lived at a distance or because they had no children. Inevitably they had to be more reliant on their own resources. Two of these marriages could be described as exclusive relationships in which the lives of both partners revolved almost entirely around one another.

Ralph Hodgkin was extremely close to his wife, who was three years younger than he was. Their happiness was centred on activities around the home, including preparing meals and engaging in various hobbies (including genealogy and collecting postcards). They had one son, married with a daughter, who visited every few months. From his own accounts, Ralph emerged as a determined man, and something of a 'loner'. Later in the study, he told us more about his life story. Both he and his older brother had begun working for their father, a painter and decorator. However, when he wanted to marry after age 30, he confronted his father with the fact that his pay was insufficient – his father would only work in good weather – and left to work for a house builder in a town elsewhere in Hampshire. Soon Ralph was able to set up his own business. He also developed the clever idea of buying up old houses at auction, which gave his men work to do indoors when the weather was bad. His father was amazed at his success, initially having questioned whether his son 'knew what he was doing' and could afford this way of doing business. Ralph retired early at the age of fifty-eight, moved back to Southampton to be near his wife's family, bought a new house and made sure all the fittings were "first class" and able to "last a lifetime."

His wife was central to his sense of self. When we first interviewed Ralph in his early seventies, his self-esteem was also based on his good health, active lifestyle and practical competence, but each was related to his life with his wife. His sense of his own significance was unsure: "possibly I'm important – but only to my wife" (later in the study he did include his son in this assessment). His health continued to be good into his early eighties apart from impaired hearing and a long-standing heart problem. His self-esteem remained positive, although he continued to question his own importance and was affected by the loss of friends and also by the fact that his "best friend was no longer interested" in him. But at age eighty-three years, he experienced a bad accident, falling from a ladder at his house which resulted in multiple injuries that he described as "a broken leg and broken right arm, dislocation of the left arm, a broken rib and twenty-seven stitches in the forehead." He spent a long period in hospital, was housebound for three months afterwards and was never able to recover his previous level of activity. We take up his story again in Chapter 8.

George Rowan and his wife had no children. He had married late at age 45 when his wife was 36 at the end of World War II. They had met before the war and agreed to marry at its end. In fact he had proposed on a mountainside in Scotland where they had gone for two-week holiday. But on the way back, they were involved in a major train accident in which forty-nine people were killed. The train went off the rails and down an embankment.

I was in hospital. Well for two months I just laid on my back. I didn't move for two months. My wife, although she had terrible injuries, she was getting about a bit . . .

His wife had badly broken bones and pelvic injuries. Both remained in hospital for the best part of a year during which time they carried on their romance by passing notes through the nurses. They still kept these notes in a suitcase.

They delayed marriage for another three years to try to maximize the compensation George's wife could claim as a working person. However, in the end, she never went back to work and remained forty percent disabled for the rest of her life. Their marriage was a happy one, marked by "tremendous companionship", which George, in one of our last interviews, attributed to their fully formed characters when they married. They did not have any children, apparently through choice. In fact, George's wife did not express a desire for any children until shortly before her death.

I never once heard my wife say she would like a family. It's only since she's been very ill that she wished she had a close relative, only the last few months I've ever heard her wish she had a family and that was because she wanted visits from a family.

George had spent his whole career working in banks, apart from war service in the gunnery. He did not enjoy this work but never found an alternative.

It was a . . . dreary type of life, particularly when I was young because it was sorting old cheques away and that sort of thing, writing entries in books, long columns of entries like that, absolutely no interest to me. . . . I remember, after I'd been in the army for four and half years and enjoyed the open-air life I did contemplate farming. There again I didn't want a farm with animals.

When he was young he had compensated for his boring work by playing a lot of sport, but marriage had transformed his life.

I have been very happy with my wife, and that is the most important aspect of my life. I was quite happy before I met my wife, but I have been extremely happy since I met her.

George's health remained remarkably good, apart from some joint problems, throughout the course of our study. At eighty-five years, he attributed this to his "loving and caring wife." From the first interview with him at age seventy-five, his sense of self-esteem was also firmly based on the presence of his wife in his life. He said that she was central to his past, present and hopes for the future. But he began to realize that, contrary to expectations based on their respective ages, he might well outlive his wife.

His heightened concerns about her began in his late eighties when she was prescribed medication for high blood pressure and appeared to feel unwell as a result. Two years later, she was required to undertake tests for her heart and was suffering from depression. George noted the change in her:

I don't worry about it all the time, concerned is a better word really. For instance, my wife sat in the chair and didn't do much else this morning, it's a little distressing, isn't it?

At this time, George's wife was present for the interview, and they seemed to view participation in the project as joint. He now did all the housework, and his wife had "trained" him to do the cooking so that he should be able to be more self-sufficient. Both had been affected by the recent unexpected death of a mutual friend. George's wife commented:

It's made a big difference to our lives really. She was more like a daughter, not really like a . . . I mean . . . a friend, a real friend, somebody that you can have confidence in . . . Life has gone. It's a big hole in our lives really.

George added:

Had we needed anyone to lean on, they [friends] were there to lean on, but we haven't got that now.

Significantly, George, now aged eighty-seven years, would not answer the written sentence completion items that required speculation about the future ('In the next few years . . .'; 'maybe I can . . .' etc), apart from:

'Later when I'm older'. . . "I wonder."

But on other items, he continued to reiterate his wife's centrality to him.

'When I feel lonely'... *"not lonely while I have my wife."*

'Most important for me is'... *"my wife."*

'The goal that I would like to accomplish in my life is'... *"to live long and healthily and happily with my wife."*

His insecurities were expressed indirectly.

'When I feel unhappy'... *"very."*

'I am afraid of'... *"cold and darkness."*

George's wife in fact lived another six years, dying of pneumonia at age eighty-four on an elderly care ward. His health remained strong, apart from a slight problem with breathlessness. He therefore was able to continue his new caring role within the household. These abilities, as well as his general importance to his wife, continued to sustain his self-esteem. He also maintained a number of interest activities, including visiting places of beauty in their car, music and reading. Moreover, a new religious element emerged in his self-ascriptions in these years.

'What do you believe in?'... *"The good Lord."*

Although in early interviews George had indicated that he attended the local parish church sometimes and that religion was 'fairly important' to him, it had never featured as a major supporting feature until his later interviews. We consider his adaptation to losing his wife in the following chapter.

Four men with strong outside interests

The remaining four married men in our sample are somewhat more difficult to categorize together. But they all, at least in their later seventies, possessed strong goals outside the family, and their sense of self at that time was largely rooted in activities related to these interests. Family life, although important to them, appeared to play a more secondary role in their lives, at least in the earlier stages of ageing.

Of all our sample of cases, **Thomas Johnson** was possibly initially the most work oriented (along with Stuart Murray, see Chapter 6). He said he was someone who got "bored" easily and preferred work to leisure. He had difficulties with the idea of retirement. In fact, he continued working for as long as he could.

He had followed in the footsteps of his father, entering the navy at nineteen years of age. His father, along with three of his uncles, from the same Hampshire village, had been killed in the Dardanelles campaign of 1915. Thomas worked in the boiler rooms for twenty-two and a half years, rising to the rank of chief petty officer. He served in the navy throughout World War II, including at the Battle of Cape Matapan, the relief of Tobruk and the Normandy invasion. After leaving the navy he got a job in the boiler house in a local rubber company and later worked as a caretaker for a construction company. When he finally retired at eighty, it was only because he was told to, after a period in which he had been unwell with septicaemia.

. . . it was one of the bosses there, I used to see him most mornings and he said 'You old bugger it's time you retired.' So I said 'No, I'm alright Mr B.' He said, 'No you ain't.'. . . I said I'll tell you what I'll do, I'll retire when I'm eighty.' When I went back to see him about six months after, he said 'Christ you look well.' I said, 'But I'd sooner be out here working.'

From the beginning of the study, Thomas had been living with his wife in a council house on a large estate on the outskirts of the city. She had also been used to a busy life, bringing up children and living with her mother-in-law while her husband was away at sea, then working in residential care also beyond normal retirement age. She too said that she missed work since she retired. They had had one daughter but had also brought up the wife's younger brother from the time he was twelve years old following their mother's death.

Although Thomas's self-esteem in his sixties and seventies had been mainly based on his various activities at work and at home, he was able to make the transition to retirement, late as it occurred, with seemingly little difficulty. In fact, as he progressed through his eighties, he seemed to become more content with life. He referred often to his role in the family, particularly with his grandchildren. He commented in his written responses to us that he had "had a good life", had "no great worries", saw himself as "free and easy" and aimed to "enjoy the years I have left." At age eighty-two, he wrote that the most meaningful aspect of his life was "that I have been lucky to have had good health and a long happy marriage" and that "my family life, grandchildren and five great-grandchildren" were what was important to him now. He and his wife were fortunate that their growing family lived in the area and were in close contact with them. They expressed the view that they were a "happy couple."

Thomas's family ties clearly became more important to him as he grew older. At the centre of these ties was his relationship with his wife. Perhaps this was understated in their day-to-day life, but it was apparent in their easy and relaxed attitude towards each other that there was a profound affection between the two of them. His wife said herself that she and her husband got along well despite the differences in their characters. He was outgoing and sociable, whereas she was quiet and did not like mixing a lot. Nevertheless, they did admit that from time to time, they got on each other's nerves.

At the same time, Thomas retained his broader range of interests. We were impressed in his middle eighties by his engagement in the world around him, particularly his belief in "helping others that are perhaps worse off than you." He also engaged actively with his interviewers, taking a lively interest in the political career of one of us and sharing historical books on the war at sea with another. He liked to reminisce about his World War II service and spoke with great pride and affection of the comradeship he experienced in the navy. But by the end of his life, his greatest interest was in showing us photographs of his eight great-grandchildren. He agreed with our written assessment of him, particularly the importance of still being able to do tasks around the house, the centrality of his relationship with his wife and the great joy he derived from the younger generation of his family.

As they aged further, their daughter came in to help them with the heavier cooking and washing. Thomas had become somewhat more concerned for his wife's well-being if he were to die before her because "she can't even write a cheque." But her younger brother had reassured him that he would look after her affairs. When we last spoke with Thomas at age eighty-seven years, his brother-in-law had just arranged for him to be flown up to Manchester for a day visit, the first time in his life that he had been in an aeroplane. He had "loved it!"

At this interview he still seemed to be quite sprightly, although he now had persistent problems with his knee and was waiting for a hospital outpatient appointment. He had broken an arm a year before after falling outside the house. More recently, he said he had become liable to topple over for no good reason but had not yet reported this problem to his doctor. Both he and his wife were in good spirits, and their house was well maintained and decorated. Their family members were continuing to provide help with the housework and gardening and generally keeping a close eye on them. Thomas and his wife clearly felt valued by their family. He expressed great satisfaction with his past life and agreed that old age was 'a happy time' for him. His self-esteem remained solidly based on his family life and his continued ability to do things. He died two years later at eighty-nine before he could be interviewed again.

Alfred Parker was still working part time as an accountant for an insurance company when first interviewed at age sixty-eight years, and he was also involved in voluntary work. Early in his career, his previous company had moved him around the country, and he had not married until age thirty. Their only child, a son, had developed meningitis at age fifteen and subsequently lost his hearing. This, Alfred said, had been the worse time of his life, which otherwise had been happy and peaceful. In his early adulthood, he had been active in politics, but he became disillusioned, and after his son's hearing became impaired, he took up voluntary work in helping disabled people.

Alfred was also a committed church member. He had left the Church of England to join the Roman Catholic Church in his forties and later in life became particularly active in his local church. At the time of our first interview, he had recently been appointed a 'special Eucharistic minister', taking communion to sick and disabled parishioners. Later in the study, he commented more on the importance to him of church life.

I enjoy the church, I've put a lot into trying to help other people in my life ... and I realize that we are here to help people to help one another and that seems to be the main objective of my life.

During our first interviews, Alfred's health was good apart from "water-works" problems, for which he had a small operation at age sixty-nine, and the long-standing effects of asthma, which he had developed as a child of ten. He had recently given up smoking because of chest pains. His wife, however, appeared to have more serious health problems. She was no longer able to walk up steep slopes or steps, and Alfred had taken over some of the heavier household chores. Their son had remained unmarried and lived elsewhere in the country. Alfred's self-esteem was mainly positive, based around his various helping activities as well as assisting his wife, but he acknowledged that his "mental processes were beginning to slow down." His main aim, he stated, was "to lead a good Christian life."

Both his and his wife's health deteriorated in the following years. Alfred had a heart attack at age seventy-two, and by his later seventies, he was needing to use a Ventolin inhaler regularly for periods of breathlessness resulting from worsening asthma, which also made climbing stairs more difficult. Unfortunately, one of the medications he took to control his heart trouble made his asthma worse. Over the same time period, his wife's situation had also become much worse. She had developed Ménière's disease, which disturbed her sense of balance and so made her liable to fall. She was also losing her sight. Alfred therefore needed to do much more of the housework and received two hours help a week from social services.

Despite his concerns Alfred was able to maintain positive attitudes both to himself and their situation. Financially they were comfortable. He expressed himself as fortunate with his happy married life and proud of his son. However, his Christian faith remained central to his self-presentation and was strongly evident in the written answers he supplied on the self-completion questionnaire when he was eighty-one years. It was an understanding of faith strongly linked to helping others, but he was also critical of the limited amount of charitable work he had done so far.

'Most important for me is' ... "my faith."

'The goal that I would like to accomplish in my life' ... "is to really earn my eternal reward."

'Later when I'm older' ... "I hope to still be fit enough to help others."

'I feel really good' ... "if I have been of use."

'I am afraid of' ... "not living up to my ideals."

'When I compare myself to others' ... "I find I am lacking in so many ways."

Two years later, Alfred's wife went into hospital for surgery. Unfortunately, a tumour was discovered, and so the surgery was more extensive than had been anticipated. Her situation became graver when she subsequently suffered a stroke. She was transferred to the hospital elderly care unit where she remained until her death five months later after enduring several more strokes. We describe Alfred's experience of bereavement in the following chapter.

Ernest Davies had met his wife when he worked as a young man on a farm. Formerly self-employed as a painter and decorator, he continued to do the repairs around the home well into his old age. Always a keen gardener, he also kept two allotments as well as a large back garden. When first interviewed at seventy years of age, Ernest and his wife, who was two years younger, also had one son living with them. Three years later, his son had married, and his wife had also come to live in their home. They lived in a former council house, which they had purchased from the council in the early 1970s.

Ernest's self-esteem was high and based primarily on his activities ("I never stop working", "I'm always on the go"). But he also mentioned the importance to him of his family (his wife, two sons and eight grandchildren) and "doing a lot" for the Deaf Children's Association (one of his sons was profoundly deaf) as well as his Trade Union. His main worries were financial ones: "I'll get by but it's a job to look forward financially."

When interviewed again at eighty-one years of age, his health problems were increasing. He was encountering trouble with shortness of breath when walking on level ground. He had also suffered a 'mild stroke' and had had to cut down on sugar intake due to suspected diabetes. He also had a major fall, which he said had resulted in swollen legs. Nevertheless, he continued to maintain his garden and allotments. He was avoiding depression and maintained a high self-esteem based on the same pattern of activities as ten years earlier. At eighty-three years, he wrote back to us:

'I'm best at' ... *"painting, gardening and have three plots."*

'I intend to' ... *"keep my allotments going – it gives me something to go out of the house."*

He said he was "proud" of his sons and was particularly "happy" when his two granddaughters came to see him. However, he acknowledged that his life was changing.

'It's hard for me' ... *"to accept I am starting to feel my age."*

We continue the account of Ernest's life as he became increasingly frail in Chapter 8.

When first interviewed at seventy-six years, **Cyril Steel** was still an active man, particularly engaged with his local bowling club. He visited it two to three times a week and helped with the maintenance of the green in summer. He also went regularly into town and took yearly holidays. He and his wife had one son and two grandchildren who lived nearby. His only health concern at this stage involved his eyes, which he said were "going." His self-esteem ascriptions were entirely positive, his usefulness based on the help he gave to his wife and "keeping the bowling green in good order." He accepted though that he was "slower physically" and said that his future depended on "keeping mobile and independent."

Unfortunately, Cyril's good health was not to last. Only one year later, his life was considerably changed. He no longer went out, even giving up his participation in the bowls club, because of cataracts in his eyes. He was markedly depressed, admitting to feeling 'miserable and sad' as well as 'irritable'. He said that he felt that life had lost its meaning. His self-esteem had also declined. He attributed his loss of a sense of usefulness to his inability "to do work because of the loss of sight." He had no longer any sense of aims in his life and to questions on the future commented in depressed terms that "there is not much future for anybody at my time of life."

The only reason for this rapid mental decline evident from our questionnaire evidence collected at the time is his declining vision due to the forming of cataracts. His and his wife's financial situation was 'comfortable'. They owned their house and had the benefits of an additional occupational pension from his previous work as an aircraft engineer. A year later, he was yet more negative about himself, denying he was important to anyone and commenting that "a lot of people have written me off." Again he expressed little hope in the future, stating "for what? I'm near the end of my life."

In fact Cyril was to live another twelve years. In retrospect, it seems a pity that neither his depression nor cataracts received treatment in this crucial period of his life. Eventually, four years later, he did receive operations for cataracts when he was aged eighty-two and again at eighty-five years, but by then, his health had taken a dramatic change for the worse. When he was eighty, he suffered a major stroke that left him almost completely immobile, incontinent, housebound and wholly dependent on his wife for the remaining years he lived. We continue an account of his life in this frail state in Chapter 8.

Meaning in the lives of our ageing married women

As with the married men, nearly all of the older women in our sample who were still married in their later seventies reported long-lasting and satisfying marriages. The main exception – Elsie Darby – had only recently remarried for the third time at seventy-five years of age, following the death of her second husband, and she was clearly less than perfectly content with her decision.

There is less to write about our older married women's lives for the simple reason that by the later stages of ageing, fewer had their husbands living, and of those ten women who were married, only one was not bereaved within a few years. As with the married men, we have tried to distinguish among them according to their principal sources of self and meaning in their later seventies. Surprisingly, perhaps, more of our older married women than men displayed strong interests outside of the home and immediate family. Given that most of these women would have to spend much of their future life alone this could be understood as adaptive behaviour on their part. However, we begin, as with the men, with those women more exclusively committed to their husbands and close family.

Four family women

Emma Lawson's family was the largest in our sample, comprising seven children, twenty-three grandchildren and numerous great-grandchildren by the time of our last interview with her. Her husband, a cook by original profession, had been disabled as a result of an accident at work in his early forties. This had resulted in a substantial reduction in their income. He had taken on various types of work to support the family, latterly as a storekeeper, continuing until he was seventy-two years old. Emma and he lived in a council house together with one son. Her self-ascriptions in her late sixties were for the most part positive and largely based on family relationships. Her aims ("to have great-grandchildren"; "to celebrate our golden wedding anniversary"), her sense of usefulness and importance ("the family all come with their worries for help and advice") and her enjoyment ("the family helps me enjoy life", "I took my granddaughter window shopping yesterday") all reflected the centrality of the family to her life. At age sixty-nine, she and her husband visited one of their sons in Australia. She told us later on in the study that her children and grandchildren had kept her busy and young throughout her life:

I had no idea what being old was... when he [her youngest son] was five, I had my grandchildren start coming... so I've always had somebody to keep me young and make me feel young.

Emma's life appeared relatively stable until her husband's death ten years later, shortly after celebrating their sixtieth wedding anniversary. Her enjoyments and sense of importance remained firmly family oriented, although she showed some slight decline in her sense of usefulness as she grew older, which she attributed to having less responsibility for caring for children. However, their eldest son was still living with them at the time of her husband's death. We continue her life story post-bereavement in the following chapter.

Dora Meadows was the one example of a woman in our case study group who benefitted, as many of the men did, from a long unbroken marriage until her death, even though her husband was five years older than she. They described themselves as financially 'comfortably off', owning their own home and receiving additional income to the state pension. They had three children, two of whom lived within easy travelling distance and one in South Africa. All were supportive of their parents.

Although Dora maintained relatively good physical health as she aged, she developed some disabling mental health problems that persisted until the end of her life. When first interviewed at age seventy-six she scored highly on the depression index, indicating that she suffered from panic feelings, felt anxious when she went out of the house on her own and sometimes had weeping spells. Her family assisted her in this situation. Either her daughter or son visited daily and helped her with shopping. However, her symptoms of agoraphobia (this seems to have been a family trait because her sister suffered from the same problems) increased over the next ten years. She became unable to walk even relatively short distances (less than one hundred yards) outside, and therefore could not visit friends or attend social functions. She received treatment for these problems at age eighty-seven years and by age eighty-nine the symptoms of depression had lessened. She was now taking antidepressants as well as tranquillizers. But her tendency to anxiety was still disabling:

I begin to feel: 'oh dear, I've got to go out. Oh dear, somebody's coming to see me', sort of 'oh deary' all the time... I get terribly worried. I get in such a state, I think what's wrong with me, I'm going to die soon or things like that.

Nevertheless throughout this period, Dora's self-esteem remained high. Her family – and to some lesser extent her friends – were the main sources of her well-being. They provided enjoyment and comfort and made her feel important; her aims in life were centred around their health and well-being. She was able to cope with the housework and cooking. At age seventy-nine, she said that her main purpose was to "look after my husband, keep my family and have good health." Even as her symptoms of agoraphobia increased through her eighties, her self-esteem did not decline. This was probably because her family situation, which she valued so highly, remained stable, and she was able to continue contributing within the home. She gave especial praise to her "kind husband", and it was obviously important to her that she could also continue to look after his well-being through cooking and caring for him in various ways.

At age eighty-nine, she indicated her wish to carry on as before in the answers she provided on the hand written questionnaire she returned to us.

'Later when I'm older'... "I still hope to carry on with everyday chores."

Her happiness was gained from:

Seeing my two daughters coming every day and doing what they can for me in the garden, shopping, one thing or another and . . . being with my husband all these years counts for a lot.

Her advice to others regarding dealing with health stresses was:

To try and cope as best you can . . . find out what's wrong with you and try and fight it . . . I'm trying to fight it, but it's difficult sometimes at my age to fight all these things, but I think as the years go on you are able to cope more.

Above all, Dora remained involved:

When we receive letters from my daughter in South Africa, it brightens me up quite a bit and I enjoy very much writing to her, telling her all the family news twice a week and I'm able to fill two foolscap papers.

She also remained in touch with the world at large through her knitting:

I knit for the Red Cross. I knit two more fashion scarves . . . And I knit cot blankets . . . always for the Red Cross . . . And that acts like a therapy.

Dora's husband provided the support she needed at home, and as they became older, their daughters came in regularly to do the gardening and shopping. Right to the end of her life, her aims in life centred around her husband's well-being and that of her three children's families. When asked about feeling lonely, she said she "never" felt lonely. She appreciated the benefits her family brought her:

When I compare myself to others . . . I am very lucky compared to some poor souls.

Her resilience in the face of the eventual death of her husband was never tested, because she died in the following year at age ninety years.

In her conversations with us, **Emily Shields** reflected much on both her past and present life. Born in Aberdeen, she had been sad to leave when her father decided to move south for the benefit of her mother's health. By then Emily was already established at work in the Scottish Civil Service, and she described how much she had missed the rich social and cultural life of Aberdeen on coming to Southampton. Her life improved after she met her husband, a policeman, who had also been transplanted from his native Northern Irish culture. They married late, when Emily was thirty-five years old, initially lived in rented accommodation, but were able to buy their own house eight years later after her father died. Her mother then came to live with them until her death. They had three children.

Emily was one of the few married women in our sample to comment in detail on her relationship with her husband (who was also part of our original study). Whereas Emily was quiet, her husband was "exuberant."

... it didn't matter what Brendan did, it was noisy. He had an aura of noise around him if you know what I mean. You always knew he was about when he came in and everything was so quiet afterwards you know, it wasn't that he shouted about or anything, it was just he had this noisiness about him.

Nevertheless, Emily felt that she and her husband complemented each other well and their marriage was successful despite his busy working life in the CID (Criminal Investigation Department), which meant that she "never knew where he was, where he was going, when he was coming back, when he was going out."

Their life changed again after her husband retired at fifty-five years, and they realized they needed another source of income. They decided to try pub work and Emily underwent training, but because Brendan had started drinking heavily, they changed their mind, and Emily sought work at a newly opened ten-pin bowling rink. When first interviewed in her later sixties, she was still working part time there. Problems with arthritic hips had led to a replacement operation on one, and she was waiting for another. Her self-esteem was largely based on contributions to her family. At that time, her daughter and grandchildren were living with them while the daughter's husband was working abroad for five years, and the family was seeking to re-establish their home in Southampton. But there was also a significant element of strongly felt inner conviction in her self-ascriptions as she described her self-confidence, her aims and plans for the future, and her enjoyment of music, books and dramatic productions.

Her life remained stable over the next ten years. She stopped work when she was seventy-five years old but remained healthy and active, her hips appearing to cause her no further problems. Deterioration in her husband's health, however, began to limit their travelling, which they used to enjoy. Emily described how she coped with life's problems by just taking things as they came. Facing up to things and working out a solution, she said, was a therapeutic activity in itself. By contrast, her husband got caught up in worrying about the worry.

In the handwritten ascriptions she sent to us at this time, at age seventy-seven (three years before her husband's death), family themes continued to predominate as providing central meaning to her life. She was proud of her three children and grandchildren, felt really good when her "family has enjoyed themselves on a visit", and believed that she could "still be of use to her family." A new theme that was emerging, however, was a hope that she would continue "to be independent and to keep in good health" and that she would "never become a burden on others in my declining years." Nevertheless, she remained "optimistic", wanted to travel more, and was considering further work in the garden. We describe her adjustment to bereavement in the following chapter.

Rita Fletcher was the youngest member of our sample when first interviewed at age sixty-four years. She was living with her husband, aged sixty-nine years, who had worked as an office clerk, in a detached house overlooking the river. They had one son and three grandchildren with whom they were in close contact. The house, which was in need of modernization and repairs, was rented from a private landlord, and they received both rent and rate rebates to help with the costs. In later interviews, Rita was to tell us about previous tragedies in her life, including the death of a fiancé in the Second World War and the loss of a four-month-old baby.

Rita's life in her sixties revolved around caring for her mother, who lived nearby and was going blind in one eye, as well as her husband, who was also gradually losing his sight. Two years later, she was having to do all the cooking, housework and shopping without assistance, as well as all of the gardening and some of the maintenance. She described her husband as having become 'very touchy', frustrated by his lack of sight, and this was making life more difficult for her. Her husband, she said, had "depressed the real devil out of me." Over the first three years of interviewing, her depression score increased. She admitted readily to 'feeling miserable and sad' and 'wondering if life was worthwhile'.

She displayed a relatively low level of self-esteem with little expressed enjoyment in her life or hopes for the future. However, she felt capable doing the housework and looking after her mother and had confidence in herself. She described herself as "not frightened of stating her opinions" and "the moving force in the family" who "had to push husband." Her aims were to continue looking after her mother and husband.

When interviewed again eight years later, both Rita's husband and mother had died, and Rita had suffered a severe grief reaction as a consequence. We take up her story again in the next chapter.

A close couple

Doris Iveson and her husband had not had children but had built a close relationship together. They had moved house a lot during their married life, from London to Wales and then along the south coast. Even in Southampton, they had lived at several addresses. When first interviewed, Doris was aged seventy and her husband seventy-five. Their present small semi-detached council house was not ideal for an ageing couple in that the bathroom and toilet were added downstairs on the back of the kitchen. Doris's husband had worked as an accountancy manager at a local department store, which had earned him a small occupational pension that supplemented their state pension. Doris herself had not worked outside the home.

In her youth, Doris had been an extremely good competitive swimmer and was proud to display various medals she had won. She had also featured in a film on British women in sport. However, by age seventy, she was becoming increasingly incapacitated by arthritis and two years later was not able to walk as far as a mile. At seventy-one years, she fell down in a busy street when her knees simply "gave way." In the same year, her depression rating increased substantially, probably as a result of both her and her husband's health problems (he also had fallen over and lost consciousness). Doris was also worried about an extension being built onto the rear of the house next door, which she feared would block light to her home. She wanted to move and had in fact applied for a council flat on the basis that her bad knees made life difficult living in a house.

Doris's increasing disability gave her cause for concern for the future, but she still expressed enjoyment in swimming, as well as knitting and sewing. Her life was centred on the home and her husband. However, they had little or no social life, making only a few visits to friends and relatives. The 'Rheumatism Club' that Doris attended was the most important feature of her life outside the home. Despite her health problems and depressed mood, Doris's self-esteem remained high in her early seventies, related to her own importance to her husband, her domestic ability and other activities.

But by seventy-nine years – in the year before her husband died – her mobility was very constrained, and she had become more or less housebound. She was no longer able to cope with all the household chores and relied on a combination of outside helpers to cope. The deterioration was due to various health problems. She had been suffering from anaemia and angina since having a heart attack in her mid-seventies. She also had a hiatus hernia and declining sight as a result of cataracts. Her depression score increased again, now including psychological symptoms as pessimist ideas and difficulties in collecting her thoughts. Her self-esteem had also declined (she replied positively to only three items) and was maintained principally by her sense of importance to her husband. However, she was worried about his fragile health. We continue with an account of her life after his death in the following chapter.

Six women with strong outside interests

As we have already noted, more of our older married women, compared with the men, had developed strong outside interests beyond family life. These mainly related to social activities in their local neighbourhood but also included involvement in churches and other social organizations.

Irene Monroe had worked when younger as a nurse and had also qualified as a chiropodist. But her identity had long been rooted in her religious faith. From their early married life, she and her husband had determined to live their Christian vocation, making the choice to live on a council estate to help others. She had given birth to twin daughters, one of whom died at forty-two years of age when Irene was seventy-one, after many years' health problems resulting from the emergence of a brain tumour in her late twenties. She had died shortly after giving birth to a child of her own. Irene described her daughter's death as "the biggest tragedy of my life" and had been determined to live until the child reached adulthood. In addition, she had two other grandchildren.

When we first interviewed Irene at age seventy-seven years both she and her husband were in declining health. She suffered from heart disease, which limited her abilities, but she remained active in her local Church of England parish. Her faith was the most prominent source of illustration for her self-esteem ascriptions, alongside her caring activities for her daughter's family and for her own husband, for whom she said she had become "essential." They had recently moved house and appeared to be economically secure, but her declining health and the growing stress of caring for her husband seemed to be causing Irene depressive symptoms. Her self-esteem also diminished in the period leading to her husband's death two years later. She said that she had "relinquished much due to heart trouble", no longer 'counted' because she "could not do the things I used to do", and felt that she "sometimes let my husband get me down." But her self-esteem continued to be sustained by her faith, getting enjoyment from "studying spiritual things" and facing the future with confidence by "looking to the hereafter."

It was eight years before we interviewed Irene again. In the meantime, her husband had died (shortly after our last interview), and her own health had deteriorated. She initially moved to a warden-assisted flat but at age eighty-seven transferred to a private residential home. The combination of angina with an arthritic condition had become so severe that she found it difficult to move at times. We take up her case again in Chapter 7.

Eva Chester had been born in Hungary and employed as a nurse there before coming to Britain to work as a housekeeper for a doctor's family. She met her future husband (also a member of our initial study) on a trip to Paris. He worked as a power-station manager but had retired by the time of our first interview. They agreed that they were 'comfortably off' and enjoyed an active retirement, sharing the household tasks and a busy social life. They had not been able to have children. In her later sixties, Eva was still doing voluntary work for the Red Cross as well as attending social clubs and societies two or three times a week. She had few health problems and regarded these years as the best of her life.

She had a strong sense of self-esteem. She enjoyed the many activities she engaged in and liked the neighbourhood in which she lived. She felt important because of her relationship with her husband. But most of all, she said she had cultivated the ability to enjoy the "small things" life brought her, such as "reading, having a new dress or gardening." She was hoping for opportunities for new activities and especially wished to travel more. She hoped that neither she nor her husband would "outlive the other" and commented that "God will take care of us." A member of the Roman Catholic Church, she attended mass regularly and commented that religion had come to mean more to her than when she was younger.

When interviewed some years later at age seventy-six, just before her husband died, her life had changed relatively little. She remained involved with her Red Cross work and kept occupied at home "with letter writing, reading, teaching Hungarian and baking." Her network of social relationships seemed to some extent to compensate for the fact that most of her relatives still lived in Hungary. She remained in close contact with Hungarians in the locality who had come to Britain as refugees after the 1956 uprising against control by the Soviet Union. Her self-esteem was still high, and her attitudes to life positive.

Marjory Evans and her husband also enjoyed an active social life after retirement, including belonging to a singing group. They were living in a pleasant bungalow, which they rented privately on the outskirts of the city. Marjory's self-esteem ascriptions were almost entirely positive in the first three years of interview, focused on her husband, her two sons' families and looking after her own house, but also stressing her involvement helping others in the neighbourhood. Throughout her later sixties and into her seventies, her health remained good, although she showed a tendency to some depressive symptoms (particularly sleep problems and some restlessness). Nevertheless, she remained an active person. When young, she had trained as a dressmaker and enjoyed making things for fêtes and bazaars, sewing and decorating hats and preparing jams and chutney.

At seventy-eight years, in the year before her husband died, they had a disturbing car accident. Another car collided with the passenger (Marjory's) side of their car whilst her husband was turning right. Marjory was taken to hospital, was very bruised but determined to continue with her daily routine.

I was all bruised, terribly bruised all down and I looked terrible. My face was all grey and when my neighbour came in, she said, 'Oh Marjory', she said, 'oh dear oh dear', and on the next morning, the Saturday, she came in with a lovely walnut cake and I had already made little cakes. I felt awful but I was determined that I would get up and do my cakes 'cause we never had any, 'cause weekends I always done my cakes, so she looked and she said, 'good gracious you been making cakes Marjory, I was going to save you. So John, my husband looked up and said, 'you know what Marjory is, Mary'.

Although this indomitable aspect of Marjory's personality was clearly an asset in regard to many aspects of adjustment to the difficulties of later life, it would prove to be counterproductive when faced with the loss of her husband.

Susan Turner had also had a happy marriage to a retired wood craftsman (a 'silk finisher'), a cosy home, which they had owned since the beginning of their marriage, and a beautiful garden. They had no children. They had worked together in their younger days to create the garden, which they continued to tend carefully. Before her marriage, Susan had, like Marjory, developed skills as a dressmaker and worked as an assistant matron at a university hall of residence, and then later, after her marriage, as a part-time school cleaner. But at age fifty-nine, she had had to stop work to devote her time to nursing her husband who had become unwell with chronic bronchitis. He later also developed diabetes and finally cancer before he died when Susan was seventy-five. She had applied for and received an attendance allowance to help defray the expenses of caring.

When interviewed in her early seventies, her own health was good, but she was clearly suffering somewhat from stress because of the increasing demands of caring for her invalid husband without any outside help. A year after our first interview she underwent mastectomy after discovering a lump on a breast. When interviewed some years later about her reactions to being told that she had a tumour, she said:

Well I was really . . . I was just . . . I can't explain it, I was worried sick . . . I didn't know how it came . . . they said it was stress and worry that I'd had.

Although the greater part of her time and attention was focused on caring for her husband, Susan kept up other interests, especially knitting and dressmaking, and enjoyed baking. Fortunately, she could drive a car, which helped her overcome, to some extent, the restrictions resulting from her husband's ill health. They were thus able to visit relatives occasionally and do the shopping together. She professed herself very happy despite the stresses of caregiving, but regretted especially that she had had to curtail activities within her Methodist church. She had particularly enjoyed singing in the choir. Although religion was still important to her, she felt that she had lost contact with her church community.

Susan's sense of self-esteem was focused on her own abilities, providing care for her husband, but also her other activities around the home and garden and her social contacts outside. However, she showed some decline over the initial years of our interviews, mainly because of her increasing confinement at home. Thus, early on she could say that she got much enjoyment out of life because

I love my home and don't mind looking after my husband as I can make him feel he's wanted – I keep him going.

Two years later on, however, in answer to the same question, she commented that she got little enjoyment out of life because

I'm confined. I would do more if I were able.

Thelma Swinton, like Irene Monroe and Susan Turner, had long been actively involved in her local church, a Baptist church. She was also a highly sociable person visiting and being visited by friends and neighbours 'several times a week'. In addition, she visited elderly people as a member of a charitable organization associated with her church. When first interviewed in her later sixties, her self-esteem was high based on her family (husband, two sons and grandchildren) and friends, as well as her church and charitable activities. Her husband was a retired carpenter who had moved with his wife to Southampton after the war because he thought there would be a lot of work with the recovery of the city after the heavy bombing it had endured. He was a railway enthusiast and had worked since retirement for the volunteer-run 'Watercress Line', the Mid Hants Railway, in Alresford.

Thelma associated her optimism and general outward attitude with her Christian faith.

I get much enjoyment from the Christian Church and a good home and family.

I'm important to others as I visit people and they rely on me.

I have an outward attitude to life – particularly when you are a Christian.

Two years later, although remaining positive, she felt she should be more involved.

I'm not awfully confident – I think I should be doing more.

Thelma encountered some minor health problems in the following years. The most significant was hearing impairment, which was corrected with a hearing aid, but also some tinnitus resulting in a persistent noise in her head. She also experienced some 'giddiness', occasional problems with 'tremors and shakes', as well as some pain in her knees. However, she still remained mobile, 'walking more than a mile a week'.

Her husband died when she was aged seventy-seven years and, as with the previous cases, we describe her adaptation to bereavement in the following chapter.

When we first interviewed **Elsie Darby**, she had in the previous year married again for the third time at age seventy-five years. Although marital problems were not referred to in the first three years of interviewing, she did indicate marked symptoms of depression, especially restlessness and irritability, and hardly referred to her husband in her self-ascriptions apart from the fact that he also attended many of the same social activities that she did. They were supported financially only by their state pensions and were living in an apartment that was part of sheltered housing for older people provided by the local city council. There was a warden in residence who could summon help if required.

Throughout her later seventies, Elsie lived an active life, attending social clubs 'four or more times a week', and also visiting friends and relatives. Her own family was a large one. She had three children and one stepchild, fifteen grandchildren and fourteen great-grandchildren. Yet her sense of self revolved principally around her social activities and her contributions to the welfare of others, particularly knitting for those in need of clothing, laying the table at the social clubs and generally "helping old folk." The social clubs also made her feel important because they "depended on" her "quite a lot." She helped out when they were short staffed and liked being involved in the committee. Her aims were also focused on her caring role, "doing what I can to help others" as well as "helping those who can't help themselves." She expanded in considerable detail on her motivation to help others but also on her own inner strength, which allowed her to "persevere with things", "keep on until I get things right." For the future, she still expected "to do lots." Unlike virtually all the other members of our sample with a large family, she made little or no reference to it, apart from a mentioning that she shared a lot of common interests with her husband.

When next interviewed at age eighty-six, she had recently divorced, and there had been a marked decline in her physical health, following a heart attack. She had moved from sheltered accommodation to a residential home, resulting in many of her previous social activities being curtailed. But she was still her positive, optimistic self. In fact, Ellen was to live a long life and in later interviews was able to explain more of her motivations and how they stemmed from her early life experiences. We take up her remarkable story of late-life recovery and resurgence in Chapters 7 and 9.

Concluding comments

As we indicated at the beginning of this chapter, our married participants, at least when interviewed in their later seventies, presented a generally highly positive view of marriage. The same applied to family life and the bonds created with children and grandchildren. The sense of continued belonging, security and mutual comfort was evident in many of these people's accounts as they described the benefits of long lasting marriages. The positive picture of the role of marriage in older people's lives was perhaps stronger in our sample of men than of women. This could be attributed to the men's greater age, and more probable dependency on their spouses in later life. Women's activities, by contrast, were more likely to be limited by their husbands' declining health.

The various benefits marriage and family life brought to older men were strongly illustrated in our male participants' accounts. The sheer delight experienced through the daily and weekly contact with his family members was most graphically described by Ted Jackson. As he said, he could "not help" enjoying life "with a family like mine." As he reviewed his life, he "could not have been happier", despite the difficult earlier parts. Of course, the huge gratitude he expressed stemmed in part from the shocking abandonment he had experienced in his first marriage. He knew what it was to be in a desperate situation, left alone with the care of four children. In return, his children reciprocated strongly what he had done for them. As we shall see in Chapter 8, his positive attitudes would remain as his health and that of his wife declined.

Leonard Johns relied on his wife and family to get through some difficult episodes in his life. He had acquired a nervous vulnerability to stress (perhaps related to his wartime experiences, although he did not talk about them), and he needed the strong guidance that his wife provided and that he accepted as the "driving force" in their marriage. He became greatly depressed in later life after his son's divorce but especially because of a disturbing dispute with his new neighbours over noise after he and his wife had taken care to prepare for themselves a comfortable retirement. Without his wife and daughter's support (which are described further in Chapter 8), he would probably not have survived his depressive collapse so well. Dennis Wilcox was also sustained by his wife as both his and his wife's health declined and one daughter died. His self-esteem also lowered. He became critical of his life's achievements but was sustained by his marriage – "one thing I've done right" – and his children's achievements. He was concerned that his wife would pre-decease him, which as we shall see in Chapter 8 proved justified.

A number of the other men also reiterated how important their wives were to them. Ralph Hodgkin all his life had relied very much on his own judgement, but his wife was his one true partner. He said he had no other real friends left. As we shall see in Chapter 8, his wife was to be by far his major support after a major injury put paid to his previously active life. George Rowan's life was similarly closely intertwined with that of his wife. Their late marriage and its underpinning romantic story made them apparently inseparable. But his wife's earlier decline and death meant that he rather than she would eventually have to live without the other.

Our older women's experience of married life was different from the men's because it was they who were generally expected to live longer and to care for their husband in his final period of life. Of our female case studies, only Dora Meadows benefitted from companionship with and support from her husband until she died. This was an important factor in enabling her to maintain high self-esteem despite a disabling mental health problem. Moreover, although our married women also reported for the most part happy marriages, a number clearly came to be restricted in their own activities by their husbands' ill health and the need to care for and remain at home with them, particularly Irene Monroe and Susan Turner. They as well as others, most clearly in the case of Elsie Darby, were to gain a new lease of life once they were free of these restrictions, however much they might continue to miss their husbands. This heavy demand on caring for older husbands, sometimes for many years, and the likely damaging effect on women's own physical and mental health, was also evident in some of our male cases, notably that of Cyril Steel. However, support from children could be an important ameliorating factor on the stress of spousal caregiving, and this issue is discussed in detail in Chapters 7 and 8.

Perhaps it should not be a surprise that older marriages tend to be happy marriages. After all, both partners will have survived earlier problems and are more likely to have come to terms with stresses and difficulties in their partnership. This is not to say that there were no signs of continuing negativity. Both Mr and Mrs Wilcox and Mr and Mrs Johnson admitted that they still annoyed one another, but that did not mean that they were not deeply attached. Thomas Johnson is a particularly interesting case because in the course of our longitudinal study, he became increasingly involved with his wife, children and grandchildren. A previous life at sea and different interests meant that they had lived quite separately much of the married lives even past retirement age, as Thomas had insisted on keeping working as long as he could. But by the end of his life, his primary concern was for his family and particularly his wife's health and how she would manage without him. His story is a good illustration of a general phenomenon we observed in our larger sample of men and women's sense of self becoming more focused on family as they aged through their eighties (Coleman, Ivani-Chalian and Robinson, 1993).

The other side of being a "happy couple", as Thomas referred to himself and his wife, is the inevitable suffering that comes with separation by death. Those whose lives were so exclusively focused on their spouse, and especially those without children, such as Doris Iveson and George Rowan, would seem to be more likely to be vulnerable to extreme grief reactions and failure to adapt to a life alone. However, this was not always the case as the next chapter demonstrates.

5   Adaptation to loss of spouse

Bereavement has remained a neglected aspect of the study of ageing, even as its significance in later life has increased. In economically prosperous societies with high standards of health care throughout life, bereavement of spouse has become more concentrated among the older part of the population. Nevertheless, there is a widespread assumption that adjustment to bereavement becomes easier with age. In some respects, this may be true – older couples have had longer to prepare for the inevitability of death – however, it is insufficiently acknowledged that the loss of a partner, particularly someone who has shared most of one's life experiences, is probably the most crucial blow to identity and quality of life that people receive in their lifetime. It is hard to imagine recovering an equivalent relationship. Bereavement of spouse thus becomes a major contributor to loneliness and depression in late life.

For many older people, the experience of ageing involves learning to live alone after many years of living together. Some of those currently old may never have lived alone in their lives, having moved as a young adult from living with parents to living with spouse. Even after the initial period of adaptation, there is a long process of learning to be undergone, not only learning of new skills but finding new ways to motivate oneself to continue to be active, to undertake tasks that previously were more externally driven. Circumstances of course vary greatly between bereaved individuals; but for current generations of older women and men in whom gender-role differentiation was more marked, women often have to learn to cope with financial matters and practical repairs, men with housework and food preparation. But more important – and more demanding of inner psychological resources – is finding a new focus in life, or maintaining a previous one on one's own, after years of being together in partnership.

Our case studies provided a rare opportunity to investigate spousal bereavement longitudinally. Qualitative studies of spousal bereavement typically begin after death and lack a comparable depiction of the person while their husband or wife was still alive. Taken as a whole, our interviews confirmed that the death of spouse in later life was experienced as one of the major losses our participants had encountered in their lives. For most them, it was also an experience that they had not been able to prepare for in advance. In the accounts that follow, we attempt to describe the process of adaptation in the participants' own words. These interviews were conducted sometimes only a few months after their spouses' death. In other cases, the interval was longer, sometimes two or more years. In this chapter, we have therefore decided to concentrate on twelve persons, eight women and four men, whom we interviewed both before and generally soon (mostly within the first year) after the death of their spouse. But in the concluding summary, we also mention some of our other participants who provided evidence on their experience of losing their spouse.

All of the twelve case examples, apart from George Rowan who was bereaved at age 93, were in 'early' to 'middle old age', between seventy and eighty-five years, at the time of their spouse's death. Reactions varied. Eight showed marked grief reactions involving evident depressive symptoms, some severe in character. Although most recovered well, the trajectory of recovery varied considerably. Comparing and contrasting the cases highlights factors that help to understand the diversity of response. The first case we present illustrates how an apparent initial positive adjustment can mask unresolved grief. In the subsequent sections, we consider factors that appeared to intensify the experience of grief and those that appeared to promote easier adaptation to the loss of spouse.

Major depression as a consequence of failure to grieve normally

Marjory Evans's husband died suddenly at age eighty-one years when Marjory was seventy-nine. The event was traumatic for her. He died in bed whilst she was making him a hot-water bottle because his feet were cold. We interviewed her a few months later.

I got the bottle and the kettle was just on boiling and I heard 'ehhhuh'... and I flew in the bedroom and he was blue from here down and his tongue was right round there and I thought oh my goodness and I collected myself together and rushed to the phone and phoned my neighbour, phoned my two sons first, my sons said 'dial 999 quick', which I did, 'and we'll be over', and my neighbour was here first. My two sons, my two daughters-in-law, the ambulance and police were in here in 10 minutes and the same ambulance lady... she came out and said 'I'm sorry my love...'

Marjory's bereavement occurred a year after their serious car accident (reported in the last chapter) to which she responded by being very active despite her injuries. At the time of our interview, Marjory was reacting in a similar way to her husband's death, performing more tasks, having taken over all the gardening as well as the housework. She had lost one stone in weight since her husband's death and was seeing her GP every couple of months to monitor this. Her weight loss, she thought, had been exacerbated by a recent dose of food poisoning, which spoiled a holiday she had taken to Jersey. She had chosen Jersey for a holiday because she and her husband had celebrated their wedding anniversary there, in the same hotel, only a month before he died. She did not tell her sons beforehand – they told her later that even their father would not have thought it a good idea – because she had wanted to prove to herself that she could do such things independently. She did consult a doctor while she was away but still tried to cope without drawing attention to her problem.

I wouldn't even let them see it when I went down to the dining table you know. As I said, I didn't go down all the time, I think it was about twice, but I just sat down there and passed it off.

The impact of her husband's death was evident from many of her responses, especially on the written self completion task:

'My life up to now'... *"wonderful up to last November when suddenly I lost my beloved husband after fifty-eight years."*

'It's hard for me'... *"to feel so full of life at times my beloved husband comes to the fore all the time."*

But her depression rating, although raised, did not indicate major depressive symptoms. Also her self-esteem ascriptions were entirely positive, based on her family relationships and sense of continuing confidence in her own abilities. The extreme positivity was evident also in the statements she returned to us:

'I am best at'... *"being a happy disposition trying to help others";*

'Others think I am'... *"marvellous in every way";*

'My weaknesses are'... *"I don't think I have any fortunately."*

Clearly for Marjory, being perceived well by others was of the highest importance:

'My appearance'... *"is first priority."*

Her religious faith also came strongly to the fore in illustrating her confidence in the future in both her verbal and written responses:

"I'm confident I can go on as long as God gives me the faith to go on and I am sure he is."

'When I think about myself'... *"how lucky I am, pray God I stay that way."*

'Later when I'm older'... *"I pray I shall still have the faith and confidence that God has given me."*

Less than a year later, Marjory was admitted to hospital suffering from major depression. She stayed there five weeks in which she received ten treatments with electroconvulsive therapy (ECT), an indication that her depression had not been responding to pharmaceutical treatment. She reflected on how she had come to be so depressed when she spoke to us five years later. She had been told, she said, that she had not grieved properly for her husband:

I was here you see, I was trying and I couldn't get over the loss of John and I wouldn't tell anybody much outside, not even when my friend and I went to town, if we met anybody I'd just say I'd lost my husband. I wouldn't put emphasis on it and the doctor said I should have emptied it all out to people. He said you might depress them, but he said you'll get better and I didn't do it you see, and this depression gradually got worse and worse and the doctors came out there, came over to me and they said 'aren't you any better' you know, come in each day and that in the end one of them said to me, 'I think you'll have to come in'.

When we interviewed Marjory eighteen months after her hospital treatment, she was still showing some marked depressive symptoms, especially regular feelings of sadness and discomfort, and she remained on antidepressant treatment. Nevertheless, she was succeeding in getting back to her busy social life, and enjoyed "entertaining my many friends." Her "two caring sons" became the most meaningful aspects of her life. They visited her every day Monday to Friday, both of them coming on a Friday. She wrote to us that she was sustained by "doing all the things my dear husband would have done" and by her "faith and prayers."

Although continuing to suffer from depression, Marjory maintained the strong sense of self-esteem that was apparent after her husband's death and even after her hospital treatment for depression. Two years later, she referred to her capabilities in looking after herself and self-confidence in living an independent lifestyle. In her written self-descriptions she posted to us on this occasion, various themes were discernible, which were consistent with the statements she had made about herself in previous years. Firstly, there was the importance to Marjory of her home and entertaining others:

'What parts of life is it most important that you stay in charge of?' ... *"My home, always has been the most important to me to be able to say 'come in, lovely to see you.'*

Together with this was her commitment to her family and friends, and above all to her dead husband:

'What is it about your life that makes you feel most alive?' ... *"Doing all the things my dear husband would have done."*

Finally there was her repeated affirmation of her belief and hope in her Christian faith, her prayers and 'the Bible'.

Three years later when Marjory was eighty-six years old, she was interviewed twice, once each by two of us. Both times she continued to present a positive self-image. The interior bungalow and the garden outside were attractively maintained. Her clothes were smart, and she herself presented with a bright expression and twinkle in her eye. She was still wearing elegant high-heeled shoes and clearly concerned to maintain her appearance. However, she had had two falls in recent years, one tripping over a rug at home and the second one in the street. In the latter one, she was with some younger people when she hurt her wrist (which had to be placed in a sling):

They took me in there (the Tax Office) and they gave me a cup of tea and that . . . they said they would get an ambulance, I said, 'Oh no, I'm not going in ambulance at the hospital, get me a taxi. I didn't want anyone to see me . . . so anyhow I went in the taxi.

The greatest problems she said she experienced were a continuing tendency to anxiety associated with her previous depression, which caused her to shake at times. She was still taking medicines to help her cope. However, the overt depressive symptoms appeared to be considerably reduced.

But a more disturbing new development was threatening her physical health. During the past year, when she had been wearing a low-cut dress, her hairdresser noticed that some scar tissue on her breast had changed (the scar had been associated with septicaemia after the birth of her younger son) and had become "just like an envelope, went like that you know how you seal an envelope up." She advised her to seek medical advice. Marjory did not take notice of this at the time, but the hairdresser persisted:

She said to me afterwards 'have you been yet?' and I said no, not gone yet. Since then when she's come, she said to me 'you know,' she said, 'you're a naughty girl, you ought to have gone in the first place.'

When Marjory eventually went for a biopsy, she was told it was cancerous. Surprisingly, she appeared not to have been terribly worried by the news.

Well, I didn't know what to feel really, I never worry about it now . . . Now it doesn't worry me at all.

She was taking tablets to treat the condition.

I don't think it makes you better but it keeps it from getting worse, this tablet does, it takes you through each day . . . I have to take it when I've had my breakfast, separately with a glass of water and I take it religiously, and on my washing machine beside the larder I've got on there, 'Take your tablet, Marjory, each morning'.

Marjory's self-esteem remained totally positive with a similar pattern of themes to previous years, emphasizing her capabilities and her sociability:

I like to be with people. I'm overjoyed when I go visiting (my family) . . . I've given so much time to people that I know – neighbours appreciate still.

She continued to emphasize her youthfulness:

I know I'm eighty-six but I only feel about 50 . . . I've got enough 'go' in me as my younger days.

A distinctive feature of Marjory's self-presentation throughout our interviews was a preoccupation with the way in which others perceived her. She appeared to go to great lengths not to 'let things show' and tried to hide her 'weaknesses' to the extent that she did not even let herself grieve properly for her husband. It was also important for her to project an image of a competent and caring person.

I don't like any one worrying over me. I will do it all myself.

She realized that her failure to 'let her grief out' when her husband died had been the cause of her problems.

She had an important resource in her two sons, and she was proud of them. They continued to visit her as regularly as before, but she told them to stay with their families at the weekend, and did not want to be dependent on them. She already had ten great-grandchildren. She had the advantage of being well integrated in her neighbourhood and went to eat roast dinner with one neighbour alternate Sundays. The other Sunday, the neighbour came to her. Her doctor, she said, had praised her and wished his other older patients living alone did the same.

Underlying her strong morale was her religious faith. When she spoke about her childhood in Southampton, she remembered especially her grandfather who was a strict member of the Plymouth brethren and would not allow his wife to work on Sunday. Although both his daughter (her mother) and she had not gone to church as adults, Marjory said that her grandfather had given her a strong example of the practice of prayer in private, and prayer had remained important to her throughout her life.

Marjory's grief had continued until our very last interviews with her seven years after her husband's death and two years before her own death. She thought constantly about him:

It doesn't matter what I'm doing you know, it comes in front of me and that. I don't know whether I told you before, like I told my sister-in-law, I think one of these days, I'm going to wake up and find it's all a dream. I know it can't be.

She also continued to have vivid dreams of her husband. He had been such a kind, caring man, who had even cleaned her false teeth for her in the mornings. At our last interview she told us how she found in his clothes a booklet on how to become a Christian. This had given her much comfort. She remembered how he had said to her that he wished he had her faith. Clearly he had wanted to believe and "was on the path."

She died two years later at age eighty-eight years before we could interview her again.

Factors intensifying grief: isolation, poor health, and the continuing impact of previous losses

Some of our other bereaved spouses also suffered from particularly painful and prolonged grief. This could often be attributed to other circumstances in their lives, particularly the absence of other close relationships and the presence of special difficulties in their situation, whether physical or social. Previous experience of bereavement, perhaps unresolved, and other memories of painful episodes in their past life would also play a role in intensifying present grief.

As we described in the last chapter *Doris Iveson's* arthritis and heart problems were greatly limiting her life before her husband's death, and she was already displaying some depressive symptoms. She and her husband had no children and had been closely involved with one another. We interviewed Doris a year after her husband's death. She was now eighty-two years old and in a poor health condition. She was clearly depressed and easily prone to tears.

Yes, I don't know anybody... [crying]... I mean we used to do everything together... it's awful, I'll never get over it... [crying]... never mind, come and we'll have a cup of tea...

Doris explained how she had become even more dependent on the help of others for many things but now had had to assume sole responsibility for her financial affairs. This had given her considerable stress because it used to be her husband's duty. Since a fall in her bedroom earlier in the year, her bedroom has been moved downstairs, and she now rarely went upstairs. To aid her mobility outside the home, she had taken the initiative to buy a sophisticated walking frame with both wheels and brakes. Through the kindness of her home help, she had also acquired a budgie, which appeared to give her some companionship. She also had a couple of friends who, as a group, provided support and assistance to each other. But she had become wary of other contacts, particularly from family, because one of her husband's relatives had been found to be abusing his status and removing property from the home after her husband's death.

Doris's sense of self-esteem had declined further, with sad illustrations to the various negative ascriptions: "I sit alone all day" and "Nothing to look forward to." A few months later, she moved out of her house into a sheltered council flat. The loss of her husband, however, remained irreparable. When asked two years later what had been most meaningful about her life, she replied: "being married to a good man." The significant aspects of her life remained only in her memory. She and her husband had been very close, devoting their lives entirely to each other. There were no children, grandchildren or even nephews and nieces with whom she could communicate and who could provide a greater relevance for her current life. She did not enjoy a good relationship with her sister or with her husband's relatives. As a result, she expressed her feelings about her current life in totally negative terms:

It's a really nice life I've had. That's why I notice it now; it's totally different to what it was before; since my husband died, I've had nothing.

For Doris the sterility of her life alone meant that she regarded only the past as being meaningful. Because she idolized her husband, her time with him continued to provide the focus for her life. Perhaps she had sacrificed her own separate identity in favour of his, and with his death, she had few of her own personal interests to fall back on. Nevertheless, she was content with her past and felt fulfilled in the life she had led, but as a consequence, her present existence was without meaning or purpose. When we next interviewed her, the frailty of her situation was already strongly evident, and we therefore continue her account in Chapter 7.

Harold Rank lost two wives during his lifetime. At age eighty-seven, he began to speak with us about his first wife, who had died of tuberculous meningitis in 1941 when he was thirty-two years old. He spoke of how much he had also loved her, that he still felt for her, that she had been taken away from him suddenly. He became tearful as he talked. Perhaps he had never had the opportunity to grieve for her at the time. Life had been tough during the Second World War. He had been working on the building of spitfires in Southampton and had seen men killed beside him in the factory.

When his second wife developed Alzheimer's disease in her late fifties, at first he would not accept the diagnosis. In retrospect, it had been possible to see that the type of early-onset dementia she incurred was a hereditary condition that had also affected her mother before and was to affect her younger sister later. But at the time, Harold could not understand, and he became greatly frustrated by his wife's increasing disability. For many spouses of persons with dementia, the disease can result in a double experience of bereavement, first of the person one used to know, whose distinctive characteristics have changed, sometimes beyond recognition, and later of actual physical death.

We were able to observe the effect on Harold in the early stages of his wife's illness as we saw him at yearly intervals in the first three years of the project. At our first interview with him aged sixty-nine, things appeared to be going well in his life. The strong sense of self-efficacy he presented was striking. He had solved many problems in his life and appeared as a person who thought he could deal with whatever life threw at him. He proudly commented that nobody "can pull the wool over my eyes." His self-esteem, however, was for the most part based on his family relationships, not only with his wife but also his children, whom he said "think the world of me." He was also proud of his own health as someone who had never had a major illness in his life.

A year later, his self-esteem was still entirely positive, but even more concentrated on his family. Illustrating his sources of enjoyment, he commented that "my wife is my life – and my children" and that his main aim was "to see my wife get better and back to normal", adding that "I've no intention of giving up yet." He also said that his confidence in the future lay in his ability to "to solve all my troubles", undoubtedly a reference to his wife's illness. A year further on, this was one aspect of his self-esteem that had become negative. He expressed 'little hope for the future' and now thought that "my wife will just get worse." His sense of capability and usefulness remained focused on "caring for my wife." But he had given up nearly all his previous other activities, and he had diminished social contacts, as he was now "full-time caretaker of my wife."

The happiness he had expressed on previous occasions had disappeared ("Old age was a happy time until my wife got ill"), and over the two years since his wife's diagnosis, his depression ratings had gradually increased. He now stated that he felt 'miserable and sad', 'got frightened sometimes', 'had weeping spells', 'was restless and irritable' and 'experienced disturbed sleep'. He also said that his memory was "not as good as it was two years ago" because of "preoccupation with my wife." He was increasingly worried about the help he would need in the future. Although not attending church, he appeared to have turned more to religion, perhaps as a solace in his difficulties. Initially he had told us that religion had 'never meant much to him' but now explicitly said that it 'meant more to him than when he was younger'.

Two years later, when he was aged seventy-three, his wife was taken into care, where she lived for another five years. When we next interviewed Harold at age seventy-nine, it was only one year since his wife had died. His own health had deteriorated. He appeared to be quite incapacitated and said he was suffering a great deal of pain from 'trapped nerves'. His depression ratings had increased further, and he no longer felt that life was worth living. Much of his previously high self-esteem had collapsed, leaving only his sense of self-confidence and his importance to his children, who gave him considerable practical support with housework, shopping and gardening. But this was insufficient to prevent his feeling both lonely and isolated. He indicated that he continued to look to his religious faith for support.

The next year, he entered hospital for a hip replacement. However, he was still left with some disability and pain. When we interviewed him a year later at age eighty-two, his inability to carry out previously normal activities weighed heavily on him. He still had the confidence but not the ability to carry out tasks around the house.

I have confidence in myself that is . . . if I got rid of all these aches and pains . . . but as it is . . . I know I'm not likely to do that.

His situation was "damned annoying because I've been an active man." More distressing still was the implication of loss of his independence, which he had always valued so highly.

I haven't coped you see, that's the point, I haven't coped, not without help, and I object to having help.

He was now also preoccupied with the fear that he might have to leave his home. He spoke to the interviewer as if addressing the world around him.

I worry if I've got to go into a home . . . I don't want to do that . . . don't break my heart . . . this is my home and this is where I want to stay.

Above all, he was still grieving the loss of his wife.

I often wish I could . . . go back to what I was like . . . what I was like three years ago . . . no, not three years ago . . . what I was like ten years ago when I had my wife with me and we were together.

His depression rating was high and his self-esteem low. Even the one area that remained intact – his importance to his family – appeared to be in doubt.

Look after your relations, your parents . . . because you only get one lot of parents [sounds very emotional] . . . look after them . . . I don't want to say what I'd like to if you've got that on.

His main aim in life was "to die."

It seemed hard to imagine that Harold could recover from such a low state of morale. The loss of his wife, the increasing sense of isolation, and now the perceived threats to his independence seemed to be cumulatively too much to bear. Yet there were still signs that he retained the strength of purpose that had helped him solve so many problems in the past. He recognized himself that if his physical health were to improve, his self-esteem might recover.

If I got rid of all these aches and pains I will be up again . . . I often wish I could go to bed and wake up and it's all gone and I shall get out of bed and jump and shout out 'Hooray' and go back to what I was like.

But despite his belief in his past ability to overcome difficulties, he felt the problems he now faced were too great.

I've had challenges all my life . . . I always enjoyed a challenge . . . but I can't say this is a challenge . . . I can't say I'm going to challenge this . . . I know I'm not going to get rid of it.

Harold needed help but at the same time seemed reluctant to receive it either from his GP or other services. Offer of assistance was easily seen as a threat to his independence. But there were positive signs in the good relationship he had developed with his home help and his acknowledgement of the importance of having a faith. His grief three years since the death of his wife was profound. He still needed to come to terms with his loss and possibly accept new challenges in life. The continuing story of his adjustment to frailty and recovery from grief and depression is told in Chapter 8.

The full extent of the experience of loss in **Rita Fletcher's** past life only became apparent to us after her husband died three years after our previous interview with her. Her mother also died in the same period, as well as a close friend and neighbour whom Rita found dead unexpectedly as she called at her house. Later, she stated that these three bereavements in close proximity had "sent her over the border" and that she "couldn't take any more." She developed a severe depression for which she was treated in hospital with ECT.

When interviewed again at age seventy-four years, Rita was generally physically fit and active, but symptoms of glaucoma were beginning to disturb her sight. She showed no marked symptoms of depression, and her self-esteem score was higher than before, although she was still indicating doubts about whether she had 'much enjoyment in life' and whether she 'looked to the future with confidence'. Two years on, however, she again became depressed. Her landlord had made major changes to the house, including installing double glazing, which resulted in a lot of stress for Rita. She developed shingles, the after effects of which caused her a lot of pain. Later she was discovered in a state of hypothermia and very depressed. She was admitted again to hospital and given more ECT.

At the time of the interview later in the year when she was seventy-six years old, she had recently fallen over in the garden and injured her left wrist; she was experiencing a slight tremor in the right hand, which she attributed to the ECT. Her depression score, although raised in relation to previous two years, was not high, but she presented to us as very nervous, and easily worked up or distressed over apparently trivial things. She needed a lot of reassurance about her ability to cope alone and was still being visited regularly by the psychogeriatric service. Her son and family were also keeping a close eye on her. Finances remained her main concern, and she was budgeting carefully.

The only thing as I said is money worries me a bit, which I don't have enough because I am not alone there . . . I have to sort it out every week, stamps for this and stamps for that, the television's due next month, we got the stamps all ready for that and me gas is due the 15th . . . I'm very methodical, I have my money on Thursdays and I sort it out and I can manage and I reckon about £20 a week on groceries. And then I have my hair done every Friday . . . that's my bit of luxury I like to have my hair done. So I don't think I work too badly. I never get into debt.

Rita's self-esteem had decreased significantly and seemed to reflect her perception that she was no longer a carer but a dependent herself. In the past, she had attributed her sense of importance to the reliance of others on her, but now her response was negative.

I'm not even asked to babysit now – my son does it for the children now – the next generation.

She was not able to complete the handwritten questionnaire on this occasion, so further self-descriptive material is lacking. We concluded, however, that as long as she was able to physically cope alone, taking pride in her house and her ability to keep it in good order, she would recover her previous sense of self-esteem. She also had the stable support of her family living nearby.

Shortly after this interview, there was a significant new event in Rita's life. She was contacted by a person who had been asked to trace the natural mother of a 54-year-old woman who had been adopted as a baby. Rita was that mother and shortly afterwards met and began establishing a relationship with her daughter. When we interviewed again three years later, she wanted to speak with us about the mixture of emotions that had marked the intervening time. Initially she had been concerned that she would lose her son's respect when he found out that his mother had had an illegitimate child. Instead her son and his family fully accepted his stepsister and her family into their lives with no loss of respect for Rita.

More disturbing, however, were the unhappy memories that were brought to the surface associated with the period when the baby was conceived. For instance, although he was not the father of the child, the death of her fiancé during the war, which Rita had previously cited as being one of the 'tragedies' in her life, happened shortly before her daughter was born.

At the start and after time went on now with this coming up, it's all raked it all up again, you know what I mean. Some of it, murky past, I'd rather it be buried and finished, but ... [a neighbour] understands me because I only talk to [her]. I don't talk to [Rita's son] like that.

However, she was now feeling able to talk openly about her early life, whereas this had previously not been possible. She was also expressing wishes tying her past to her future plans. Her dead fiancé was uppermost in her mind.

I've got his last letter. You wouldn't think that was possible, would you? Well, I have. It's there. I want it in my coffin too when I'm gone. I've asked that they put it in. I hope they will.

Now at the age of nearly eighty, Rita's physical health had remained relatively stable since the last interview. She was starting to experience some weakness in her limbs, she continued to notice the tremor in her right hand, and her eyesight remained a major concern, although it was not noticeably worse. However, her depression score was markedly raised on this occasion, with symptoms of loss of appetite in addition to sleep disturbance, and increased feelings of sadness and being tense. Surprisingly, her self-esteem instead was also raised on this occasion. She seemed to be feeling more important to her family than before and expressed confidence in speaking with people and being in their company. On this occasion, she did return to us the self-completion questionnaire, which indicated the overwhelming importance to her of her family.

'What is it about your life that makes you feel most alive?' . . . *"Seeing the family and going on outings with my daughter."*

'What is it in life that gives your hope?' . . . *"Hope that one day I shall see my mother and all those of the family I have lost."*

The theme of an 'afterlife' was strongly expressed together with her belief in God.

'What do you believe in?' . . . *"God and another life."*

After this interview, we reflected on the significance for her of being reunited with her daughter. Until she had come back into her mother's life, Rita had been obliged to hide a part of her past from her son, his family and her friends. Although she had been able to speak of the death of her fiancé, the circumstances surrounding their relationship had never been fully explained. The suppression of her previous pregnancy must have been particularly disturbing at the time of her second son's death. Now that her daughter had re-entered her life and the truth had been shared with and accepted by her son and his family, she had been able to acknowledge an important part of her life.

Her daughter's reappearance had therefore provided the linkage that was necessary to enable Rita to articulate her full life story. She was now able to speak about elements of her life history that were previously taboo, and in doing so attempt to come to terms with what she described as her "murky past." Her current preoccupation with her memories indicated that she was working through the process of coming to terms with her own life history at an accelerated pace to that which would occur in normal circumstances. Her heightened depression seemed to us to be an outward indication of the inner turmoil that was taking place. We wondered whether she would be able to resolve the struggle.

When we next interviewed Rita two years later, although her mental health was improved, her sight had deteriorated to the extent that she was in considerable danger of going blind. She had also experienced a serious fall. We therefore continue our account of her life in Chapter 7.

A lifelong search for love

For ***Eva Chester*** the death of her husband when she was aged seventy-six years came as a major shock. It was preceded two months earlier by a serious accident in which she fractured a hip and thighbone, which kept her in hospital for three weeks. At the time of the interview a year later, she was "trying to carry on" with her household tasks but was experiencing a high degree of depression. She looked dispirited and reported difficulties in sleeping and starting activities. She had to "force herself" to have an interest in people and her surroundings. With no children, she was reliant on outside help with the garden and the housecleaning.

Her self-esteem was lowered. She felt that she 'did not count anymore'. In the past, she had gained a great deal of self-esteem from her relationship with her husband as well as from her voluntary activities. Now she could neither say that she felt confident nor unsure of herself as her confidence "comes and goes following the death." Nevertheless, she showed signs of recovery. She was getting some enjoyment out of gardening again, feeling capable due to her cooking, and she described her aim in life as "to begin to be interested in the future again." She agreed that she looked to the future with confidence, "hoping for better health and improvement in walking." She had taken the initiative earlier in the year to travel to her native Hungary for additional clinical treatment (physio- and hydrotherapy).

Eva gave a considered picture of herself in the written answers to the self-completion questionnaire she later sent back to us. 'Most important for her' was "to feel in good health and good spirits." 'Hard for her' was "just to look after myself, not having someone to discuss my problems with." She was thinking purposefully about the future again. 'If possible' she would "remain in the house where I live now and be able to keep it as it is now." 'In the next few years' she would "try to make friends." 'Maybe' she could . . . "still be able to travel." She 'liked to dream about' . . . "travel to far away places." After her recent losses, she was seeking actively to reconstruct her life.

When we next interviewed her two years later, Eva's recovery seemed complete. Her depression rating was much lower, and her health generally was improved. She still experienced some pain and stiffness due to the accident she had four years earlier and commented on being short of breath when walking. However, she reported travelling to town more than once a week and being able to walk up to a mile. She spoke about spending her spare time 'gardening and chatting to neighbours' and had been travelling even as far as Australia.

Eva's self-esteem had recovered almost to its high pre-bereavement levels. She felt capable through her housework and also gained enjoyment from the media as well as "playing a game of cards and laughing with her friends." In particular her confidence had returned so that she felt able "to cope with whatever comes in my way." Her recent travels also appeared to give her restored interest in life, derived from the companionship she found on her journeys and from being able to visit new places: "I feel if I'm in good company I come to life – as a result of travelling."

She also revealed herself in the second self-completion questionnaire she sent back to us as a person who derived inspiration from human relationships, involving the giving and receiving of affection. For instance, to the question what 'kind of things she enjoyed doing', she responded "preparing for guests – especially I like baking." For what she 'believed in', she wrote "love, love, love" and to what was 'important' in her life today, "a few faithful friends." What 'made her feel most alive' was "when I am among friends; when I'm alone I like to listen to good music." She also referred to her relationship with her husband as being "the most meaningful" aspect of her life so far. Loss of relationship was also reflected in the one aspect in which her self-esteem had not returned to pre-bereavement levels, namely her feeling that she did 'not count anymore': "I live alone, of course. I don't feel that I belong or am very necessary to anybody." The recent death of her sister had intensified these feelings.

It was at this interview that Eva began to review her life with us. Its theme was her lifelong search for a full-hearted relationship. This had its roots in her early childhood where she did not experience "much of a family life." She described her past voluntary activities for the Red Cross as "the major contribution she had made in life." Indeed she said that she believed her main role in life was "to try to make people happy who allowed [her] to." Since her husband had died, she appeared to have been making a great effort to restore her sense of 'belonging' through forming new and meaningful relationships with others.

My search for love and friendship is perhaps more intense as I haven't got a husband to focus my affection on.

In fact her recent interest in travelling and particularly sea cruises was central to her search.

Because I was rather lonely, I found it very interesting to observe so many people from different parts of the world in one big ship – watch the behavior and watch them in different moods and, of course, my great love of the sea.

She had begun to search for new companions to compensate for the loss of her husband and other close friends. This had led her on one cruise into a romantic relationship from which she had only with difficulty extricated herself when she found herself actively pursued by an older man.

Although her relatives in Hungary had died she had recently found friendship through being contacted by Hungarians that she helped resettle in Britain in the 1950s, which gave her the additional satisfaction of being able to keep in touch with her cultural roots.

More people who I helped in 1956 when there was the uprising in Hungary ... these people who I helped settle in this country, they're coming back now that they are older, they seek my friendship again.

Two years later, when she had reached eighty-three years, we interviewed Eva again, on three occasions. Her health had shown some deterioration. She was experiencing increased problems with breathlessness and also dizziness, which she attributed to angina. Her means of coping was to ask assistance from local people to take her up the hill when she went shopping; she found that she still could make the return journey alone. She had a strong sense that whatever happened, she could "always cope." Her depression rating had not increased. She was still able to maintain her own home with the assistance of a private home help three days a week for cleaning and a gardener to help with the lawns. She continued her active social life with a network of friends in the neighbourhood in which she lived.

A new element in her life had resulted from a change in her allegiance from the Roman Catholic church to a Pentecostal movement in the vicinity of her home. She explained her attachment to this religious group in terms of feeling wanted by them:

The biggest help is that I am included in the activities. Age is never a barrier.

Her relationships with younger people from the group also provided her with a sense of continuity from one generation to another.

I especially appreciate the friendship of younger people [from the church]. It compensates for me not having had a family. I take interest in their progress in life... It gives me a new interest to follow daily life... they have babies, they have studies and exams... most of them are teachers.

She especially liked the genuine approach of these "born-again Christians" who "really cared for one another", although she would have liked them to have more ritual in their religious practice (she found Roman Catholic ritual excessive, however).

Eva's self-esteem was high. She felt 'useful' being able to welcome people to her home "giving them food and smiles." She enjoyed her various activities, gardening, reading, watching TV and listening to the radio. Nevertheless, she remained feeling somewhat lonely and with a sense that she was "not really important to anyone."

The element of life review in Eva's conversations with us continued. She spoke a lot and very positively about her husband, how they had met in Paris, and how she had been lucky to have such an 'understanding' and 'considerate' husband. For example, she remembered how he would say "their loss" if people rejected her. She had come from Hungary to Paris just before the war to learn French but then could not travel back. She went to Lourdes, where she prayed for a husband. She had met him soon afterwards, and felt therefore that she could not turn him down. It seemed that Eva needed to get the love she missed in childhood, where she said she "did not know the love of a true mother." She had not wanted children – perhaps because of this need of hers to be at the centre of attention.

For many years, she said, she had been keeping a diary, which she found not only helped her to reconsider the past but also as a means of expressing herself. She valued it greatly:

To write down my feelings which are my very own. It's nice to look back on happy days and not so happy days – which doesn't seem so important after a few years. I couldn't do without that diary.

A further source of inner strength was derived from reviewing how she coped with past problems, which seemed to help her to look at the present in a positive light.

Definitely – it gives me satisfaction that I was on my own and had to make my own decisions, guide my own destiny.

I look through and am surprised at what I've accomplished. I come to terms with past events – I glide over the nasty things and my sense of humour prevails all the time.

She also had a religious conception of life.

I believe you are helped through life by God. I try to help myself but I feel that someone is directing my life – which is God.

She had loving memories of her husband but had surprised herself by how easily she had adjusted to her loss of him.

Lots of things remind me of him. It was the first time in my life I had somebody whom I had loved and lost and I was surprised I quickly adjusted . . . He had a quick passing . . . a happy long life . . . but my loss it wasn't so big.

Eva seemed to have come far in resolving her striving for love:

My philosophy in life is to be content with what you have got. I think that is most important – to be content and not desire something which is unreachable and just a dream.

She was "ready to accept if I can't fulfil all my plans." But she still enjoyed life.

I think the world is beautiful. I like to see as much as possible of the world and meeting people . . . I love people as you know.

The world is so beautiful. I'm very happy to watch the sea in different moods – the moon over it; the sun rising and the sun setting.

She had even come to terms with the idea of death.

I treat my husband's death as a happy ending. I'm happy myself to be reaching the end of the road of life.

Preparing for an exit from this life. I'm not afraid of death. I'm hoping it's going to be better than this life. We find it difficult to visualize, but in the end we will see it. It's like an adventure – I'm looking forward to it.

Nevertheless, there remained a void to be filled.

I don't dwell on the past – I look to the future but I still feel upset that no one really needs me.

All my life I look for love – I don't find it . . . but I'm contented.

At the time of these interviews, a Hungarian friend had become "very much a part of my life."

He is so alone and men can't take it. I know I give more than I get but I am interested in his life. We are important for each other.

We interviewed Eva once more when she reached eighty-six years. There was little evident change in her health. She was still performing most activities of daily living without help. Her mobility was slightly further reduced because of problems with her heart, but she continued to walk up to a mile a week. Her depression rating remained low, but she was beginning to find occasional difficulty collecting her thoughts "especially when baking." Her close friendship had continued, and her self-esteem remained high. In fact, for the first time since her husband's death, she said that she 'felt of importance to others' because of a close friendship with a male companion. He gave her "something to live for."

I always feel bucked up when my friend comes to see me. A friendly atmosphere makes me cheerful.

She remained optimistic. Although she said that religion did not mean as much now to her as when she was younger, she also said that she was "lucky as God is looking after me."

However, a year later, when she was eighty-seven, Eva experienced a series of minor strokes. We kept in informal contact with her over the following years but did not conduct formal interviews. Social services became involved in her case and considered that she would be in some danger if she remained in her present home, especially because of her use of open fires and electrical equipment. After a meeting with a social worker, Eva decided that she would like to relocate to a flat in a nearby town by the sea. By the following year, she had moved and daily carers were employed to attend to her needs. During the day, she also attended a private residential day facility and was escorted there and back by her carers. She enjoyed their company as well as the regular activities at the day centre, including hair dressing, dancing and social events. Eva celebrated her ninetieth birthday there and was even able to visit Hungary as she had long desired.

Unfortunately, the next year she had a fall at the day centre and broke a hip. She was admitted to hospital but never regained the ability to walk. Placement in a residential home became difficult due to her mental as well as physical deterioration. However, her previous Catholic parish priest who had maintained contact with her over the years was able to arrange a place for her in a nursing home run by parishioners in his new parish. Eva lived there comfortably for a further eighteen months, but her heart had begun to fail and she died peacefully just after her 93rd birthday.

Supportive factors: family, personal beliefs and ongoing commitments

Although the other participants we interviewed both before and after their spouses' deaths incurred less severe grief reactions, bereavement in all cases had a significantly negative effect on their sense of well-being, at least in the short term. It is only in comparison with the preceding cases that it is possible to identify protective factors. The close support of family, especially children, clearly played an important role, as did personal beliefs and continuing ongoing commitments.

The significant role of family is well illustrated in the case of *Emma Lawson*. The loss of her husband weighed heavily for many years, but her family's continuous devoted care secured for her a long and happy old age. Emma's extensive and close family relationships were described in the previous chapter. At the time of her husband's death, a few months after they had celebrated their sixtieth wedding anniversary, her eldest son was still living with her. Emma was then aged seventy-nine years. We visited her two months later. The family had continued to be supportive. For fifteen months after the death, she had two of her sons living with her at the same time. She had learned to take over all the cooking (her husband had been a cook by profession), and the family had bought a microwave oven to help her. She was doing all the housework and shopping. She was encountering some difficulty sorting out her pension arrangements, but a daughter was helping her resolve the issues. Her health problems included arthritic pain in the neck, which was being treated effectively by painkillers, and heart problems for which she had been taking medication for five years. She was beginning to suffer from shortness of breath, which meant that she had to stop a little at intervals even walking on level ground. Also, despite the family's considerable support, which she said had helped to 'cushion' her since her husband's death, her self-esteem was lowered and her depression score was raised as a result of increased sleep disturbance. Nevertheless, despite her recent bereavement, she partially completed and sent back to us the written self-completion questionnaire, which demonstrated the great significance her family had in her life. Her goal she wrote was that "my family has a full and happy life as I and my husband did."

Emma succeeded in visiting her son's family in Australia a year after the bereavement but was greatly saddened by the death of another son, her eldest, who was living with her at the time, a few months later. As with her husband's death, she did not have the opportunity to 'say goodbye' to him, which caused her added grief. Because her son had bought the house under the 'right to buy', Emma had now inherited her home. Another of her sons whose marriage had broken down then came to live with her.

When interviewed a year later at age eighty-two years, Emma showed more depressive symptoms. She reported herself being weary of life at times, with reduced sleep and appetite, and looked somewhat dispirited; she admitted to suffering from depression over the preceding years, which she attributed to the death of both her husband and her son. She was also beginning to encounter problems with weakness and pains in her joints, including her arms, knees and feet.

Her self-esteem was somewhat diminished but still solidly based on her family, her usefulness to them, her enjoyment both of her children and grand-children and her plans to visit Australia again and see the 'first Australian baby'. She now had twenty-four grandchildren and fourteen great-grandchildren with one more expected soon. She spoke to us directly about the importance to her of her family.

The family. It's the most important thing I've done. They've turned out marvellous, they haven't all made a load of money, but they have all turned out good. I've had no bad ones in amongst them.

Her responses on the written self-completion questions also highlighted her relationships with her family.

'What is it about your life that makes you feel most alive?'... "Having my great-grandchildren visit me."

'What do you believe in?'... "To help where possible and give plenty of love."

'What has been most meaningful in your life so far'... "Bringing up my family and knowing that they have all been well behaved etc. etc."

At eighty-four years, Emma was for the first time living on her own, her son having bought his own place once his finances had been settled after his divorce. But when interviewed a year later, she was in the process of trying to sell her house as she was planning to live in a 'granny flat' attached to the house of another of her sons. She felt that it was costing too much to satisfactorily maintain the house and that it was too big for her alone. She was excited about the prospect of the move and hoped that as a result, she would have enough money left over to visit Australia yet again (she had visited a second time the previous year). Her son was in the process of getting consent for an extension to his house, and he was able to finance this until his mother sold her own property. She spoke in detail about the plans.

I don't have to wait until it's sold, if the place is built for me I can move in... when I sell the house and I get the money from this house I shall pay him what it cost to have the place put up and then I can say it's my own flat... I shall have an entrance that goes straight into their dining room so I haven't got any stairs to climb or anything like that, that's something to look forward to.

Emma was incurring increasing health problems. Her sight and hearing were beginning to deteriorate, although not enough to worry her. More significantly for her quality of life, her joints, particularly in her hands and knees, were painful, and also her neck gave her a lot of pain at times. She was taking tablets for her arthritis and also 'water tablets' as she was retaining urine but this also had the consequence of sometimes causing her to be incontinent, especially if she was out and took too long to reach a toilet. Her depression score was still quite high, and she remained tearful about the death of her husband.

I very often wake up crying because I never said goodbye to him, that's the only thing.

Nevertheless, her self-esteem remained high, illustrated by her relations with others, neighbours as well as family. She was also looking forward to a better future.

I've got a bright future coming up. I'm going to live with son and his two girls. I will have my own two rooms and bathroom but will eat with the family. Have a lot to look forward to.

We did not interview Emma again, but after her death were given a positive account of the latter part of her life by her son, who with his wife had been her principal carer. In fact, Emma had lived another twelve years with them, dying at age ninety-seven. Throughout she had remained cheerful with a good quality of life. She had liked watching TV, especially the 'soaps', also listening to music and reading. Only in the last two years did her eyesight and hearing become very poor, and as a result she could not get the same enjoyment from life as before. She had a number of hospital admissions to sort out medical problems and in the final year was in a wheelchair. At the end, she had been ready to die, saying to her family, "Dad wants me to be with him."

Fred Hobson's adjustment to the sudden death of his wife when he was aged seventy-seven years was especially remarkable because his health condition was so fragile. He had suffered further heart attacks since his previous interview and was now, a year after his bereavement, experiencing a combination of problems when walking due to his angina, being unsteady and breathless. He had also suffered a stroke in the last year, which had resulted in his being in hospital for a period of three weeks. He had recovered well from the resulting paralysis and speech difficulties, thanks to his own efforts he said, but also, he acknowledged, the strong support from his son and daughter. Nevertheless, it was still striking that he had such a low depression rating, given his poor health and the recent loss of his wife who had previously been his main support. He did indicate 'sometimes having weeping spells' as well as sleeping difficulties in the year after his bereavement, but two years on even these symptoms of grief had disappeared.

Fred's sense of self-esteem, while showing a small dip in the year after the bereavement, had also fully recovered by age eighty. He regarded himself as fully involved in life around him, enjoying outings, meeting people, expressing his opinion, finding things amusing and still being able to perform some activities of daily living, as dressing, making his bed and preparing breakfast. What might have seemed simply a routine existence was for Fred still meaningful. Most important, his family remained central to his existence. His aim he said was to "to know how [his] grandchildren are" and "wanting to see them settled." His religious outlook had also remained an important part of his life, and he was to speak more about this in subsequent years as his frailty became more pronounced (see Chapter 8).

Thelma Swinton was interviewed again after a gap of eight years, but only one year after her husband had died. In the same year, her younger son had divorced and come to live with her for a period of time. She indicated signs of a depressive reaction (increased problems with sleeping and with nervousness) in the year after her bereavement, but these had disappeared at the interview two years later. By then she was aged seventy-nine years. Her self-esteem and morale seemed unaffected by the recent changes in her life. Her health was also relatively good, apart from some tinnitus and hearing impairment, which had been corrected by a hearing aid, and occasional feelings of 'giddiness', which had been alleviated by taking medication. Her main concern was financial because she had no other income than a state pension. This emerged in her answers on the written self-completion questionnaire.

'I'm afraid that' ... *"I might lose my home if a small income runs out now that I am widowed."*

But she was determined to carry on as before.

'I intend' ... *"to keep going in my home as long as health and circumstances allow."*

Thelma acknowledged that in fact she had experienced more freedom since her husband had died and was enjoying various indoor and outdoor activities, including housework and visiting neighbours and friends. She attributed her maintained confidence to her "Christian faith", both in her answers to the self-esteem items at the time of oral interview and also later when she returned the self-completion questionnaire:

"I seldom feel lonely – a Christian faith helps."

In fact she was to live thirteen years in relatively good health after her husband's death, strongly supported by her two sons and their families. At eighty-two years, she was still doing all the housework, cooking and shopping and visiting friends and relatives two or three times a week. She particularly enjoyed reading but also regularly attended a local history society as well as church meetings and took weekly trips to the city centre. She believed that she was 'very active for her age', yet at the same time on her self-ascriptions indicated that she felt she should be doing more.

"I'm trying to think up what I can take up as a new activity."

Otherwise her self-esteem remained high, many of her ascriptions being illustrated by her faith which she said gave her both confidence and enjoyment in life, as well as by her continuing involvement in the life of her family.

Three years later, she continued to have no problems with mobility and caring for herself but was allowing one of her sons to provide help with the gardening. Her self-ascriptions remained similar, related to her sense of competence and her contacts with her family and her church. Her Christian faith in particular gave her a sense of security, and she identified it as the major feature of her life past and present:

"My Christian life, I guess. Definitely important. I've always been a Baptist, for years and years right back in my teens."

She had been attending the same local church for forty years. She attributed her faith to her mother, who had attended Salvation Army meetings and had bravely brought up two children alone and unsupported, after her husband left the home.

Thelma was also proud of her home and its associations with her husband, who was a builder and constructed their first home. Her only significant health problem was with her hearing, but this had been largely overcome with one of the new type of hearing aids. She had also become more satisfied with her somewhat less active life.

"I get much enjoyment out of having a simple life."

Two of us saw Thelma during this year, and although she spoke relatively little, we were both impressed by her smiling, cheerful and unassuming character.

Two years later, at age eighty-seven, Thelma's health had remained almost unchanged. She was still living independently, apart now from receiving Meals

On Wheels on a daily basis. She was going 'to town' as before, once a week accompanied by a cousin, and was walking 'up to a mile a week'. Her sons continued to visit several times a week, and she again she stressed the importance to her of membership in her Baptist church. Her sense of self remained stable. She was peaceful and was never lonely, noting that although 'she liked people, she was also content to be on her own'. She felt thankful for her life and had no worries because her "family would help if need be." She repeated her admiration for her mother who had provided her with a good example, having had "a sad but courageous life."

At age ninety, Thelma fell and needed to spend two months in hospital following a knee replacement, followed by another two months on the elderly care wards. She then moved to a residential home, where she lived for another two years before her death at age ninety-three years.

Some of our participants dealt with bereavement without a religious faith but with a well-considered view of the meaning of life and death. *Emily Shields* was perhaps the best example of such a reasoned attitude. When we interviewed her one year after her bereavement at age eighty years, she explained how her husband had been suffering from cancer for about two years. For the final couple of months, she had chosen to care for him at home with support. She had minimal notice that he was actually dying, and the end seemed very quick to her. The formalities were, she said, the only thing that kept her going after the death. The police welfare organization had also been helpful. However, for a while after his death, she felt very empty. Within the previous six months, she had also been worried about the health of one of her sons who had suffered a pulmonary embolism. Nevertheless, many features of her life had remained the same. She continued to visit friends and also to attend theatre and concerts. Her self-esteem remained high, again largely based on her family and her continuing independence. She repeated twice her wish to 'go back home' – to revisit Scotland and particularly her birthplace of Aberdeen again.

That she had a clearly conceptualized and wide-ranging view of her future life was evident also in the written answer to the self-completion questionnaire she returned to us after this interview. They highlighted her sociability, her family, her independence and activities, her enjoyment of the performing arts and her belief in the future – in young people.

'What is it about your life that makes you feel most alive?' ... *"Mixing with people."*

'Who is important to you in your life today?' ... *"My children and grandchildren."*

'What parts of your life is it most important that you stay in charge of?' ... *"My faculties."*

'What kinds of things do you like working at?' ... *"Organising things."*

'What kinds of things to you enjoy doing?' ... *"Going to theatre. Listening to music. Reading."*

'What is it in your life that gives you hope?' ... *"Young people."*

Two of us interviewed Emily three years later at age eighty-three. She continued to present as an active and independent person well able to look after herself for the most part. At the time of both interviews, her eldest son was living with her while house hunting, as he was taking on a new job teaching at a school not far from Southampton. Her health was good and mobility satisfactory, although she had to take painkillers as a result of a long-standing hip problem. She was able to do the housework and the day-to-day shopping on her own, but to do the bulk of the shopping, she was relying on lifts in her daughter's car. A year earlier, she had been able to fulfil her ambition to revisit Scotland. She and her daughter had taken a two-week motoring holiday visiting Aberdeen and the area where she had spent her early life. In particular, she was delighted to have found her grandfather's grave.

The same year, however, Emily had fallen in the garden and cut her leg badly; more worryingly, she had been unable to summon help. Fortunately, her son and his children happened to be staying at the time, although out for the day:

I slipped on a pebble underneath my foot and I fell face forward between the path and the lawn, and there's an edging to the path of upright stones you know and they slashed my leg open . . . there was no-one in the house . . . I shouted . . . but I couldn't get anyone to hear. I decided to try and get down the path to the patio so that I could try and lift myself on some of the garden furniture you know, but when I was about half way down, sliding down on my bottom . . . one of my grandsons who'd come back from the seaside who went and got his father and I was whisked off to hospital, where I resided for ten days.

She did have an Alarmline that connected her with an emergency control service, but she had not been wearing it at the time. She said that she would not now move without it. She was also employing a gardener to look after the garden.

Emily's self-ascriptions remained largely positive based on her continued independence, involvement with her family, and enjoyment of cultural activities. She was still going regularly to the theatre, ballet and opera. One of her grandsons had come to her recently to ask for information on the police as, like his grandfather, he was thinking of joining. Nevertheless, some elements seemed less positive than before. She no longer had aims in life or looked to the future. She said that she was "just chugging on" and that

I don't look to the future a lot. I'm rather fatalistic. I'll just wait and see what happens.

At the first interview, she reflected on her character:

It's funny how life sort of sorts itself out. It made me very self-sufficient, I never felt lonely, I never do feel lonely you know. I'm quite comfortable in my own company, get a hold of my book and that's it. But it's no trouble to me at all. I never feel lonely . . . I like being here, I like going out in the garden and sitting on my own . . . it's lovely.

At the second interview she also reminisced about her young days in Scotland. She spoke of the 'beautiful white sands' upwards from Aberdeen, how she used to swim from 'Dee to Don' with her friends on Saturday mornings and go dancing in the evening. It had been a good life there, which she had missed when she came to Southampton.

At this interview, she also reflected on how her views on religion had developed when she was young. She had studied the world's various religions and found them interesting, but also saw them as the causes of a lot of conflict. Animal species, she said, did not have religion and fight among themselves as humans did. She had had direct experience of religious division in Northern Ireland. Her husband had been an 'Orangeman' and gone back every year for the parades on the twelfth July. Emily had accompanied him and described vividly the drumming: the sounds, different for each group, but 'like jungle drums', and the sight of the whips beating time on the drums. Her husband had strongly identified as a Protestant (and as a consequence disliked being taken for a Catholic, which often happened). Sectarianism was so ingrained in Northern Ireland, she said, and she had come to the conclusion that 'they should be left to it.'

She described herself as agnostic since she was young, believing she could not know whether there was 'a God guiding the world'. Nevertheless, she had been brought up in the Episcopalian Church of Scotland and still attended and enjoyed the services when she went back to Scotland but did not feel at home in an English church. Her clarity of view in regard to religious matters was striking. The local minister had been taken back when she told him not to pray with her after her husband died as she 'would feel uncomfortable also for him.' Nevertheless, she had brought up her children to go to church, and one son still attended. She claimed no special philosophy or principle of life, "just making the best of it." But she was still curious, still interested in hearing other people's views about religion.

Emily was interviewed again when she was eighty-six and then again at eighty-seven years. She was requiring treatment for detached retinas in both eyes. Waiting for the operation was a particularly anxious period for her as she enjoyed reading so much. Otherwise, her health remained good, apart from some increased problems in mobility, with stiff legs if she stood for too long and difficulties stepping up onto buses. Her main concerns were for her family and particularly that of her elder son. He was still living with her as his marriage had broken up and his wife and children had remained living in the town where he worked before. His older children came to stay part of the time during the school holidays, including Christmas. Sad though it was, Emily seemed to have come to terms with the situation. Another concern was the ownership of her home, which was complicated as it had been left jointly to her and her sister, which meant that if she ever needed to move into a care home, her financial situation would be complicated.

She surprised us by speaking more about missing her husband than she had on previous occasions. She admitted to becoming somewhat depressed on the anniversary of his death every year. It had occurred eight years earlier, but she was still not used to his absence. He had been such a vivid presence in her life.

Nevertheless, her strong sense of self remained, particularly centred on her usefulness and importance to her family. She could cook, clean and mend and 'boss people about if she needed to'. She could manage her own financial affairs well and her expressed confidence in her ability to cope with difficulties was striking.

Nothing troubles me. I could cope if we had another burglary. I don't scare easily.

Compared with the previous interview she was now thinking more positively about her own future, even speaking about her wish to travel to Egypt. 'It was no use looking back'. Rather it was good 'always to have a goal even if it doesn't come to fruition'. 'There was room for surprises', as she had experienced in her recent holiday to Jersey. Age, however, detracted from the value of experience. How good it would be to have 'the body of a twenty-year-old with the acquired knowledge of a person of her age'.

Nevertheless, she wanted to continue the review of her life that she had begun in previous interviews. She talked more about her early life, especially about how she had been unable to pursue medical studies due to poor health when she was young. Her parents had been advised to concentrate on her brothers' education. Clearly this had been a disappointment to her and reflected in the answers she gave to the life attitude inventory she subsequently completed for us as part of a pilot for another research project. 'In achieving life's goals', she said she had not 'felt completely fulfilled'. She also indicated a lack of sense of coherence and direction in her past life, although scoring highly on present sense of personal control and acceptance of death.

She spoke extensively again about her religious education, how she had wanted to become a nun when she was thirteen years old, how she had enjoyed the debates about the meaning of life when she attended the Unitarian church with her friends when she was older. They had broadened her mind. There was so much about traditional Christian beliefs that she could not accept, including belief in life after death. Interestingly, she had encountered a 'near death experience' after a first child was stillborn and the afterbirth became lodged and septic. The experience was most vivid, a feeling she was 'going towards the window', that there was 'someone the other side', a 'tract of water between her and a woman', that this woman 'on seeing her was coming towards her'. She seemed like her deceased mother-in-law. Indeed, the nurses with her at the time had thought that she had died at this moment. The vision had disappeared when the light was put on and she was taken to the operating theatre. Perhaps surprisingly but consistent with her questioning and skeptical frame of mind, this experience, although highly memorable, had not changed Emily's views. She had found it neither pleasant nor unpleasant and 'could not understand what it was all about'.

Unfortunately, we did not interview Emily again, even though she lived another twelve years until age ninety-nine. However, we did obtain a detailed account of her last years from her son, who lived with her throughout this period. He agreed that she had been easy to talk with, a 'wonderful' person whose 'mind never wore out'. She had continued to enjoy going to the theatre for many years, and it was only in the last one to two years that she needed some support in the home from social services. He had some criticism, however, for the health services, which had repeatedly refused a knee operation because of the risk of blood clot that had been noticed at the time of the earlier hip operation. But he thought she would have greatly benefitted from the increased mobility this would have given her. She would have so much liked to have done more in the garden.

Although Marjory Evans had been unwise to so rigorously try and carry on with her life as before, a strong personal agenda could in some cases provide the necessary motivation. This was certainly the case with **Susan Turner**. She did not have children but was part of a large close-knit family with ten surviving brothers and sisters. Her position as the oldest child meant that she had a 'mother' role for her remaining younger siblings with whom she was in regular contact. As was described in the previous chapter, she had been caring for her husband for many years, and his death, when she was aged seventy-five years, was expected. Although still grieving for him when she was next interviewed four years later, she had resolved to benefit from the new opportunities she was given. One of her first major projects, the same year as her husband's death, was to take a trip to Canada to visit relatives whom she had never met. By the time of the interview, she appeared to have adjusted well to her husband's death. She admitted to grieving deeply for some time but now no longer did so.

I don't think he'd wish it, and he used to say to me . . . we did everything together and we were both very happy and kept no secrets, and he said if I go first he said I'll go out of this world a very happy man to know you're provided for.

Learning to manage the finances was a priority task for Susan, and in doing so she tried to follow her husband's example, being methodical and keeping precise records. She took advice from others when reaching important decisions. She decided to use some of her capital to install central heating and managed interest payments to finance planned maintenance on the bungalow. In fact, the need to keep the bungalow in good order seemed to represent a monument to her life with her husband.

We have five thousand [pounds] each, that's how we came by ten thousand. I thought, he wouldn't want his house to go, he was so particular over it and he used to decorate and do everything, one room a year and the outside, and I thought I must keep it up.

Two years before the interview, Susan had given up her car, partly because she wasn't using it and partly because it gave her too many memories of her husband. Interestingly, she continued to think of the money in terms of a fifty-fifty share.

So I thought what money I paid for the car, I can... em lose his share... and I sold it for two thousand five hundred I think, so I got my share back didn't I... I paid five thousand for a little Fiesta.

Indeed, Susan admitted that learning to cope with the finances over this period had been one of her greatest challenges, even more significant than her health. At age eighty-two years, she appeared to be in generally good health. She did have a slight disability in her arm and shoulder associated with her mastectomy, which limited her activity to some extent. Her depression rating was raised but no higher than it had been before her husband's death. Her self-ascriptions were mainly positive, and she appeared proud of how well she had emulated her husband in caring for the house and garden as he would have wished.

However, there were also signs that whilst her ability to preserve the lifestyle and home as a memorial to her husband and their relationship were fundamental aspects in her morale, she had also been able to develop a raison d'être of her own, which may have been able to continue her positive self-esteem even if she was not longer able to maintain the home. Her written answers on many of the sentence completion stems indicated this:

'Maybe I can'... "do something to help others."
'It's hard for me'... "to refuse to help people."
'I plan to'... "do the things I love."
'If possible I would'... "entertain people or friends."
'The goal that I would like to accomplish in my life is'... "to keep happy and well."

Susan showed remarkable resilience in continuing to cope with the challenges that she faced living on her own in the years after her husband's death. At age eighty-three, she underwent what became a major operation for hysterectomy after she had to return to the operating table when the internal sutures collapsed after the removal of her appendix. While she was in hospital, a much-loved sister-in-law died, which caused her considerable distress, and she developed cystitis, hindering her recovery. Then while still in hospital, she fell down in the toilet, breaking her wrist. Visited by one of us at this time, she was happy to speak about her recent experience. She had decided that when she went home, she would accept the help of others in looking after herself and her home and garden. It had been arranged that her sister would come to stay and look after her initially and that later she would accept home help. She had also decided to accept the help of her neighbours with the gardening. It could be understood that she was seeking new ways to ensure the upkeep of her home, which had been a major priority for her since her husband died. Her companions on the ward commented on her tenacity and viewed her kindly.

The recovery was not an easy one, and for a while Susan was not expected by family and lay observers to do well. Two years on, she did not feel well enough to be interviewed but was eager to participate again at the next round three years later. She commented on her recovery:

But do you know it took me two years to get over that [operation].... They told me to take things steady, and I did but I couldn't get my strength back, and so I took what they said, two years easy.... I came straight back here and got on with it... I won my way through, I found I would get stronger, each day I got stronger and you can't beat your Bible can you and your prayers at night.

Now eighty-eight years old, she was still living in her own bungalow and looking after herself with little outside assistance. She was able to walk to the local shopping centre and back, although she relied on a neighbour to do the heavier shopping for her. She even made the journey into the city centre by bus three times a year to go to the Civic Centre to pay her Council Tax.

She did all her own housework, using a timetable of one room every day. She also did some of the lighter work outside, such as pruning the roses in a garden, which she was still proud of. She employed a gardener to do the heavier tasks.

I wouldn't go a bull at a gate like do the house all through, so I thought I've got to, I'm not strong enough that one room a day will be sufficient for me and finish at lunch time. I get up, I have my breakfast, I have Ryvita, three Ryvita with my own home marmalade, I always make my marmalade for the year and then I prepare my lunch, then I do my room or I might to Bitterne, it all depends what I want but I don't make myself go if I don't, no more than necessary because I find the walking a bit much.

She had also continued to carry out maintenance to her property, following in her husband's footsteps. Within the previous few years, she had had the rear fence rebuilt, double glazing installed and more recently had the drive resurfaced with bricks. She decided to have this job done for her own safety after falling on the broken concrete at the end of the drive. She was also making sure that the interior was kept well decorated. She had also taken a decision to sell some of her silverware, which was surplus to her needs and to buy a new automatic washing machine and fridge freezer.

Not surprisingly, her self-ascriptions were largely positive, supported by the examples of her housework and gardening – "I dig the garden if I want to. I still do the housework and polish. I do all my baking and cooking" – and her continuing role in the life of her wider family and with neighbours. Her pleasure in her home was closely associated with memories of her husband:

I've got a lovely home. I'm living with Mr Turner's memories, which make me happy.

Her aims were understandably health related:

To enjoy good health as long as I can. To be given the health and strength to carry on.

However, there was a new element of uncertainty and lack of confidence in her self-ascriptions related to a sense of declining activity and worries about her health. She was especially afraid of falling and 'breaking something'. A recent 'funny turn' had worried her in particular:

I sat here and all the room went round and round, the windows were upside down, everything, I thought I was going to fall out of this chair it was so violent and I didn't like that at all. . . . I thought I'm not going to live until my birthday and I felt so ill, I really did feel ill . . . the next morning I woke up . . . I felt fine.

She consulted her GP after this incident, who explained that it had been the result of high blood pressure. He was reviewing her medication. Another significant health event had been the breaking down of her mastectomy scar during the past year. This had been treated by radiotherapy but remained troublesome. Further close bereavements had also affected her in recent months. One of her supportive neighbours died suddenly in the Post Office. A brother had also died of cancer. Susan was especially upset that although he apparently knew he was terminally ill, he did not forewarn any of his family.

Susan died two years later at age ninety years, but before we were able to interview her again. Her GP's report indicated that she was in the early stages of dementia, and a move into residential care was in the process of being arranged.

Adjustment to successive spousal bereavement in late life

As mentioned in the previous chapter, *Alfred Parker's* wife remained in the long-stay wards of the elderly care unit for five months before her death. In that period, Alfred's life was centred around his wife's well-being with him spending from midday to around 7.00 p.m. with her at the hospital every day. In fact, as he admitted himself he 'overdid' his visits, and on one day in which he had undergone minor surgery on one of his ears, he had to be admitted to the unit himself one evening for an overnight stay.

He agreed to an interview with us during this time. At this interview, he admitted that he was not expecting his wife to recover from her condition, although he did not anticipate that she would die while in hospital but be transferred to a nursing home at some point. Despite the strain, he was experiencing, he still appeared fit and cheerful. His belief in preordination and that life was a prelude to something better meant that he was able to take a pragmatic attitude to his and his wife's circumstances. All the same, he was sad to see his wife in a "vegetative" state but was comforted by the fact that she was so confused that she was unaware of her condition.

His own health now at age eighty-three years was fine. His vision and hearing were good, and he had only slight problems with his mobility. His depression rating was slightly raised because of sleep problems and some other mild symptoms. His son, who was now living even farther away in the north of England, was keeping in contact by telephone, making use of the new technology that allowed easier communication for those with hearing impairment.

In his answers to the questions on self-esteem, Alfred indicated that his continued sense of usefulness was now focused on his ability to help care for his wife. But in other ways, his self-esteem appeared diminished because he was not obtaining any enjoyment from life and could see "no future at the moment." His wife's impending death had given him also a sense of his own mortality.

I've had a good life and am coming to the end of it. There's no point being alive just for the sake of it.

But there appeared to be no self-pity in these responses, merely a statement of his present situation. His Christian perspective on life after death came out both in the interview and in his subsequent answers on the self-completion questionnaire:

"I know that when I am called, that's not the end of me, that's the beginning of things. I'm quite happy about that."

'What is it in your life that gives you hope?' . . . "The belief that there is an after life. Our life on earth is only a trial for things to come."

Despite his current difficulties, Alfred was happy to review his life with us.

For the whole of life, I think I can honestly say that it has been enjoyable. There have been ups and downs, like going back to when our son had meningitis and lost his hearing. That was a horrendous time for twelve months. Otherwise it has been quite a happy, peaceful life. We have been married for goodness knows how many years – never had a quarrel. We don't know the pleasure of making up yet. We have always agreed to disagree. It has been most happy and uneventful in a lot of ways.

He reflected on his beliefs and how they influenced his actions.

'What do you believe in?' . . . "My faith and God. Being true to yourself and helping when you can."

As expected, Alfred made a good adjustment to his wife's death. Two years later, he spoke about it calmly and reflectively.

Quite frankly it was a great sense of relief because I knew she was where she wanted to go, she wasn't afraid to die. She was quite prepared for the life which had been prepared for her. She was no longer suffering, and it was really a great relief and happiness that she was happy and there was no sense of being morbid and worrying about it.

Although he had been lonely from time to time, his deeply held beliefs and pragmatic attitude enabled him to face up to his own continuing needs.

I did put a little bit in the newsletter that we mustn't be sorry for ourselves but happy for her, and people remarked at the requiem [Mass] that I did seem quite happy, not too distressed at all, which was strange enough what I was feeling . . . I was only lonely when I was here on my own, which I was sometimes.

A surprise for us, however, was that by the time of this interview, Alfred had married again. A lifelong friend of both him and his wife (who had been a bridesmaid at their wedding) came to stay to help sort out his wife's clothes, and a close relationship developed. Six months later, they married. At the time of the interview, he was looking remarkably fit and well, and he described himself as "rejuvenated." His new wife shared his Christian commitment, although she belonged to a different denomination (Methodism). They both attended each other's churches and led active social lives centred around them. They also both shared a rekindled active interest in the National Trust, and Alfred organized outings to its properties. Of particular joy to him was his new extended family. His wife had many children and grandchildren from her first marriage, and as the families have been long-time friends, the children on both sides were well known to each other. He and his wife received frequent visits.

His self-esteem was high. His usefulness continued to be illustrated by his church activities, which had increased as he had also become involved in his new wife's church. In his own church, he was now reading the first and second lessons at Mass. The extension of his family life was also something that gave him more reason to enjoy life. Beyond the present existence was also another life.

Even if it's not in this life, there's the next to look forward to. I'm convinced that destiny is being controlled. God is there controlling things.

However, he explained that he was not looking forward to death in the same way as he was before his remarriage. It was not so much that 'his philosophy had changed' but that he had 'so much more to live for now'. He and his wife had just booked a coach-touring holiday of Ireland for the summer.

We interviewed Alfred on three occasions in this year, also to check our account of his life and the basis of his sense of self. He commented favourably on its accuracy. He stressed again how hard it had been to experience the last illness of his first wife and that for him religious belief was essential in coming to terms with suffering and the thought that the person suffering was going to a better place. He had been ready to die himself but now to his surprise had plenty to live for.

It was three years before we visited Alfred again. In that time, his second wife had been diagnosed with Alzheimer's disease and prescribed for a time one of the new anti-dementia medicines but had stopped taking it because of the side effects. A couple of hours before the interview, she had gone out in her slippers to post a letter and had slipped and fallen over. She had wounded her forehead and damaged her glasses. They had been to the surgery to get it dressed. He explained that his wife had had a succession of falls in the recent months. Nevertheless, she seemed alert and in good humour, and he presented the same positive self that he had done at previous interviews, his self-esteem ascriptions illustrated not only by his care for his wife but also their compatibility of interests and enjoyments. He remained optimistic about the future and repeated his belief in what he described as 'predestination'. God was 'in charge' and would 'let him know when his time was up.'

Alfred was interviewed again two years later at age ninety. His wife had died earlier in the year, but he remained serene in his attitudes and displayed a high sense of personal meaning with many sources of interest in his life from his church activities to interests in history and nature preservation. He spoke at length about his religious attitudes. God, he believed, was "looking after us", and if we listened we could receive his advice. He described himself as talking to God every day. As he got older, he felt more strongly God's presence near to him. All that happened to us was "pre-ordained", but we could count on God's support to "bolster us up." So it had been with the death of his wives. Without God he said he "would be nothing." He described himself as praying "constantly" and "usually got a reply" to his questions. He considered that we were "on trial" in this life and how we did here "determined our afterlife." He did not speculate what form that life would be like but thought it would be a "pleasant surprise." He had felt the presence of both his first and second wives after their deaths. He had actually seen his second wife come into the room. Although this had given him a "nice pleasant feeling", he had been "mystified" by the experience. He could not see "what the point" of it was. He was not after all someone who needed 'reassuring evidence' of survival after death.

When we exchanged Christmas greetings later in the year, he wrote that he had "taken the plunge and moved to sheltered accommodation" to be near his son in Yorkshire". He was positive as ever.

It was an effort to leave X . . . road after fifty-three years, but after a week I am almost settled in and find everyone very friendly. My new parish priest called on me the day after I arrived, and my doctor is just across the road within two hundred yards. I hope you enjoy the Christmas break. Kind regards to your team.

Alfred died a year later, two weeks before what would have been his ninety-second birthday. His son wrote to tell us this and that his health had been deteriorating for some weeks with angina and fluid in both lungs that was causing him difficulty in breathing. He knew that his father had been pleased to have been involved in the project, and he had shared the various reports and correspondence that he had received with his son.

Coming to terms with bereavement at an advanced age

Alfred's second wife had died when he was already in his ninetieth year. *George Rowan's* wife died when he was aged ninety-three years. Their lack of children or other close supportive relatives suggested a severe grief reaction was likely even though his wife had been in poor health for some years. When we next interviewed him, she had only just died in hospital of pneumonia a few weeks before. Nevertheless, he wanted to talk to us. He described himself as "heartbroken." He was still in remarkably good health, apart from some loss of hearing, and was carrying out shopping and housework as before, but he had lost incentive.

I can't say I enjoy doing anything at the moment. I still do the odd jobs, and I still am doing them but without enthusiasm. I do them merely because they have to be done. I used to tell my wife I was always doing things for her and that's how I felt. It was a true incentive. That's gone now.

George's grief was profound. It appeared that he and his wife never really fully discussed the implications of the death of one or the other of them, despite some encouragement from their GP. He seemed to be quite unprepared for her death.

It's at the back of one's mind but we never really discussed it. Her doctor mentioned it to her once or twice... about two and a half months ago he said suddenly... 'what would happen to me if something happened to her' and she said deliberately 'he would die of a broken heart'.

He said that the hospital could have done more to communicate the severity of her illness to him. He felt angry that he had not been told of the seriousness of her situation. Indeed, he had been preparing for her return home.

She's not been able to go out anywhere since then, and at Christmas time she had a cough and on the New Year this developed into pneumonia and on the tenth January she went into hospital with pneumonia, which we understood was being effectively treated with antibiotics but apparently was not so and she died on February third. She got very frail indeed while she was in hospital.

The prediction of a severe grief reaction seemed correct. Despite visits from friends who wanted to be helpful, he felt very lonely. His depression score was also high, considering himself "better off dead" and with "no feelings at the moment." He described his outlook as "bleak" and said he could not wait "to get up there with her." Also his self-esteem was diminished, although he retained his confidence and sense of capability. He felt he was coping well in existing from day to day as he believed that this is what his wife would have wished him to do. He was taking sleeping tablets at the time but no other medication. He would appear to be allowing himself to grieve in a healthy manner and expressed a desire to have someone (preferably a woman) with whom he could talk things through. He was especially in need of reassurance that he had acted in his wife's best interests in complying with medical advice during her depressive illness. He feared that medical intervention had done her more harm than good.

Despite the presence of some positive signs, we did not imagine that George would regain his old level of morale. Indeed, there seemed a risk that he might become more dispirited and isolated. Yet, when another of us visited four months later, he was looking much brighter. His house was tidy and in good order, and he was also well dressed and smart. His health was good, he said, apart from the "heartache" he felt. He cried easily, but smiled and regained control of himself quickly. He wanted to reminisce about his life, especially about his wife. He described how he had met his wife: "how lovely" he thought she looked when he first saw her standing in the bank where he worked, within a shaft of dusty sunlight; how they had met again playing tennis; the war years and the train accident of 1945, her resulting serious injuries, and how this led to the three-year delay in their marriage. Their marriage had been one of "tremendous companionship." They used to sit together in the evening, holding hands, watching the sun go down across their back garden. He never wanted to be away from her.

They had benefited, he said, from being "fully formed" characters when they married (an important factor perhaps also in his ability to survive the loss of his wife). He "thanked God" for their happy married life. His religious faith, he said, now meant more to him than before, although he had always believed in the "Good Lord." He was no longer angry about her death at the hospital, but rather grateful that he had been with his wife when she died. Although he no longer enjoyed going out without a purpose, he did go out sometimes with friends and regularly to communion service at the local parish church. But coming home alone was difficult. His wife's ashes were buried in the churchyard. He looked forward to joining her. Although he was still grieving strongly, there were many signs he was leaving depression behind. He said that he looked forward to us visiting again. George was to live another seven active years, and we take up his story again in Chapter 9.

Concluding comments

Besides the twelve persons whom we had begun interviewing from before their spouses' deaths, there were other members of our study sample whom we had interviewed relatively soon after (although not before) their bereavement. In these cases, we could gauge something of the effect their spouses' deaths had had on them. Although these persons will be only properly introduced in the next chapter among those who were living alone from the beginning of our study, we should comment here briefly on the additional evidence they provided on the impact of bereavement.

Mavis Dawes was first interviewed in the year following her husband's death and her move to Southampton to be near her two sons. Her marriage had been troubled as her husband had suffered from mental illness, and she had some difficult memories to contend with. She continued to show somewhat elevated depressive symptoms throughout the first years of the study but expressed herself pleased to have moved to Southampton. Both John Otterbourne and Stuart Murray were also interviewed in the year after their wives died and seemed protected by their Christian faiths, which had grown stronger during the course of their adult lives. Charles Kitchen and Hilda Smith were first interviewed three years after their spouses' death. Both had by then recovered well, although Hilda showed some signs of depression, and Charles's depression score was raised two years later after his son's death. Both, however, seemed protected by their high levels of self-esteem, Charles's based on his active and varied lifestyle and Hilda's by her involvement in her large and devoted family. Other cases were interviewed at too long a distance from their spouse's death to draw any solid conclusions about processes of adjustment.

What in general do our case analyses suggest about adaptation to bereavement in later life? They firstly demonstrate how deep and long lasting the effects can be. Even someone as happy and well supported by her family as Emma Lawson could wake up crying five years later because she had not said goodbye to her husband. Sudden and especially traumatic deaths such as that of Marjory Evans's husband could be especially hard to come to terms with. This is a well-established fact in the bereavement literature, as also the difficulties of the double bereavement over time suffered by those, such as Harold Rank, whose second wife was diagnosed with dementia, and the debilitating effects of poor health evident both in Harold's case and that of Doris Iveson. Rita Fletcher's case, as well as Harold's, also illustrates the impact of long hidden loss and grief on an older person's mental health.

The notion that adjustment to bereavement becomes easier with age does not seem justified. That its long-lasting pain could be demonstrated in a well-adjusted sample of older people with higher levels of family support and religious belief than is likely in the next generations gives food for thought because both these factors clearly promoted adjustment. The positive role of faith in a future life for their loved ones and an eventual reunion was well illustrated in a number of cases, especially with Alfred Parker and Thelma Swinton. However, that a well-thought-out humanistic approach to life may also be sustaining in the face of death was illustrated in the case of Emily Shields, and more comparative study is required (Wilkinson and Coleman, 2010). Her case also illustrates how the pain of bereavement can return years later, however, sometimes unexpectedly.

A more positive conclusion is that bereaved older people can also recover well, even as in Marjory Evans's case after a severely pathological reaction after her attempt to carry on as normal. The most damaging factors in the long run appear to be lack of supportive resources, both external in terms of other sustaining relationships, and internal in the shape of meaningful life goals and aims. Doris Iveson lacked both: in the absence of children of her own, she had devoted all her attention to life with her husband. The great value of such loving partnerships while they last has its counterpart in the pain of eventual separation.

Of course, the main goal of our case studies has been in showing not what is 'normative' behaviour after the death of a loved person but rather what is 'possible' and in suggesting possible explanations for the variety of human responses to bereavement. Marjory's failure to grieve following her husband's death and her attempt to show principally to herself that she could carry on as if nothing had changed in her life had been paralleled the year before in her behaviour after a car accident. It reflected her strong sense of self, which could be beneficial in other circumstances and clearly would be again later in her life as she recovered from depression. But one practical lesson that could be drawn from her case is that some of her reactions could have been predicted by those who knew her well and perhaps even forestalled by closer monitoring of her plans and actions after her husband's death.

Susan Turner shared some of both Marjory's and Doris's characteristics, a previous life that had been based principally on intimate couplehood and a strong wish to continue as before, yet was able to avoid the negative consequences that they suffered. Her purposeful planning of new types of activities and altruistic reaching out to others clearly benefitted her. She kept up the high standards of her house and garden, which she had begun with her husband, but unlike Marjory she also went travelling to new places important to her but unassociated with her husband. Emily Shields and Eva Chester did the same. Of course, Susan, Emily and Eva had the strong sense of self and good health in the years after bereavement to be able to plan a new way of life and to make a success of this, which Doris sadly did not have.

George Rowan's resilience shown in his relatively quick recovery in his nineties from a strong grief reaction was particularly surprising. Should it have been? He lacked other obvious means of support. The absence of family or other friendly support was also against him. Yet the memory of how blessed he had been in his marriage turned out for him to be more of a positive than a negative factor, and he was able to draw on the resources of a Christian faith and hope that had been somewhat hidden from us beforehand. To a degree these same factors also supported Marjory after she had recovered from her depressive illness.

6   Ageing alone

In this chapter, we introduce the fifteen participants in our study who were already living alone when they entered our case study sample in their later seventies. These were predominantly women. In fact only one woman among our twenty-three female cases (Dora Meadows, see Chapter 4) predeceased her husband. In contrast, eight of our seventeen men predeceased their wives. As already mentioned in Chapter 3, all of our participants had been married at some point in their lives. In fact, it is possible to differentiate between them in terms of the period of their life when their spouses died or in a few cases separated from them. A significant minority of our women had begun living alone well before the standard age of retirement, sometimes even in early adulthood.

Widowhood has been a common experience for women in European and other societies, and concern for the financial plight of widows in particular has been a prominent feature of the work of religious bodies in earlier historical periods and for welfare organisations in modern times. Nevertheless, support from children has always been and remains the major resource widowed older people can draw on. But with smaller families and the greater mobility of children, the family has become a declining resource for supporting persons in old age. Our participants, born mainly in the early twentieth century, varied considerably in the size and spread of the families they had generated, and the consequences are evident in the character of their contacts in later life. Some of those ageing alone lived lives that were closely interrelated with that of their children's families and received strong practical as well as emotional support from them after their spouses died. There were others whose lives remained in practical matters at least independent of children or other members of their family.

The greater part of the chapter therefore deals with eleven older women who had been living alone since before age seventy-five years. We consider them in sections according to the period of life in which they lost their husbands. There is a final section on the four older men in our study who had been living alone since their middle to later seventies and whose lives when married we had not been able to consider. In presenting each of these case analyses, we again pay particular attention to the participants' expressed sources of self and meaning, but we also consider how their balance of needs especially between independence and relationship were negotiated with their families and other close friends.

Older women living alone

The women in our sample had started living alone at diverse ages. Eight of our twenty-three women had been widowed or separated before age sixty-five years (six before age sixty years). It might be expected that because they had had to make the adjustment to living without a partner relatively early in the process of ageing, they would experience the challenge of living alone as they became older and frailer differently from married women who had been living at home with a spouse until beyond the normal retirement age. They would have needed to have identified earlier in life ways of sustaining meaning for themselves independently of their spouse and as a result been better prepared for living alone in the later part of life. We begin with the cases of three women who had been living alone since middle adulthood, before considering those who had been widowed before and after retirement age.

Alone since early adulthood

Three of our women had lived without a husband since the end of the Second World War. One of the husbands had been killed in the war. The other two husbands had left their wives early on in the marriage. All three women had been left with young children to care for and so were not strictly living alone at the time of this major change in their life. But they had had to make major adjustments also because of the need to provide effectively for their children as well as themselves. All three women seemed as a consequence to have developed a strong sense of their own ability to cope with challenges and difficulties.

Vera Wright had a degree in chemistry and had worked as a pharmacist both before and after her marriage. She had brought up her two sons alone, after her husband left her for another woman, whom he had met during the war, when Vera was thirty-four years old. Tragically, one of the sons had died young while Vera was still working (she had taken time off work to nurse him in France where he was living at the time). She had only retired a year before our first interview with her when she was sixty-five years old. However, she missed work and had already taken up a new position as a part-time secretary at the local general hospital, which she converted to full time in the following year. At this stage of her life, she was extremely active, caring for her granddaughter at weekends and regularly shopping for her elderly mother. She also participated in a yoga class once a week and attended adult education tailoring classes as well as a retirement club. Although her life circumstances had prevented her from buying a house, she had sufficient income to live comfortably and was able to run a car of her own.

Her self-esteem may have been lowered by the experience of retirement but improved over the first two years of interviews, probably as a result of her increased activity. Her sense of importance to others had also increased, and she had begun to develop aims again, particularly relating to travelling. There was also a strong element of 'philosophical' realism in her attitudes to life. These appeared, for example, in her answers in successive years to questions about the future:

There's only death, isn't there?
There's a time to live and a time to die – while I'm alive I will do all I can.

Through her seventies, Vera continued to enjoy an active lifestyle. Health problems had increased somewhat, with both her eyesight and arthritis in her knee, which eventually required her to use a walking stick. She also underwent an operation for hiatus hernia. But at age seventy-eight, her self-esteem remained high. She elaborated on its basis in her written responses to the self-completion questionnaire she filled in at this time.

'I feel really good' . . . *"when people appreciate the help I've given and it's been successful."*
'Most important for me is' . . . *"to keep mentally active and involved, especially in politics and world affairs."*
'I am best at' . . . *"managing my own affairs."*
'The goal of my mental development' . . . *"is to keep astute and active and never give up."*

Although she had given up her work at the hospital, she was now a member of the governing body at two schools and had some employment as a part-time teacher. She said that he had 'clear aims' "to go abroad again and get a job if possible." She remained somewhat anxious about the future but again adopted a philosophical stance:

'A wise person' . . . *"accepts the things they cannot change."*

In this and other statements she expressed an attitude to life that she said had been influenced by reading Rudolph Steiner's philosophy: 'to be wise is to learn from the mistakes one makes in life.' Although, as she was to explain later, she had rejected the Christian faith of her upbringing, she had retained a belief in God.

Two years later at age eighty, Vera had a serious fall that necessitated a hip replacement. Nevertheless, she was able to maintain her independence for a few more years, even continuing to drive her car, although she had had to discontinue visiting the centre of the city. At our interview a year later, her depression rating was low, apart from appetite loss (she had lost two stones in weight), which she attributed to the fall. Her self-esteem ascriptions also remained high, focused on her involvement with others, her participation in activities and her sense of inner strength. Again she elaborated more on her sense of self both in the actual interview and her written responses to the second self-completion questionnaire.

"I'm game for anything, I don't give up. I have hope not despair."

'What is it about your life that makes you feel most alive' ... *"Overcoming difficulties and dealing with problems."*

"If you get any experience, you gain something from it, good or bad."

Her view of the future remained negative and realistic, but still resilient.

There is not much of a future ... but I won't give up – otherwise I would take an overdose.

Activity continued to be a key element in her life.

Oh yes, inactivity is the worst thing ... I cook for other people ... I make cakes ... I have to go and clean.

When I can serve no useful purpose anymore, I shall pass out quickly.

After this interview, we wondered how she would cope if her health continued to decline as seemed likely but predicted that her evident resilience would buffer her as long as the decline was gradual. We continue Vera's case description in the next chapter.

Nellie Moreton was faced with demanding responsibilities early in life. Her mother became seriously ill, and as a result Nellie had to leave school at age twelve years to help look after her six younger brothers and sisters. She remained looking after them when her mother died two years later until it was considered that the task had become too much for her and they were put into homes. But Nellie continued to play a significant role in their upbringing by visiting them regularly in the homes and also later by trying to secure them employment. Her responsibilities meant that she did not get married until she was twenty-nine years old because she "didn't have time before that." Although she had two children, her husband, a merchant seaman, left her during the war after only five years of marriage. She was faced with the task of again bringing up young children alone and on a very low income. Later she was to review her early life experiences with us in more detail. Eventually she was able to obtain training in catering and for most of her working career was employed as a cook in a school for 'handicapped children'. She retired at sixty-two years as a result of increasing back pain due to an osteoporotic spine (cervical spondylosis).

When we first met Nellie, she was aged sixty-six years and living in a privately rented ground-floor flat, receiving assistance for paying rent and rates. She was also receiving two hours home help a week from the social services department because of her back problems. Her depression score was raised, and she said she was increasingly worried about the help she would need in the future. She did not feel at home in the area in which she was living and had minimal contact with her neighbours. However, her self-esteem was positive, and supported by her references to frequent visits both from and to family members, her role as secretary in a society for children with learning disabilities, her active membership of the Roman Catholic Church and various other social activities.

At age seventy-three Nellie moved to another ground-floor flat within a sheltered housing scheme operated by the Royal British Legion, for which her husband's work in the merchant navy made her eligible. She settled well there and within a short time had become chairperson of the scheme's social club. She was interviewed three years later and again a further three years on at age seventy-nine. Her move to sheltered housing had reduced her fears about the future, but her disability was increasingly marked. At seventy-six years, she was still able to go out and about shopping regularly but three years later could only manage small distances, as a result both of pain and unsteadiness. She needed an aid to walk and a bath seat to take a bath. Her breathlessness on exercise had also grown worse, and she now had to stop for breath when walking on level ground. Nevertheless, at the time of the latter interview, Nellie was in full swing organizing the Christmas festivities in her housing scheme. Our conversation was continuously interrupted by visitors and phone calls. Her living room was filled with various items of handicrafts for fund-raising sales.

Her self-esteem had remained constant over the years, with ascriptions focused on her family, but also her neighbours who seemed to have become a significant factor in maintaining her positive self-image. Also satisfaction in her own personal abilities and their maintenance seemed to play a significant role.

'I feel useful'... "we've just had a sale and I made so many things and I made about fifty pounds from my individual effort."

However, it was family identification that dominated her responses, especially in her written replies to the sentence completion task.

'I am very proud of'... "my family."

'Most important to me is'... "that I have lived to see my children and grandchildren grow up."

Similarly, a sense of regret about the family life that she clearly feels she had missed out on was apparent.

'I like to dream about' ... *"what things might have been had my parents lived longer. Mother died aged thirty-six, Father forty-five."*

The difficult times in her life were also evident.

'My life up to now' ... *"plenty of problems, but always overcame them."*

Nellie expressed an awareness that she was not allowed to develop her full potential because of her family commitments.

'I believe that I' ... *"would have been reasonably clever if I had had the chance of an education."*

Nevertheless she did not harbour a grudge but expressed pride in the skills which her family equipped her for.

'I've found that I' ... *"originated from a family of tailors and tailoresses and am pleased to have inherited some of their skills."*

Indeed these were the foundation for those skills which were the greatest value to her now.

'I am best at' ... *"cooking, sewing and knitting. I also like organizing fetes, jumble sales etc."*

Nellie had to make further adaptations as her physical health continued to decline. Her life through her eighties is described in the following chapter.

Mary Morrison was widowed during the war when she was in her later thirties and also had the misfortune of losing her house to bombing. She had brought up her son alone while continuing to work.

I used to have to go to work in the old days, I got nothing for him [her husband] from the war, you know. They never gave any pension.

When she retired from her work as a shop assistant, she became involved in voluntary activities, helping especially at the local hospital.

Mary was seventy-three years old when first interviewed and at the time living with her brother and sister-in-law, sharing the household tasks, such as cooking, shopping and housework. She appeared in excellent physical health. Her mood was also positive, although she reported some memory problems, having more difficulty remembering where she put things and sometimes forgetting what she was doing. A Roman Catholic like Nellie, she attended Mass at her local church regularly.

Her self-esteem was high and illustrated by her practical work and social activities, including helping her son and his family. Similar to Vera, she also had a strong sense of her own strengths, feeling that she could "do anything for herself that she wanted to", "think for herself and solve her own problems" and "do whatever she wanted to do in the right way." The only negative element in her self-ascriptions related to her "bad memory", which made her no longer feel so 'bright and alert' as before.

By the time she was interviewed at age eighty-three, Mary was living alone again in a rented apartment. She stressed her greater isolation now that she was "alone every day and night." She was also encountering more financial difficulty, needing "to watch every penny." But her health remained good apart from experiencing shortness of breath when walking hurriedly. She was continuing to go to church regularly. Her self-esteem had also remained high. Two years later, however, she had a serious fall and fractured her hip. Her self-esteem was lowered as a result. We continue our account of the last years of her life in the next chapter.

Alone since middle adulthood

A further eight of our ever-married women were already living alone when they entered our study in 1977–8. They comprise additional examples of women who had developed strong coping abilities as a result of the difficulties they had faced. We begin by describing the lives of the five of them who were widowed in middle adulthood. All displayed remarkable strength of character in dealing alone with the often-demanding nature of their later lives.

Margaret Baker's life had been limited by the circumstances in which she found herself. The first half had been largely spent caring for her invalid mother, especially after her father died when she was aged seventeen years. After her mother's death, Margaret sold the family home in Northern Ireland and moved to Southampton to marry a businessman she had first met twenty years earlier, who she said had initially been a "confirmed bachelor." But by now she was almost fifty, and her husband already sixty. Sadly he only lived another seven years. The latter part of her life was thus lived alone in a new country. She had considered returning to Ireland, but too much had changed and many of her family and friends had also died.

When we first interviewed Margaret, she was aged sixty-six years and recently retired from a clerical job. Although she had by then worked for many years, she had no income other than a state pension and lived in a rented ground-floor flat in a house overlooking the river. At the time, she was concerned about the recent discovery of an ovarian cyst, but this was removed by the following year, and her health remained good over the succeeding years. She lived an active and sociable life, visiting friends and social clubs regularly. She obviously benefitted from these social contacts, agreeing with the statement on our loneliness scale that 'the only time I feel alive is when I'm with others'.

Margaret was unusual within our sample of cases, and also among the larger sample, in that even at a relatively young age, she expressed a low opinion of herself. Throughout the study she consistently scored at a minimal level on the self-esteem measure we used. Already in her late sixties she described herself as feeling 'useless', commenting that "in comparison to what my friends seem to do, I do nothing." She considered that she did not 'count anymore' because "no one depends on me" and "it wouldn't make any difference if I died tomorrow." Her negative view of herself was exacerbated by feeling 'unsure of herself'. She enlarged on this by stating that she was frightened to tackle anything new, refusing promotion at work because she did not feel up to it. She was even anxious about going to the theatre and clubs alone. She also saw herself as "indecisive."

By her later seventies, her external situation had changed little. Her mobility was somewhat reduced because of stiffness when walking and problems with her joints. She also had trouble with her left foot due to a stunted growth caused by poor-fitting shoes in childhood. At seventy-six years, she indicated notable depressive symptoms, especially 'pervasive feelings of sadness and gloom', 'reduced appetite' and 'difficulty starting activities'. Two years later, the depression was no longer evident, and her attitude to her health was also more positive. But her self-esteem continued to remain low. She repeated what she had said ten years earlier that she "feels useless when she sees what others achieve" and expanded on her views of self in her written answers to the self-completion questions. She felt "very inadequate" in comparison to others, "unsure" of herself in company and that she "depended too much" on others. However, a more hopeful note was struck by comments that her goal in life was to be "a good and true friend" and that she "could talk herself out of it" when she felt lonely. She also derived positive feelings from being "able to do the gardening." Furthermore, she was actively making plans for her future, stating that she "intended to take more interest in local events" and "planned to join in more groups." Thus, although Margaret clearly had a low sense of self-worth, she did not take a defeatist attitude to life.

As she entered her eighties, her health seemed to stabilize, her mobility even to improve, and her depressive feelings to decline. However, she did not find it 'nice to grow old' and agreed that 'old age is not a happy time'. At age eighty-two, she expanded again on her views of self in her written responses. "Friendship" was what made her feel most alive. "Going out with a friend to the ballet" was the peak of enjoyment in her life. She had also become more proud of her housekeeping and cooking abilities, especially baking. Perhaps most significantly, she showed resilience in regard to the future.

Regarding my health, I've got through to eighty-two and I'm sure I'll get through the rest.

She also projected a positive view of the future, focused not so much on her own life but on that of the next generation. It was "the care and kindness shown by so many to those in need" that gave her hope. Despite having no children herself, "children and young people" were her special concern.

At eighty-four years of age Margaret's health problems had increased but not sufficiently to threaten her independence. She experienced more unsteadiness when walking (which she again attributed to childhood problems with her left foot) and also some shortness of breath, as well as blurred vision due to the beginnings of glaucoma. However, she was still walking quite long distances, 'well over a mile' each week. She rarely visited the doctor, only seeking a consultation 'once a year' on average. She continued to avoid depression and showed a similar interest in life as before, particularly enjoying the occasional outing.

It was in her early eighties that we spoke to Margaret on various occasions about her life. She seemed ready to engage in more detailed 'life review'. It was particularly noteworthy that she did not see her life 'as a whole' or in terms of 'a story'. Rather it had "really been a series of events." This seemed to be due to two factors: first that there had been a number of upheavals in her life that had precipitated a high degree of change, and second that she had had little control over these changes.

It is a case of during life you have a certain choice and then some [events] which you have no control over.

These events included the death of her father when she was aged seventeen years, resulting in the "big change" through which she became the sole carer of her invalid mother who later also went blind, and the early death of her husband, which left her alone in a new country, especially as "within a couple of years all his family had died too."

Margaret was also perhaps unusual in that she did not identify strongly with the caring role that she had had to adopt. When asked whether caring had been an important activity in life, she described it as "something you more or less have to do but you don't take up, like voluntary work." Although she admired the ability to care in others, it was not a quality she attributed to herself. In Ireland, she said with humour, mothers kept daughters close, they "tied them to their apron strings." Although the memory of her husband's death was obviously painful, she refused to consider herself 'unfortunate'. A man who got a stroke at age thirty-six was unfortunate, so was a family that lost a young child.

She engaged with comments about her seemingly unusual combination of characteristics: at peace and not depressed but thinking little of herself and with a negative attitude to ageing. Her view was entirely rational, she said. She would not be missed, and ageing had more negatives than positives. For her the loss of friends was the hardest fact of ageing. She agreed though that some of the positives were important, including a greater independence of mind. Her concern was for young people and the kind of world they were growing up into. She regretted the loss of standards.

I think it's lovely when you see a family close together... I always feel terrible when I hear mothers and daughters talking about how they can't be bothered going home.

She was now attending services at the United Reform Church. She said she did have a belief but did not have the faith that she saw in others. She particularly admired those who could withstand disasters because of their strong faith.

We came to the conclusion that her low self-esteem probably dated from childhood and that she had been raised to be reticent in talking about herself. Indeed, she readily directed questions away from her own life and on to the world outside including the project we were conducting. She had volunteered for many medical research projects and wanted to know whether they had been useful. What would ours deliver?

Despite her chronic low self-esteem – she persisted in comparing her abilities unfavourably to others – her life satisfaction remained relatively high. Friendship was the main source of enjoyment in her life, despite the pain it brought at death, and she was certainly open to forming new friends. She spoke about the value of her relationship with a previous neighbour in the flat above her home, a student, with whom she kept in contact.

She gives a different outlook on life... I really get great fun from her.

Other neighbours provided practical help and 'tended to look upon her almost as a relative'.

The young pair that come, not really young... between forty and fifty... he's quite good, you know, come in and change the bulbs or anything like that.

Her continued independence was also a major source of satisfaction.

But paradoxically it was her lack of self-esteem, or more accurately her lack of self-pity, that seemed the key to her continued resilience in the face of missing a fulfilling family life that she so much admired in others.

There's no use grumbling... or moaning about anything... there's a pub with a good saying on the wall, 'I grumbled because I had no shoes till I met a man who had no feet' – I think that's really good.

We should not be kind of self-centred... we often get trapped in our little worlds and that in a way's wrong.

We interviewed Margaret once more at age eighty-six (two years before she died). She was still in reasonably good health, visiting town on a weekly basis.

The only major problem was blurred vision, linked to both glaucoma and cataracts. In the previous year, she had fallen and had subsequent problems with her back, probably as a result. The main problem in her life, however, remained her loneliness. Sometimes she felt very lonely. Nevertheless, she expressed herself satisfied with her life although continuing to feel 'useless.'

I don't seem to be doing anything.

Her focus remained on the outside world. She was disturbed by the continuing bad news from Northern Ireland. She remembered 'the troubles' there from her young days. Born into a Protestant family in Belfast she did not meet Catholics until she was in her twenties and began working. But her father's stories, as he told them coming back from work, of men being thrown in a river, and of a woman telling of how six of her seven sons had been murdered, remained with her. These dreadful events were more important than any of her own personal disappointments in life.

Agnes Coombs was widowed at age fifty-eight. She and her husband, who had worked as a stevedore in Southampton docks, had brought up five children, including two children from her husband's previous marriage. At the time of our first interview with her when she was aged sixty-six years, she already had eleven grandchildren. She lived in a council house and was receiving help with her finances from the local council and regular visits from a social worker because of her financial difficulties, recently having been unable to pay her electricity bill. She appreciated being able to confide in the social worker and over the next two years she came to consider him a family friend.

At sixty-six years, Agnes's poor eyesight was limiting her activities, and she had recently fallen badly, cutting her head and eye and breaking her glasses. At this interview, she indicated a high depression score, including symptoms of restlessness, panic attacks and anxiety when leaving the home, which subsided over the following two years. Her self-esteem, however, remained high throughout as illustrated by her strong relationships to her family and their ready support to her, as well as by her ability to get about, do things for herself and enjoy life. She was also optimistic about her future, looking forward to what might be "in store." One of her unmarried sons was living with her at the time of the interview and taking her out two or three times a week to visit others or to the pub.

Eight years later Agnes's eyesight had deteriorated further – she was now more or less blind – and she was using a white stick outside the house. Depressive symptoms were less evident, and her self-esteem remained strong, and illustrated again by references to her family and friends, as well as her continued activity. She was living alone again but receiving a lot of support from her family. Three years later, now aged eighty years, she was finding walking more difficult but was still able to look after herself with help from her family. She rarely saw her GP and had been annoyed by a recent incident when she had been visited by a locum GP who was not happy about her living alone and had her admitted to hospital for tests. She was indignant about this and thought it quite unnecessary.

... well they say it was a chest infection but other than that I was out within forty-eight hours. They said they didn't understand why this doctor got me to go into hospital ... it was her, she wanted me to go into hospital, I suppose to make them more work. I was perfectly alright!

Her attitudes to life and her self-esteem remained positive, based on family, friends, her ability to continue doing things for herself and her interest in life around. Most striking was her note of confidence in herself: "If I was to hurt myself I know I'd get over it." Unfortunately, her visual impairment meant that she was not able to complete the handwritten questionnaire on self-perception.

Although there was no dramatic shift towards loss of independence in the coming years and she was able to cope well with her increasing frailty with the support of her family, we continue our account of Agnes's life through her eighties in the following chapter that focuses on adaptation to frailty.

Helen Procter had been divorced at age fifty-nine, seven years before she entered our study. Her marriage had been childless, and she had no relatives but in her late sixties was clearly leading an active social life, visiting friends 'four or more times a week'. She acted as secretary for a club for the divorced, separated and widowed and was spending three to four evenings a week carrying out this work. She had formerly been employed as a buyer of cosmetics and jewellery for a large department store in London and was continuing to give sales parties. She also was attending dancing lessons once a week. Nevertheless, she said that she sometimes felt very lonely, and agreed that her life could be happier than it was. Her club work appeared to be important in sustaining her sense of self-esteem, referring to it to illustrate many of her positive self-ascriptions during three interviews in this period. She had distanced herself from the religious faith of her childhood and did not belong to any religious organization.

Up until her next interview at age seventy-six, Helen's health remained good. She rarely visited her GP and remained active, both physically and socially, although continuing to live alone. But two years later, she fell, fracturing her pelvis, from which she recovered at home with the help of friends; a further year on, she was diagnosed with cancer of the right lung following symptoms of breathlessness, which she thought were due to hay fever. When interviewed at seventy-nine, she was in the middle of radiotherapy treatment for her illness. Her mobility and social activities were greatly reduced. She was also taking antidepressant medication but at the time of interview was not showing marked depressive symptoms and had retained a high sense of self-esteem, illustrating her ascriptions with her housework, knitting and shopping activities.

At this time, Helen provided further evidence on her sense of self in her written answers to the self-description questionnaire. 'Most important', for example, were her "friends of thirty years." It was also interesting that her recent severe health problems had contributed to, rather than detracted from, her self-esteem.

'I am very proud of myself'. . . "for not giving in to an illness."

'I believe that I'. . . "have managed to win over the ups and downs of life by not giving in."

Also in looking back over recent years, she had pride in her achievements.

'When I think about myself'. . . " I realize I've beaten giving in to twenty-two years of loneliness."

She had also come to realize that there was some form of gain by facing up to challenges.

'One becomes wise'. . . "by making mistakes in life."

In referring to coping with health stresses, she advised others with similar problems to "fight it". . . "don't give in, I don't believe in giving in." She continued to have hope for the future, stating, "I do look to the future . . . having a good life, being able to do things, joking with friends." In her written comments, she indicated her aims for the future:

'The goal that I would like to accomplish in my life'. . . "is to live a jolly life of 100 years."

Helen was interviewed once more at age eighty-two. Her health had continued to deteriorate, and her weight had dropped from eight to six stones, but she had continued to maintain herself in her own home, rather than moving to sheltered housing, which she was considering two years earlier. She was experiencing breathlessness even when walking on level ground. Still, she was keeping depression at bay, although she acknowledged some pessimistic thoughts because of what she described as a "fear of death." She stressed again that she was a "fighter who doesn't give in" and had adopted a fatalistic attitude towards her health and life in general, explaining that "what will be, will be." She had acquired a new dog to replace the one that had died three years earlier, and was caring for "a lot of plants." She managed to have a daily walk and was using taxis to travel further.

Her self-esteem was well maintained not only by her own daily activities but also by the help she provided to others. She was *always there for someone to share a problem with.*

An emphasis on relationships and mutual support was also evident in her written responses to the questionnaire we left with her at this time.

'What do you believe in?'. . . "People who are willing to do helpful things."

'What is important in your life today?'. . . "My cousin, his daughter and friends."

Helen spoke with particular enthusiasm of two long-standing friends whom she referred to as her "special ones", and her cousin's daughter with whom she could reminisce, possibly allowing her to integrate past features of her life with the present.

'Do they [your relatives] give you a feeling of connection with the past?'. . . "Yes, especially my cousin' daughter. We go to a restaurant and we sit out and have our lunch and we talk about the old days . . . She says, 'I don't know half these things' . . . and I say, 'Well, it's all right, I know'.

Nevertheless, she acknowledged the void she experienced due to the loss of her husband's companionship and affection following their divorce, which she described as "the biggest turning point" in her life and as "very hurtful."

I think a lot of that [lack of love] was what caused my depression . . . when I found out about the tumour on my lung. I came home and thought, 'Wouldn't it have been lovely to have had somebody here, put their arm around me and say, 'Don't worry dear, you'll be all right'.

Possibly as a form of compensation, Helen derived particular satisfaction from identifying with the role of confidant herself, claiming this as her 'major contribution to life'.

Helping other people . . . I'm still there if anyone wants to come and talk.

It was remarkable that Helen had not lost but gained a stronger sense of self and meaning in her life as a result of her recent struggles with cancer.

'What has been most meaningful about your life so far?'. . . "Fighting the tumour on my lung and not giving in."

She had also retained a future perspective.

'What is it about your life that makes you feel most alive?'. . . "Looking forward to being one hundred as long as my brain stays alive."

Helen seemed to have adopted a personal philosophy regarding life that reinforced her well-being by identifying herself as a strong person, someone who was determined to remain positive throughout any adversity.

No point in being miserable, any rate. It makes your life worse.
I'd hate to give in. Just sit in a chair and be a poor little me. No thanks.

Even though she was now sometimes experiencing panic attacks, she was able to draw on her inner strengths to combat them, using speech as a form of reassurance.

I talk to myself and say, 'Don't be stupid, get rid of that panic'.
When I've been going up the hill, I've stopped, hanging on to the fence. 'It's no good giving in.' So I stop for a few minutes, 'Come on, on your way'.

Helen died a few months after this interview.

Evelyn Norris was widowed at age sixty-two years and was interviewed for the first time eight years later. Her husband had worked in the aircraft industry, and she later described how happy their married life had been. Throughout her seventies, her health remained good, and, supported only by a state pension, she was managing to live in her own home. The most important relationships were with her one child, her daughter and her daughter's family, as well as her sister who lived next door. She related her usefulness to the fact that she could help others, such as looking after her grandchildren to assist her daughter as well as helping a friend. She looked to the future with confidence.

I'm fit. . . I've got my grandchildren. I want to see them grow up.

At eighty years, Evelyn incurred 'a mild stroke' but was not obviously impaired by it. Of more immediate concern to her were increasing symptoms of arthritis in her hands and left knee. However, she showed no signs of depression and continued to have a high self-esteem, based on her family and friends and her ability to be active and independent. She said that her religious faith had become of increased importance to her. Three years later, her health was becoming worse, but she was coping with the problems.

Getting worse really but, thank God, I can still keep going.
I don't worry [about health] . . . you've got to accept it.

She remained mobile, going to town 'once every fortnight' and walking 'more than a mile a week'. She had confidence in her abilities and was still able to do some house decorating. The company of her friends gave her a feeling of importance. She enjoyed going out playing cards with them. This contributed to her sense of 'alertness' and made her feel "full of life." She was fully involved in her family and especially interested in her grandsons' lives. This was emphasized in the written illustrations she sent back to us after the interview, but also the theme of her hopes for continued independence.

'In the next few years' . . . *"I hope to see my grandsons married with children."*

'When I'm older I wish' . . . *"to keep fit and stay in my own home."*

In the following three years, Evelyn had a succession of further minor strokes that also affected her speech. Her mobility deteriorated and was increasingly hampered by unsteadiness and shortness of breath even when walking on level ground. She also developed problems with her sight due to cataracts. We continue her life story in her later eighties in Chapter 7.

Ethel Willis was aged nearly seventy-five years when first interviewed and had been living alone for thirteen years since her husband died at age sixty-three. She had one son and one daughter. She had responded to her husband's death by going back to work part time, helping in a friend's shop and in the Post Office for six years. She gave up the job after the birth of her grandson so she could spend more time with her son and his family. Ethel was clearly well settled and content in her area of Southampton. A small supplementary income left to her by her husband meant that she was able to continue maintaining the house, in which she had been living since she first married fifty years earlier, and employ help for repairs and decoration. But she was still able to do all the housework and gardening herself. Her major outside social activity was the Conservative Women's Association, which she attended every month. Until the year before our first interview Ethel had been the secretary for this organization, but otherwise she was not very active socially, instead spending a lot of time listening to the radio, watching TV and above all reading both books and newspapers. She also continued to use her skills at dressmaking, which she had learned when young.

She had no major physical health problems in her mid to late seventies but consistently indicated some depressive symptoms, including sleep problems, restlessness and feelings of sadness. These were especially marked at the first interview when she had recently lost a sister and another close friend. Her self-esteem was also not consistently positive. She commented especially on her lack of enjoyment, comparing it negatively with earlier stages of life, and seemed to lack a future perspective. She had 'no aims left in her life'. Her sense of self was based mainly on her family, her ability to do things for others and to maintain her home environment.

There were no dramatic changes in her health over the next ten years, although by her mid-eighties, Ethel was complaining of hearing impairment and weakness in her limbs, restricting her activity to some extent. Her depression score was diminished and her self-esteem largely positive. However, she continued to report little enjoyment in life. Her main concern was over her son, whose marriage was breaking down. At age eighty-five, she incurred a series of major health problems after being admitted to hospital with a throat infection. We take up her case account again in the next chapter.

Alone since retirement

Three previously married women in our study were bereaved in their later sixties and seventies but before entering our study. In each case, relations with their children and families appeared as the most important factor determining well-being.

Olive Reid was widowed at age sixty-seven and by her middle seventies had developed disabling health problems as a result of severe arthritis and consequent weak joints. Like Ethel Willis, she had one son, who lived in London, and one daughter. However, her daughter had emigrated to Canada many years earlier. By the time of our first interview with Olive at age seventy-six, she was confined most of the time to the house despite an operation on her legs in the preceding year. She was greatly concerned about her health and worried about her future. Initially, she had a high depression rating with symptoms especially of 'weeping spells' and 'not sleeping easily', but these had diminished two years later. She had received a boost from being able to visit her daughter in Canada in the preceding year. Her friends and neighbours were supportive, visiting her regularly throughout the week. She had developed strong interests in indoor activities such as reading, knitting and crocheting and playing solo games as Scrabble and Patience, as well as watching TV and listening to the radio. Her Church of England minister brought communion to her at home.

Her self-esteem remained relatively high throughout this period, supported by her interests in her family, her friends' visiting and her general interest in world affairs. Her enjoyment came out of "hearing about the grandchildren and what everyone is doing" and her sense of importance because "people tell me they like visiting and I do them – I have lots of friends." Visiting her daughter in Canada had clearly been most important to her, and her main aim she said was to go back there. She remained optimistic thinking that she would "come out on top eventually."

However, two years later at age eighty, her condition had deteriorated sufficiently that she had to give up her house and enter a residential care home. We continue with an account of her subsequent life there in the next chapter.

Hilda Smith had the largest family of all our case study participants, with five surviving children, sixteen grandchildren and five great-grandchildren already at the time of our first interview with her. She was then aged seventy-one years and been widowed for the previous three years. Her husband, as Agnes Coombs's, had worked as a docker, and Hilda believed in retrospect that he had died of asbestosis caused by the cargoes that he was required to unload during his working life.

Both at first interview and the next year, Hilda showed somewhat raised depression scores, probably related to her still recent bereavement, and feelings of loneliness. The depressive symptoms – sadness and weeping spells –

along with the loneliness and also worries about her memory had subsided a further year on. Otherwise she was healthy and also considered herself to be a very active person for her age. However, she was beginning to show signs of angina, which made some cleaning chores difficult and as result accepted some assistance with housework from her daughter. The next year, she moved into smaller accommodation, a council flat, which made life easier.

A lot of her time was devoted to her family. This included walking her daughter's dog every evening, helping with child-minding whilst their mothers were shopping, and she also added that she had been known to provide a refuge for her grandchildren when they were "in disgrace." She said that she loved to have a house 'full of children'. Although she did not seem to go out to visit friends nor to receive visits from friends and neighbours, in the first year of our study, she appeared to be visiting her family every day, and also to be visited by someone within the family just about every day. Her high self-esteem was illustrated almost entirely by references to her family. She described her life as "wrapped 'round children, grandchildren and great grandchildren" and said that she had "plenty to look forward to with all the kids growing up – more weddings." Sadly one of her grandsons died two years later.

Hilda's life continued relatively unchanged over the following ten years, apart from a further move into another council flat nearer her original home. Her family continued to be supportive to her, visiting several times a week. But by age eighty years, she was experiencing a number of health problems, needing to take medication for thyroid problems, and also suffering from diverticulitis. She had recently suffered three transient ischaemic attacks. She was also experiencing some pain on walking, mostly as a result of pain in her joints, and noticing pain in her limbs. She had fallen off a bus in the last year but apparently without major injury. Her hearing and eyesight were becoming impaired as well. Nevertheless, she did not feel that any of these health problems adversely affected her lifestyle. She still shopped for herself and continued to go into town.

However, by age eighty-three years, although she continued to be mobile both inside and outside the house, several additional health events had given the family more reason to keep an even closer eye on her. We continue our account of her life in the next chapter.

Mavis Dawes had moved from Lancashire to charitable communal housing in Southampton in the year before her first interview at age seventy-two years. She consistently described her past life as 'hard', and in her interviews in her early eighties gave a detailed account of the various losses and disappointments in her life.

I've had a sad life, you see my mother died when I was nineteen. She died when she had a baby in her charge. She was forty-four. I had to give up work then . . . I was left at nineteen with a family and a young baby to look after.

Mavis had possessed academic abilities, winning a scholarship, but as a result of ill health had been unable to progress her education. She would have liked to have become a schoolteacher.

I started with a rheumatic disease, then I was off to school for four months but I didn't get a chance. I was going in for the Oxford exams at the Higher Grade school and I had to go out to work at fourteen.

She had been close to a sister who was only nine months younger. In fact she felt that they were like twins. Her sister had died when she was only twenty-four, and to Mavis the loss was even worse than losing her mother.

Her marriage had been troubled because her husband had psychological problems. He had a 'breakdown' at some point. Mavis said that she had had to bring up her children – two sons – almost singlehandedly. From age fifty, she ran a successful corner shop for thirteen years but had to give it up because of lung trouble. She allowed her younger son and his wife to take it over but it failed within a year.

When her husband died, one of her sons encouraged her to come to down to the Southampton area where both sons were living.

I wasn't well at all – chest trouble, asthma I had. He brought me here. He took me to his home . . . but his wife didn't want me of course . . . so he tried his best to get me a flat.

Subsequently her son tried to start his own business, in which Mavis invested her money, but that was all lost when the business failed.

Mavis initially settled well into her new life in Southampton, visiting family regularly every few days, attending church and older people's clubs. Her physical health improved, although her depression scores remained somewhat elevated. She felt herself that she had adapted well to the move south and gave many examples as illustrations to her self-esteem ascriptions.

I've gone into Southampton from the start, looked around and made myself known.
I enjoy going to my clubs, meeting my friends, seasons, trees in greenery.
I make people laugh, have OAPs [Old Age Pensioners] in stitches.
I'm in better health than was. Love every day in the flat.

But difficulties continued. Her younger son was sentenced to prison for some months and continued to have a lot of problems, primarily as a result of alcohol abuse. This was a major ongoing concern for Mavis. Depression also persisted in being a problem, as did related difficulties with sleeping for which she had to take sleeping tablets. As she entered her eighties, her physical health began to decline noticeably. Her eyesight deteriorated but improved after a cataract operation. She was also experiencing difficulties in walking because of stiffness in her legs and suffered from breathlessness even when walking on level ground. We therefore continue our account of her life in the next chapter.

Older men living alone

There was a small group of four men in our sample of cases who had been widowed before, or in one case very shortly after, they entered our study. They were all already in their middle to later seventies. They are therefore somewhat distinct in age and experience from the rest of the men we have presented in Chapters 4 and 5. Two of them had even experienced some service in the First World War I. For the most part, they displayed good health and lived long lives, in two cases beyond one hundred years. None of them became significantly frail before they reached their nineties.

Stuart Murray lost his second wife, to whom he had been married nearly ten years, early in the first year of our study when he was aged seventy-four years. He appeared to adapt relatively easily to this loss. This seemed at least in part attributable to his strong religious outlook. He was a Baptist and consistently stated that he derived great strength from his faith. When he was interviewed a few months after his bereavement, he expressed himself secure in his belief in life after death.

As a Christian I have no fear of death. There is a resurrection.

His self-esteem was extremely high, which he illustrated with his various activities in addition to his religious faith. He was still in full-time work as a solicitor's clerk, cycling to his office every day. He also had numerous interests and hobbies, including going to football matches and collecting stamps, and was secretary of the local bowls club.

I enjoy work and recreation and make the best of everything, every moment of the day.

At seventy-six years, he stressed the continuing importance of the work that he was doing.

I feel useful as I do a good job of work and don't know what they would do without me.

Stuart had an independent spirit, the origins of which he was to explain in depth much later in the study. The son of travelling theatrical artists, he had first worked as an actor too, but when he was seventeen, he walked out on his parents and, declaring himself a year older than he was, signed on for the army ("which was pleased to have me"). He served in the 'Black and Tans' regiment to counter the Irish rebellion after the First World War, was then posted to Asia Minor during the Greek-Turkish conflict and finally to India, where he met his first wife. He lived in India for thirty-five years, transferring at some point from the army to the Indian Civil Service and staying on after Indian Independence. Eventually he returned to England to join his first wife and two children who had left India earlier. For some years, he worked in India House in London and then obtained a job as a clerk in a solicitor's office, which he still held.

When interviewed again at age eighty-four years, Stuart was still continuing to work in the solicitor's office full time. He described his health as excellent, despite having had a 'mild stroke' and a 'broken leg' the year before! Two years later, he was still cycling to work and walking "more than twenty miles a week." His attitudes to ageing remained positive. Even the broken leg had not deterred him for long.

I carried on as usual . . . I only lost a week at the office.

He was not worried about his health in the future, he said, as he "lived day to day." He surprised us though at this point in the study by telling us that he would only agree to continuing being interviewed if he received a clinical assessment from one of the doctors in the Geriatric Medicine Department similar to that which he had obtained in the first years of the project (we arranged this for him).

His self-esteem remained extremely high. It was again his work that made him 'feel capable' as well as getting 'enjoyment out of life'. It also made him feel 'bright and alert' and gave him 'clear aims'.

I get the best out of life and aim to be employed usefully.

He was, however, beginning to stress more the importance of his relationship with his son and daughter and their families. Indeed, his main concern at the time of the interview was for his grandson, who had experienced complications following an operation. His faith remained his bedrock of confidence in the future.

I look to the future with confidence – whatever it holds – due to my faith.

[Stuart appears not to have sent back a completed self-description questionnaire after this interview.]

Remarkably, three years later at age eighty-nine, Stuart was still working full time as before. His health remained good, the only problems he mentioned being the metal plate in his previously broken leg causing some discomfort and stiffness in his neck, which he attributed to rheumatism. He continued to use his bicycle and walked 'more than a mile' each week. He was less engaged in leisure activities outside the house but enjoyed TV and reading, "especially religious books." He visited his children's families less than once a month but kept in touch by phone. He remained concerned about his grandson who had been badly affected by what Stuart put down to a "medical mistake."

His self-ascriptions continued to be entirely positive as before. He still attributed his sense of usefulness to his ability to remain in active employment.

Everyone depends on me at work. I open and close the office and distribute the mail.

Stuart's work-based identity was also illustrated strongly in the life story interview conducted at the time as well as in the written statements he sent back to us afterwards.

My own individual progress has been entirely due to my interest in success in the job I have to do.

'What is it about life that makes you feel most alive?'... "Opportunity to work and make a contribution to society."

'What has been most meaningful about your life so far?'... "That I have succeeded in satisfying my employers – I'm never out of work."

Family and friends also reinforced his feeling of well-being. He was concerned "to pass on the benefits of my own experience to my family – spiritual gifts rather than material." When asked to identify a very meaningful moment in his life, he referred to "the conversion to belief in God", which occurred while he was a young man in India. He said it had "transformed the whole outlook on life." He was later to explain more.

Stuart finally retired from work at age ninety-one years. We interviewed him again a few months later. Retirement had clearly left a void in a life in which work had been the central part of identity. Nevertheless, he was still in excellent health for his age with no problems with his sight, hearing, mobility or breathlessness.

He had adjusted to his new life with determination, replacing his tasks at work with household duties, doing all his own housework, cooking and shopping. He continued to cycle to the shops about a mile away from his home. He had also increased his involvement with his bowling club since retiring, attending twice a week, not actively playing but helping with tasks where he could, including getting the green ready for the new season. His indoor activities had increased, especially reading religious books, and he enjoyed the visits of his son (every week) and his daughter (every month). Inevitably, his sources of self-esteem had changed with his ascriptions being illustrated with various home and outside activities and relationships rather than work-based ones. His religious faith appeared to have become of even greater importance to him.

I look to the future with confidence. I hope to have a Christian end to my life – I'm never alone – God is always with me.

The only event that he reported as disturbing his life in the last period had been the tragic murder of his former employer.

Stuart agreed to a second interview in which he commented in detail on our 'theory' of the bases of his identity. He approved our view that independence as well as active contribution to society were central aspects of his life past and present.

I'm quite happy and content being alone. I don't seek help unless I'm medically unfit. I don't need help, I don't look for it.

A strict daily routine was the basis to his view on maintaining a healthy life.

In all things I like a routine – getting to bed and getting up at the same time – it's vital. We are like a machine – if you put your oil in the wrong place – something will go wrong. You will pay the penalty – you have to treat your body as something wonderful and keep it that way.

We wondered how he would react to rapid health deterioration, but he indicated awareness of this as a possible future issue for himself.

I like to boast that I'm self-reliant – I'm not dependent on anybody. . . . I do everything – I can't be bothered with anyone to help. Of course, I suppose the time'll come when I'll need it.

He had succeeded in adjusting to retirement by keeping himself occupied with indoor tasks, in fact he was very busy.

I never wake up in the morning and say 'Well, what have I got to do?' . . . I'm still sorting out the bedroom from when my wife died . . . if it's in order when I die, I shall be very satisfied.

I've got so much to do – I find it difficult to entertain – to fit in people – as you have to be prepared.

Membership of his bowls club provided further continuity, but as he grew older, there were fewer members he knew well.

I was secretary there for ten years . . . I see one or two friends. . . . There are a couple of members I know – not many have lived as long as I have. . . . I've been a member for over thirty years.

There were also some activities he missed, particularly chess.

If I had someone who plays chess I would be very interested to have them . . . a lovely game . . . I enjoy it.

His identification with his family was also important, an aspect of his self that appeared to us to have increased in importance over the years. He was looking forward to the return of his granddaughter from Australia the following week, and he had made special financial provision for his grandson who had particular health needs. However, he was determined not to allow his family to reduce his independence. Referring to his son and daughter-in-law's weekly visits, he commented: "Oh yes, he only stops for one hour ... I don't let them make a meal out of it."

He agreed that his religious faith constituted his prime source of identity, acting as a form of reassurance and a guide to living.

There is nothing else to live for – you need something to hang on to. I believe in God more than anything else – it assists me if I have any pain or troubles ... Guidance is sought – guidance is given – you can't be reliant on yourself, you've got to be reliant on God.

At the same time, he felt it increasingly difficult to identify with contemporary British society, in particularly its changing morality, which he attributed partly to immigration.

I'm rather disgusted with the whole way this country is moving ... the speed, the drugs, all the alcohol, burglary ... I've no patience with young people who can't behave properly.

We are heading for a crisis – God will not be mocked. But the country as a whole is doing everything to mock Him.

Stuart was pleased to have another of us visit him a few months later when he was ninety-two years old. In fact, he prepared a full meal, with sandwiches, cakes, desserts and fruit, all covered with a cloth, a habit he said he had begun in India because of the flies. He was happy to present his life story in some detail. He spoke in particular about his conversion to Christianity by an American missionary in India when he was in his early twenties. He came back to the subject of faith later on in our conversation, saying that he had nothing to fear as he saw his life as having been "written by God." He showed the well-used books he had used throughout his life to meditate on the Bible. There were certain passages that he read regularly. Reading alone though he agreed did not make one a Christian; one's life as a whole did. We spoke a lot about India, exchanging family memories of places there. He had known Nehru, India's first prime minister after Independence from Britain. The climate had not worried him. He had worked in temperatures of 100 to 105 Fahrenheit without a fan.

He had plenty still to occupy himself, he said, pointing to bags of stamps that would 'keep him busy for the rest of his life'. He also said that he would be pleased to see us again. However, a year later he incurred the first of a series of strokes that left him with speech problems, and at the next interview point would not agree to a visit. He died two years later at age ninety-six, having recently entered a residential home after admitting to himself that he could not live on his own anymore.

We obtained this information from his daughter-in-law shortly after Stuart's death. She stressed what an independent man he had been, expressing strong beliefs not only in religion but in all he said and did. She and his son had set up care packages for him in his last years to keep him at home. Disability and dependency had been difficult for him, as we had predicted, and she said that his problems with speech after his strokes had particularly annoyed him.

William (Bill) Blackburn, when first interviewed, was aged eighty-three years and living in a small semi-detached privately rented house in the centre of Southampton without a bathroom or indoor toilet. He had only social security payments to supplement his pension, but he did also receive a rent and rate rebate. His wife had died eight years earlier after fifty-seven years of marriage. He was looking after himself without any help and appeared to be perfectly content with his lifestyle.

Brought up in Lancashire, he had left sail training school at aged fifteen and a half years with various seagoing skills but otherwise had received no further formal education. Although he spent some time at sea, he seems to have worked principally as skilled labourer in the motor transport section of naval stores. He became involved in the Trades Union Movement in an official capacity and later in life worked as a bookmakers' clerk.

Bill's health was good at the time of first interview, and he was not depressed. He pursued an active social life at the local pubs and labour club. In response to one of the self-description questions, he acknowledged that some of his social activities, particularly the combination of drinking and gambling, were 'foolish'. He confessed to us at eighty-five, two years later, that he had overspent as a result of gambling. Horseracing was a major interest for him. His self-ascriptions were consistently positive (apart from the reference to 'foolish' behaviour). He was important and helpful to his "neighbours", doing odd jobs for them, and "to the publican of the local" – 'who got his money!' He enjoyed life and was "always smiling."

Over the following years, Bill continued living in his familiar but increasingly unkempt surroundings. His activity and independence decreased as he experienced a number of health events, surgery on his prostate gland when he was eighty-five and again at eighty-nine years, diverticular disease, cataracts and viral infections to chest and bladder. At age ninety-two years, he was admitted to the elderly care wards at the local general hospital because his strength was disappearing. This might have seemed to be the prelude to his final decline, as with many of the other cases, particularly given that while he was in hospital, he fell and broke his shoulder and pelvis. But in fact he was to recover from these injuries and to reach his century. How did he achieve it? We describe his life in his nineties and past one hundred years in Chapter 9.

Charles Kitchen was widowed at age seventy-nine years. He described to us how he nursed his wife through her final illness over a period of four years. Although he had assistance from the District Nursing Service and access to respite care to allow him rests, he said that he looked after her practically totally himself. Caring for her had been a great challenge to him, and her consequent death (at home) a great loss.

He was aged eighty-three years when first interviewed, living in a bungalow on the outskirts of Southampton. He had left school aged just under 13 years, after passing the 'labour exam', to become an apprentice baker. But less than a year later, he joined the Royal Navy as a stoker and remained in the service for twenty two years, rising to the rank of chief stoker. He was later to tell us many stories about the interesting missions in which he had taken part. He had clearly found much satisfaction in his role. After leaving the navy, he joined the customs service, based in the ports of Liverpool, Newcastle and finally Southampton, where he chose to retire. He and his wife had three sons and numerous grandchildren. He had a number of outdoor activities, principally relating to sport. He played golf and bowls and was a regular spectator at both football and cricket matches. He did not consider himself any less active than in the past and had recently taken an extended holiday to Australia to visit family.

His health was good when first interviewed, and he showed no noticeable signs of depression. However, two years later, one of his sons died, and when interviewed a few weeks after, his depression score was raised – besides sleep disturbance, he also showed symptoms of restlessness on this occasion. However, his self-ascriptions remained positive in all respects, based on his many activities and the help he was able to give to others. He was also confident about the future.

I feel well and look forward to meeting old friends again at bowls this year.

There was little change in Charles's situation over the next few years and into his early nineties. He had a cataract removed from his left eye when he was eighty-nine. The main change in his lifestyle was that although he still enjoyed watching and playing sport, he had given up his 'Saints' (Southampton Football Club) season ticket. This was because of his awareness of the risk of personal injury as a result of the increasing trend in the 1980s towards violence at football matches. We take up the account of his life through his nineties in Chapter 9.

John Otterbourne was also widowed at age seventy-nine, a year before he entered our study. He was then living in a self-contained unit in the home of his daughter and son-in-law. Two grandchildren were also living with their parents. The arrangement was such that John could look after himself, including doing his own cooking. Nevertheless, he seemed to have a close relationship with his daughter and said that he could confide in her. He said he enjoyed his own company and spent his time mainly on indoor activities, including playing the piano one hour a day and looking after the greenhouse. He did, however, regularly attend the local Baptist church and said that religion now 'meant more to him than when he was younger'. He has formerly been employed as a ship's office and clerical worker and had lived for many years in South Africa, working for the town council in Johannesburg, and after his return to England doing similar work in Hampshire.

He had good health and, apart from increasing problems with memory, found it 'nice to grow old'. His self-esteem was also high, derived from his various activities and also his contributions to others such as "helping financially" and "keeping my grandsons in order!" He had valued friends in South Africa and elsewhere in England with whom it was important for him to keep in contact. His hopes for the future centred around his strong Christian faith and his belief in 'eternal life'.

God has provided well for me in this life and the afterlife is well catered for. . . I look to the Lord and Saviour with confidence.

His only concerns related to his future health as he felt increasing physical weakness and also deterioration in both his hearing and sight. By age eighty-three, he was also a little concerned about memory failings but at the same time suggested that he had always been a little forgetful. The same year, he was also in hospital for a prostate operation.

John's health deteriorated as he approached ninety years. At age eighty-five, he fractured his left leg and at eighty-nine broke his pelvis. His hearing also became more impaired. But sustained by his daughter's family, he remained active and independent with a high quality of life for a number of years more. We describe our last interviews with him in Chapter 8.

Concluding comments

Just as our chapter on marriage while growing old has been more about men, so our account of living alone has been more about women. The few men we have described who were living alone when they entered our study had been bereaved relatively late in life but were also all rather unusual cases. We will return to two of them in our account of older people living with a high quality of life in their nineties in Chapter 9.

Although there were a few other men described in Chapters 4 and 5, such as Harold Rank and Fred Hobson, who lost their wives earlier than they might have expected, the experience of early bereavement and separation set out in this chapter has been predominantly a story about women's subsequent lives alone. What is striking is how well most of these women coped with the sudden and unwanted changes they experienced in their lives, whether they occurred in early or middle adulthood. Most of them were able to discover new sources of self-esteem and meaning separate from their previous marriages. Vera Wright and Nellie Moreton, whose husbands had left them, both had to find work in early adulthood to support their children but at the same time developed rewarding careers and obtained fulfilment through work and helping others. Their varied activities and the confidence they had gained continued to benefit them into later life. Those who had found themselves alone in midlife and without children, such as Helen Procter and Margaret Baker, still managed to make a new life for themselves focused mainly on friendship and social contact. Both had been particularly unfortunate in the events that had befallen them, but showed no sign of self-pity. Helen was to encounter yet another blow with a sudden diagnosis of lung cancer when her life was flourishing again. But she showed the same resilient spirit in battling this as well.

The saddest story was perhaps that of Mavis Dawes who was handicapped by the legacy of a troubled past life and difficult relationships that continued into the present. But she had demonstrated considerable coping ability in intransigent situations. The question for her and for many of the other women described in this chapter was how they would cope with the problems arising from likely increasing frailty. The next chapter analyzes the experience of frailty and its consequences for sense of self and meaning in the lives of these older women as well as in those already described in Chapters 4 and 5.

7 Women becoming frailer

Becoming frailer is central to the meaning of ageing. Whereas the presence of disability can be lifelong but also unchanging, the essence of frailty is fragility, a liability to further deterioration. A person who becomes frail is more vulnerable to illness and sudden death. There is a sense of being constantly at risk, of encountering a serious accident or fatal change in bodily condition, whether through incurring infection, becoming weaker or remaining too long in life-threatening conditions of exposure and isolation. Disabled persons and those around them can adapt more easily to a stable situation of need, but frailty requires a different type of adjustment. Regular or constant monitoring often becomes necessary.

Frailty is of course a relative matter, as is the need of personal monitoring. We are all vulnerable to gradual or sudden changes in bodily, environmental or social conditions, and in modern societies, we have become even more dependent on others to provide certain essential daily services for us. But there comes a point in most people's later years when the probability of damaging change occurring increases, particularly because of a decline in physical and mental abilities. Various negative outcomes become more likely: injury as a result of falling, weakness from failing to maintain adequate nutrition and inability to manage the household, competently carry out personal care tasks or move outside the house safely without fear of hurt or becoming lost.

In this and the following chapter, we consider the lives of those members of our sample from the time in our study that they began to become noticeably frailer. This usually implied that their continuing survival and welfare was dependent on the support provided by other people, generally their spouse or child(ren) (or both), and in some cases social care services. In fact, most of our sample became very frail before they died, if only in the last weeks or months of their lives. But here we consider those, still a majority of our cases, who came to live in states of significant frailty and whom we interviewed during this part of their later life. Most of these participants reached this condition at some time in their eighties, some did so earlier in their seventies, and some did not reach this state of life until their nineties.

The analysis we have conducted examines how our participants adapted to their sense of increasing frailty. As in previous chapters, we present the evidence we collected on their perception of self and meaning in life. We focus here predominantly on cases of increasing physical frailty, rather than mental frailty, and thus exclude from consideration those who suffered from chronic depression and anxiety as Rita Fletcher (see Chapters 4 and 5) until her physical condition also deteriorated, and Dora Meadows (see Chapter 4) who learned to cope well with a moderate to severe psychological condition of agoraphobia thanks largely to the support she received from her husband and children. Dora in fact died before physical frailty became an important element in her life, and in her last years gained a sense of usefulness by being able to care for her more physically frail husband.

Because our aim was to study adaptation to living with frailty longitudinal observations over time were necessary. In both our female and male cases, we begin with those who were youngest at onset of increased frailty and continue in succession to the oldest. A few of the latter could not be described as having become properly frail until their nineties and are therefore left for consideration in Chapter 9. Of the twenty-three women in our sample of cases, we interviewed twelve after they had become significantly frail and followed all of them as they became yet frailer. We can thus comment with some confidence on the evidence for changes in attitudes that these women showed over time and the factors that might explain them.

Becoming frailer before eighty years of age

In the preceding chapter, we described *Olive Reid's* life in her mid-seventies when she was already suffering from severe arthritis in her leg joints, was worried about the future and had become noticeably depressed. However, a visit to her daughter in Canada appeared to give her encouragement – her depression ratings subsequently declined – and when interviewed at age seventy-eight, she was hoping to visit Canada again. Despite the depression, her actual self-esteem scores had remained high throughout this period and she could clearly rely on some important personal resources, both internal and external, that she had acquired throughout her life. She was proud of the families both of her son and of her daughter. She had reliable neighbours and friends who visited her regularly, as did her Anglican minister. She had also developed a number of indoor hobbies that allowed her to entertain herself well at home, while maintaining a strong interest in the outside world.

We were not able to interview Olive for another eight years, by which time she had reached eighty-six years of age. Six years earlier, her physical condition had led her to enter a residential care home. Since then, she had become considerably more incapacitated, needing help also with bathing and unable to leave the home, which was privately run. However, she had maintained the same interest in the media, including reading newspapers, watching TV and listening to the radio. She had also maintained her previous activities of knitting and crocheting. Old friends and neighbours visited as before, 'several times a week'. Two years later, her daughter visited from Canada and with the aid of St John's ambulance (a British charitable service), Olive was able to go and stay with her for some days. When interviewed later in the year, she also referred to the woman who sat next to her in the care home as a "great friend."

In the two interviews we conducted with her at the ages of eighty-six and eighty-nine years, Olive presented the same contrast in indicators of well-being that she had shown ten years earlier. She had continued to show the same tendency to become depressed and yet retained a healthy self-regard at least at the times she was not severely depressed. Before her interview at age eighty-six, she had been hospitalized for depression with suicidal thoughts and treated with electroconvulsive therapy (ECT). She needed hospital treatment again for clinical depression two years later. At both interviews, she presented with a high depression rating, indicating 'persistent feelings of sadness and gloominess', 'fluctuating ideas of failure', and admitting to 'feeling miserable and sad' and 'having weeping spells'. However, she showed some improvement at the second interview, no longer indicating she was 'weary of life' and becoming 'tired for no reason'. This positive development was also reflected in her self-esteem ascriptions on the two occasions.

Olive attributed her problems with depression to her increasing disability. This also made her feel 'useless', she said at eighty-six years, because she could not offer any help in the life of the care home. She "wanted to do things but could not." She amplified her comments on herself in the self-completion questionnaire she filled in for us at age eighty-nine.

'Often my mood is'... *"depressed due to my inability to walk or move freely."*
'I am afraid of'... *"becoming helpless."*
'It would be nice if'... *"I could have kept my home and not rely on daily help."*

This last comment in particular reveals just how important staying in her own home had been to Olive. At that time, she had been living in a care home almost ten years.

Nevertheless, aspects of her self-esteem had remained strong. She said that she 'had always felt important because of her family' and her aim in life was to 'see her grandchildren grow older'. She was also sustained by her memories of her family.

'I like to dream about'... *"my family and happy home life."*

There was also evidence that she now gained even more support than before from her daily activities and interests. At eighty-nine years, she said she felt useful because she "looked after herself", enjoyed life due to "reading and playing cards" and felt capable because she "knits and crochets." She had aims because she "looked forward to doing things."

It appears that Olive had been able to substitute some of her earlier investment in family and social relationships with the activities she was still able to pursue, as evidenced by some of her other written statements.

'Most important for me is' . . . "to read or knit."

'When I feel unhappy' . . . "I try to interest myself in reading good books."

She also continued to be involved in the world around. She 'still felt bright and alert' because she was "aware of all that's happening." Her hope for the future was that she would "find things better in the world." When asked as part of the interview whether 'life had remained meaningful' she responded:

I think I've retained my interest in life . . . I feel so lucky to be so well in my brain, which I'm really thankful for.

Yet the losses in recent life had clearly been hard for her to bear, and her efforts to continue to accomplish things and communicate were meeting increasing obstacles. She was unsure of doing anything now "out of routine", and her recent loss of voice meant that she could not speak to her neighbours in the sitting room of the care home.

I have been rather worried because I can't talk across the room.

Her inability to carry out tasks independently had resulted in her feeling at times that "everything was a burden" and that she "wanted to die." She also expressed her fear of dependency on the written questionnaire she completed for us.

I am afraid of . . . "becoming helpless."

Although her daughter's recent visit had given Olive a boost, it was clear that her last years had been a valiant but never-ending battle to maintain her self-esteem and ward off depression. She had struggled hard to find more meaning in the activities she could undertake in her chair-bound state because wider goals could no longer be imagined. To the sentence stem 'In the next few years', she had answered laconically, "I do not look ahead now", and in the open interview, she had commented on the role of prayer in sustaining her:

Well I pray, I just pray for the strength to get me through each day.

It seemed a great pity that more was not being done to help Olive lead a more engaged life, joining in group activities both inside and outside the home, that would have helped meet her expectations of her later years. She died two years later before we were able to interview her again.

In Chapter 5, we described the devastating impact that the loss of **Doris Iveson's** husband had on her sense of self. Aged eighty years, she was already in poor health as a result of arthritis, other health problems and depression. In the year after her husband's death, she also experienced the dramatic onset of glaucoma, which led to emergency surgery. She described the event one year later.

It happened really suddenly. I was quite alright and I walked to about here and I got to here and just had a terrible pain, and I went ooh... whatever is happening – and everything went black. I didn't collapse or anything or pass out, it just happened – a terrible pain and my eyes went dull, went off, you know, couldn't see. Terrible. Eventually I got the sight back. Oh it was awful. I was vomiting for ages and ages and ages.

Before this interview, she had also injured the same foot twice, resulting in a cracked bone, which was still giving her considerable discomfort. Her depression score was now quite severe, with continuous feelings of misery, decreased ability to enjoy her usual interests, fluctuating ideas of self-depreciation and fleeting suicidal thoughts. Without a family of her own, she could not rely on help from children or other relatives. Her only close friends appeared to be as frail as she was. Her sense of loneliness following her husband's death was already acute.

Fortunately, Social Services intervened soon after this interview and encouraged her to move into a sheltered council flat. According to Doris's own account, this followed an incident when she fell whilst a social worker was visiting her. When next interviewed, she had been living in sheltered housing for two years. Her health had continued to deteriorate. She was dependent on outside help to get by from day to day. Although she was able to carry out the basic tasks of dressing, feeding and toileting herself, she needed help with bathing, housework and the preparation of her main meals.

She still had her wheeled Zimmer frame but had now also been provided with a wheelchair. Indeed, problems with her joints, especially her knees, meant that she could not move far on her own. She was clearly continuing to suffer from heart problems, experiencing breathlessness on exertion. She was receiving some help with housework from a woman who had been on her husband's staff at the department store in town. She had made these arrangements after being dissatisfied with the standard of service she used to get from the home help sent by Social Services. Other recent health events included a bout of bronchitis and a blocking of her tear ducts, which she thought might need surgery to correct. She was seeing the doctor every couple of months. Although her sight was impaired, it did not seem to have deteriorated over the previous three years. Her hearing and speech were also unimpaired.

Her score on the depression scale had decreased little since the last interview. The highest scores continued to occur for the elements related to feeling tense and sad, as well as problems with sleep and appetite. Her attitudes to health and her experience of ageing continued to be negative, but she showed some increasing acceptance of her chronic health problems. Another close friend had died, as had her budgie. She had been extremely fond of the bird and was upset as much by the way it had died – in pain from a tumour – as by the actual loss. She had subsequently acquired another budgie but had given it away as they did not get on.

She found it difficult to get about and so stayed in most of the time. She did get out every now and again to visit friends, but her major social contact was to go to a weekly luncheon club and to attend a Red Cross club. She received Meals On Wheels every day except luncheon club day. The telephone was another important source of social contact. During our interview, she received a lengthy call from a friend. She complained that the people in the housing complex were not sociable, but she did accept the company of a Jehovah's Witness neighbour who seemed to be unwelcome elsewhere. Doris kept the TV and radio on much of the time, more for company she said that for entertainment. She was still able to do a little reading, especially newspapers, and also tend plants around her flat.

At the time of interview, Doris had just returned from a Christmas respite stay in a Social Services residential care home. She said she was glad to get back to her own home because she had found the company in the care home tiresome. By the end of the stay, she was starting to get 'as bad as' the permanent residents. She had not found the food very appetizing either!

Despite her generally negative attitudes, Doris was still clearly in control of her life. Although her self-esteem ascriptions remained generally negative, there had been some movement. For example, to the question whether she was as 'bright and alert as ever', she said:

I'm OK, but other people do not have the same interests as me.

One of the most striking wishes she expressed was to take up swimming again. It would have been good to have made that wish achievable for her.

She struggled to complete many of the handwritten answers about herself on the open schedule we gave her, but the answers she did give were revealing. For example, to the question, 'what has been most meaningful about your life so far?' she answered:

Being married to a good man.

The importance to her of social contacts also came out clearly in many of her answers.

'What is it about your life that makes you feel most alive?' ... "When I get visitors."
'What kind of things do you enjoy doing?' ... "Going to clubs."
'Who is important in your life today?' ... "Friends."
'Who or what do you especially care about?' ... "Friends and visitors."

The most significant aspects of Doris's life remained only in her memory. She and her husband had been very close, devoting their lives to each other. She appeared after their marriage not to have continued to develop an identity separate from him. That is why her reference to 'taking up swimming again' was so surprising. There were no children, grandchildren, or even nephews and nieces who could provide a greater relevance to her current life, only her friends and neighbours most of whom were ageing fast. Her present life lacked meaning in comparison to her past life. She had been fulfilled in that life but was now left without any significant role or purpose.

It's a really nice life I've had. That's why I notice it now.
It's totally different to what it was before.
Since my husband died, I've had nothing.

Doris died before our next interview aged eighty-seven years.

Nellie Moreton's life story provided a strong contrast with Doris's. As described in Chapter 6, Nellie had delayed marriage because of responsibilities to her six younger siblings after her mother died when Nellie was twelve years old. Her marriage only lasted a few years, ending like Vera Wright's as a result of separation from her husband during the war. Like Vera too, she had then had to seek work again to look after her two children. An osteoporotic spine leading to cervical spondylosis had led to earlier retirement than she would have wished and created worries for her future. But she had felt securer once she moved to a sheltered housing scheme, where she took on a very active role as chairperson of the scheme's social club.

Her health continued to deteriorate, and by age eighty years, her mobility outside had greatly declined, although her active and appreciated role within the housing scheme as well as within her own family had helped keep her self-esteem high. She was interviewed again at eighty-two years of age, by which time her physical decline was more accentuated. She could no longer walk more than a few hundred yards, and she admitted that she 'could no longer do all the things she used to' because of weakness in her limbs. However, her earlier problems with breathlessness on exercise had been improved by the fitting of a pacemaker. In the previous year, she had been admitted to hospital as an emergency when her heart problem was finally diagnosed. Nellie herself admitted to occasional problems with depression, although her actual test scores were not high. The main change seemed to be an increasing weariness about life, reflected for the first time in negative expressed attitudes to the experience of growing old.

Nevertheless, she was still maintaining her independence as far as she could, and although no longer chairing the scheme's social club, she was still contributing to its fund-raising through the making of handicrafts. She had regular contact with her family, neighbours within the scheme as well as attending a luncheon club two or three times a week. She was also going on occasional theatre visits and day trips. Her self-esteem ascriptions and handwritten responses to the open questionnaire on life strengths were now illustrated mostly by references to her family, her care and concern for them, as well as their care and concern for her. She had obtained particular pleasure from the birth of her first great-grandchild within the past few months. Handicrafts were also important elements. She described herself as doing work for bazaars and charities and also 'helping her daughter with sewing for a drama group'. But she also in her self-ascriptions and illustrations indicated a satisfaction with the mental faculties, strong qualities and happy memories that she still possessed which augured well for the future.

'What is it in your life that gives you hope?' . . . *"That at my age I can see, hear and have a fairly good memory".*

'I have confidence in myself' . . . *"If I set out to do a thing, I usually do it."*

'What parts of your life is it most important that you stay in charge of?" . . . *"My faculties, remembering the good times."*

'What has been most meaningful about your life so far?' . . . *"My survival against great odds."*

Nellie regarded her life as a struggle, being made up of a series of events, things that had happened to her that were out of her control and yet had had significant effects on her life. This started with the early imposition of responsibility for her siblings as a result of the death of her mother and then the struggle to being up her own children when her husband deserted her. Despite such a harsh fate, she derived personal satisfaction from the task of bringing up her children and in focusing attention on those less fortunate than herself. Indeed, in doing this, she was able to develop a positive attitude towards her own misfortunes.

Working with her [a child she visited] you just think how lucky you are to have normal children.

She continued to use this strategy in her working life by getting employment at a school for children with special needs.

Now, in later life, Nellie was enjoying a kind of security that she never experienced as a young woman. She had been able to bring together the skills she acquired throughout her life to settle herself into a respected position in her community. However, without a doubt, her family was the most important aspect of her life.

Well, it makes me appreciate what I've got now. I appreciate my family. They are all good to me, and my own brothers and sisters, they are now repaying me for what I did for them. Can you understand what I mean? They are concerned about me. They wouldn't see me go without things.

Her children and their offspring were also the most meaningful facets of her life.

Well, my children I think (are meaningful) because I had to bring them up – four months old and two – I was there for them, and they were there for me and we've never lost touch. They married good partners who are also good to me . . . So in that way I feel very lucky.

From the way Nellie spoke about it, her family appeared important not only for its own sake, but also because it allowed her to achieve vicariously the secure and happy family which she missed. It was striking that she was actively aware of the importance of maintaining relationships and not taking her family's love and loyalty for granted. The recent birth of her great-grandson was the culmination and reward for the lifelong effort of devotion to others indicating that Nellie had achieved both generativity and integrity.

These were the conclusions about her sense of self at age eighty-two years that we composed at the time. But in fact Nellie was to live another almost ten years. As Erik Erikson and his wife Joan asked towards the end of their long lives, is there another stage beyond integrity? The concepts Erikson had formulated to describe successful ageing in the 1950s no longer seemed adequate for societies where post-retirement life expectation had increased by a further ten years. How should one describe the meaning of these extra years? Gene Cohen, whose ideas about ageing we mentioned in Chapter 2, has described it using the theatrical term of 'encore', a reassertion, perhaps expressed in new ways, of previously asserted values. But could there be genuinely new elements in the longer lives of older people as they became frailer?

We interviewed Nellie on another three occasions, twice at age eighty-four. Her situation was little changed. Her family remained the central feature of her life. A second great-grandchild had brought further joy and pride in her offspring. Her health continued to be a trial for her, particularly her back problems, which reduced her mobility, but also a referred pain in her left leg. She was receiving home help and assistance with shopping three times a week and still attending the luncheon club as before. She was also hoping to have a shower fitted in the near future.

However, she had suffered two disturbing events in the previous two years. Her confidence in health care had been badly affected by an unfortunate experience over her pacemaker. After the initial one failed, the procedure to fit a replacement had not gone smoothly, resulting in a painful and unpleasant experience for her.

Presumably it was only a faulty valve, but when they opened it up it was the whole pacemaker that was wrong and they couldn't find the key to get a new one out of the cupboard. There I was laying there... the surgeon was getting all het up, and in the end he said, 'I've had enough of this'. I said, 'So have I'... and by the time they did get the pacemaker the anaesthetic had worn off and I felt every stitch.

Subsequent to this, Nellie had been offered the opportunity to have an operation on her back. A combination of an assessment of the risk involved and the remembrance of her previous experience led her to decline.

The other negative event was a walk-in theft a few months earlier. A sum of £200 was taken from her flat, and the unsettling effect on Nellie had been considerable even though she was not the only resident who had been affected. She felt keenly the sense of individual violation.

I felt pretty awful. I think it was more to think that someone had been in here. The loss was dreadful, but the thought that someone was able to get in here....

The money was only there because she had just collected her pension and so was needed for paying bills and day-to-day living. Happily her family was able to rally round and pay for her without any problem.

Nellie's self-esteem remained high, illustrated principally as before by her family and valuable position within it. However she no longer regarded herself as 'capable of doing a lot' and no longer had aims or hopes for the future.

I do everything I can now – at eighty-four you don't expect to do much more, do you?

The constant back pain was affecting her morale, leading to broken sleep pattern and sluggishness in the morning. The pain was also leading her to ask questions of her Christian belief.

... but I also ask myself what I've done to deserve all this pain.

Nevertheless, she continued to be a regular attender at her Catholic parish and helped with fêtes and bazaars as much as she was able.

Most interesting was her reassertion of her family role. She saw herself still very much in a position of responsibility, looking out for her family's welfare, and she was of the view that the family continued to 'take notice' of her.

Don't get me wrong, I don't interfere in any way. Not with the husbands and wives and the way they bring up their children because everybody has their own ideas, but I do like to know what's going on and I like them to involve me, which they do.

Similarly Nellie was confident of their help and support if she needed it, even though she had no desire to become a burden on her family.

She readily agreed that her life's mission was complete with the birth of her great-grandchildren. However, it impressed us that the satisfaction she expressed was not because of her own achievement in realizing four generations but because of her own daughter's sense of fulfilment.

I know my daughter was dying to be a grandmother for one thing and by golly she's a grandmother, a very, very devoted grandmother.

The continued happiness of those for whom she has battled throughout her life was of supreme importance to Nellie.

A new element in her self-disclosure at this interview, which she enlarged on in an interview the following year, was a reconsideration of her husband's role in her life. It was thanks to his work in the merchant navy that she had been eligible for British Legion sheltered housing. She said that she may at times have done him an injustice because he had been so entirely dominated by his mother. It was almost as if she perceived him as not being in control of his own life. She had found out later from her sister-in-law who lived across the road that her mother-in-law had kept the money her husband had put by regularly for the upkeep of their two children. Her feelings of bitterness were directed at her mother-in-law. Yes, she said, she had forgiven her but could not forget the hardship she had been caused. She wanted to stress how much harder these actions had made her life, for example, that she had had to take her very young son and daughter with her to work, whether cleaning or embroidering.

Neither her son nor daughter, she thought, had suffered from not having a father, because they had never known him. But he did ask to see them when he was dying. He had written to his daughter at work, not at home. She was then eighteen years old. When she had asked her mother's advice, Nellie had said that she might regret it if she did not see her father. So her daughter did visit him, accompanied by her brother, although they did not go to the subsequent funeral.

Nellie also reflected more on her early experience of her mother's illness and death and how at age twelve she had had to take care of the family. It had been especially hard because her father drank (as her husband did too). He died seven years later, and the family could not afford a proper service of burial, nor pay the rent on the family house. Because Nellie could not cope, the family was dispersed. Her two brothers and two sisters were taken into care with the local Catholic sisters, while Nellie went into service and her older brother found work. But she had continued to look out for them as they grew older and was still in regular contact with her two surviving sisters and one brother.

Nellie reiterated at this second interview how proud she was of the new family she had built. Yet one element of continuity with the old family was in the practice of the Catholic faith. Nellie reminisced how her mother, even though not a Catholic herself, had always encouraged her to walk to Mass at the Catholic church in the city centre. She took sandwiches with her to eat afterwards because of the long distance. Now she was taken to church, on Saturday evenings to the Catholic church in the neighbourhood (her daughter also helped in the local Catholic school), and during the week to a luncheon club in the hall of the old church in the city centre.

All the family lived in the city and visited regularly, her daughter on five days in the week. There were many photographs of them around the room, and most telling of the family's centrality to her own identity was that Nellie wore a small photograph in a locket of her first great-grandson on a chain around her neck. She said she was sad for older people when they told her how they did not see their families for weeks. She seemed to imply that she who had been so unfortunate in her family early in life was extremely fortunate now.

Nellie was interviewed for the last time at eighty-seven years. She remained very much the same, but had lost weight, was somewhat unsteady on her feet and clearly got dizzy quite easily. Her life had changed little externally. However, she had been left money by one brother who had died, which meant that she now for the first time in her life had plenty of money to spend. She agreed that these were the best years of her life. She continued to be taken to luncheon club and to church services. Strangely, her home help had recently been withdrawn by social services, and Nellie was most displeased about this. Despite social services claiming that she had been reassessed, she was not aware of when and how. She was now paying someone privately to do the housework, although she had not yet established a reliable service. [Our comments at the time were as follows: "If an eighty-seven-year old with a history of heart problems, chronic back pain, arthritis and who is disabled enough to use a wheelchair from time to time isn't entitled to a home help from social services, then who is?] Nevertheless, Nellie still greatly appreciated the sheltered housing scheme in which she lived and was particularly pleased with the service she received from the warden.

When we next contacted Nellie three years later, she had moved to a residential care home and shortly afterwards admitted to the elderly care wards at the local general hospital. She died in the following year, aged ninety-one years.

Becoming frailer in the early eighties

Mavis Dawes's health was declining in her early eighties. When she was interviewed at age eighty-three, her oldest son, who had business interests in Scotland again, was asking her to come back there with his family. But Mavis was reluctant to agree because of continuing friction with her daughter-in-law. Also, her younger son in Southampton had become dependent on her financially, and she worried about his failure to care for himself properly. She remained active socially, attending the local Baptist church regularly, as well as the Salvation Army and the local community centre. She was waiting for a shower to be fitted in her flat because she could no longer use the bath. She had had a fall recently during the night and received some physiotherapy sessions for her arthritic knees but had given them up because she felt they were more trouble than it was worth. She was now also getting short of breath even when washing and dressing.

Although there were some negative themes in her self-ascriptions, related to her increasing disability, strong themes remained, especially related to her role within the family, both to her remaining sister and to her sons. She described her eldest son as "very kind." But her youngest son was the focus of concern.

'I have a clear aim in life' . . . *"I want to live to be able to still help my youngest son."*

Her written self-descriptions conveyed her understanding of herself at this time, stressing in many the importance of good health.

'Later when I'm older' . . . *"I don't mind living much longer so long as my health doesn't get worse."*

'It would be nice if' . . . *"I hadn't had arthritis, but I suppose I might have had something worse."*

'I've found that I' . . . *"have spells of depression, mostly when I'm not well."*

'In the next few years' . . . *"as long as my health doesn't deteriorate, I shall be alright."*

Positive aspects of her appearance were also clearly very important to her.

'I am very proud of' . . . *"my skin for my age."*

'My appearance' . . . *"I have a very good appearance except for my arthritis."*

Some new and positive themes emerged from her life review at this time.

'When I think about myself' . . . *"I have had a fair amount of courage to stand my life."*

She also clearly harboured fond memories of her earlier years.

'I like to dream about' . . . *"the happiness I had before my husband took ill and when my sister was alive."*

Her answers indicated again how her family remained her major concern.

'The goal that I would like to accomplish in my life' . . . *"always to see my family well."*

Her religious faith was also evident in some of her answers.

'When I feel unhappy' . . . *"I believe in prayer."*

'Maybe I can' . . . *"thank the Lord for the good things."*

Unfortunately, later the same year, Mavis fell again, this time with much more serious consequences, breaking her hip and femur. Altogether she was in hospital for almost four months. We interviewed her again two years later and seven months after she had been moved into a downstairs flat. She was now eighty-six years old and suffering from multiple health problems. Both her sight and hearing were considerably impaired and affecting her quality of life. Her physical disability was related to continuing problems with arthritic joints as well as weakness in her limbs. She also was still encountering breathlessness, although this did not seem to be as severe as the last time she was interviewed. She continued to have bladder troubles (cystitis) and experienced urinary retention. She was also suffering from bleeding piles. However, her problems with depression had not increased and what symptoms she had concerned difficulties in dropping off to sleep and a slightly reduced appetite.

Mavis was now quite disabled. She was no longer able to do any shopping and had become almost housebound. Within the house she could no longer climb stairs and walked with the aid of a Zimmer frame. She needed help with some of the housework and was receiving Meals On Wheels as before. Besides self-care activities, she spent her time reading, listening to the radio and watching television and also occasionally playing card games and looking after houseplants. Her only outing was once a week to a social services day centre to which she was brought either by the day centre's own transport or by her son.

Yet despite her awareness that her health had continued to deteriorate and that she had become much less active than she used to be, she appeared to have developed a more positive set of attitudes towards her present life over the previous couple of years. She denied being troubled by health problems and expressed the opinion that these were in fact the best years of her life. In fact, she agreed with the statements that she 'found it nice to grow old' and that 'old age is a happy time for me'. Also, her self-esteem ascriptions had become more positive. Even negative statements were illustrated with comments that were not indicative of low morale.

'I get little enjoyment out of life' . . . *"I'm content in myself."*
'I have no aims left in my life' . . . *"I'm nearly eighty-seven!"*

She referred to her importance to her son, her usefulness in helping friends at the day centre, and her confidence in meeting and talking in front of people. She expressed a heightened sense of inner contentment.

'I look to the future with confidence' . . . *"Because I'm satisfied with life as it is. I'm quite happy in my flat. I enjoy food and will be having my sister to stay for two weeks soon."*

The meanings she perceived in her life came out clearly in the answers she supplied to the self-completion questionnaire on life strengths. Her activities, both social and mental, were dominant themes.

'What is it about your life that makes you feel most alive?'... "When I am being useful to somebody. I am taken to... Day Centre each Thursday, sit next to a blind man and help him."

'What parts of your life is it most important that you stay in charge of?'... "Keeping my sense of humour and being optimistic."

'What kinds of things do you enjoy doing?'... "Watching television, reading good books, listening to radio."

'What is important to you in your life today?'... "Keeping my brain active."

Her family and her present home also hold a significant place in her identity.

'Who or what do you especially care about?'... "Always my family."

'What has been most meaningful about your life so far?'... "Having my lovely little flat and being able to get up each morning."

Underpinning meaning in her life is provided by her religious faith.

'What is it in your life that gives you hope?'... "Christianity."

'What do you believe in?'... "The Lord Jesus Christ."

She continued to have worries about her younger son, whom she described now as an alcoholic and in poor health because of having only one lung. She had recently been having arguments with him as well. Considering her older son was in the process of moving to Scotland, it seemed remarkable that Mavis was so serene in her attitudes. The state of inner peace she had now reached and her positive attitude to growing old were in striking contrast to the negative descriptions of the hardships of her past life.

Mavis died three years later at age eighty-nine years shortly before we were due to interview her again.

Rita Fletcher was interviewed again on three occasions at age eighty-two. She could be considered now both physically frail because of her deteriorating eyesight resulting from glaucoma as well as vulnerable to a recurrence of depressive illness. Although she had largely overcome the psychological turmoil that had troubled her since the period of her husband's and mother's deaths, her determination to maintain her previous level of activities had resulted in major problems. She had been encouraged by her health advisors to start using a white stick to indicate to others that she had visual problems. Understandably, she was reluctant to accept this advice because she felt that it would signal her vulnerability to people who might pose a threat to her. But she had been daring too much. Earlier in the year, she had fallen down the length of an escalator during a shopping expedition to the centre of the city and been lucky to survive with minor injuries.

Well I went up, got to the top alright, but just at the top I panicked. I put the wrong foot out for the landing, that's where I went wrong. I panicked and fell back, right back on my head, and she [a friend] came down on top of me ... I remember getting down the bottom and seeing everybody's feet down the bottom and anyway, they said could I stand, and I said, 'Oh don't ask me to stand' and they said, 'She's hurt badly.' I wasn't, I just felt I couldn't stand straight away.

At the time of the interview, Rita's depression rating was not high. She was sleeping well with the help of sleeping tablets. She was, however, weary of life at times, questioning whether it was worth living and admitted to fleeting suicidal thoughts. She stated quite emphatically that she would not want to continue living if she went blind. She was still being visited at regular intervals by the psychogeriatric service.

She appeared to have settled down into a pleasant relationship with her new-found daughter (see Chapter 5). She had been recently invited to her daughter's sixtieth birthday party, which was clearly an important occasion for her in that she took care to buy a smart new dress for the occasion (it was while she was shopping for her outfit that she had her fall). She described the moment when her daughter noticed Rita and her son's family at the birthday party.

You should have seen her when she was in that hall, she came in with her family, and we were sat down in the corner together, but when we got up, oh boy, didn't she go mad. She thought it was lovely to see us and of course a lot of introducing then, you see, yes, introduced me to so many.

Her son had taken a beautiful present of a china doll for his stepsister, and the fact that her daughter and her son got on so well was a source of pleasure to Rita.

And now what I think, he's got someone when I'm gone, hasn't he?

As reported in Chapter 5, Rita had never really demonstrated high self-esteem. The apparent improvement noted two years earlier when she was 'discovered' by her daughter had not been maintained. She continued to feel 'capable' in her housework and 'important' to her family, and she also had some hopes for the future:

I hope to live long enough to see Labour in ... If Tony Blair gets in, I'll have a big increase in my money. Things can't get any worse at the moment.

However, the fall she had recently experienced had damaged her sense of self. She said that she had "lost confidence since the fall." The discontentment that she felt about her past life remained.

I've never had a good life, what I mean I've never had a life when it's been cheery. My brother brought me up, life was dull then, there was only Grandma and I so I never had a really what-do-you-call-it life.

She seemed to be constantly worried about the poor state of repair of her house. However, the evidence from the effects of previous maintenance work would suggest that any renovations should be avoided. She was also concerned about her finances, saying that she had to "watch every penny." Her family remained the most meaningful feature of her life, and she was currently very worried about her granddaughter's baby, whose health was precarious. Nevertheless, Rita was coping with her present situation, primarily with the help of her son and daughter-in-law, and so long as her sight did not deteriorate too much, there was hope she would maintain her current level of well-being.

Because of Rita's vulnerability, we did not think it right to cause her possible distress at the follow-up interview by drawing attention to some of the details in the case study we had written about her. We therefore summarized sections and sought her comments instead on her early years and changes in her social circumstances since the study began. She provided additional information on the period in which she suffered several bereavements and a spell of severe depression. She also spoke about the help given by her son and daughter-in-law in looking after her house and the problems with her eyesight. Her concerns about the house were evident. She said that she no longer had the confidence to go down the steps into the back garden in case she fell. But she was clear that she wanted to die in that house 'just like her husband did'. She repeated her assertion that she did not want to live without her sight and that she was now "so scared of falling down."

When another of us came to visit her a few months later, she was pleased to go again through the events of her life from her upbringing in the Cotswolds to her reunion with her daughter. She spoke about her fiancé who had died in an accident during the war, how she still had his last letter and wanted it to be buried with her. She also spoke about her husband and how he loved working the garden sloping down to the river. She was sad she could not go walking down there now because of her eyesight. She had been told that if she fell again, she could lose her sight completely, so she had to be careful. She also described in detail the multiple bereavements that had led to her depression, and praised the psychogeriatric service for the kindness shown to her. She emphasized how the same consultant doctor still visited her. She was particularly pleased that we had received so well the story of her discovery of her daughter and encouraged us to visit again. She showed the beautiful view from the back of the house. It was like a "fairyland" she said at night with the lights on the river.

Two years later at age eighty-five, Rita collapsed at home and was admitted to hospital by her GP, who considered that she had not been eating properly.

However, on return home she fell again and was not found until the next day, by which time she was suffering from hypothermia and had to be admitted to hospital again. Her son and daughter-in-law subsequently took over all her domestic care needs, including financial responsibilities, and at the time of our last interview two months later, they were calling every day to see her. She was also wearing an Alarmline pendant that could connect her to emergency assistance and using a Zimmer frame to walk. Although her depression score had not increased, her self-esteem remained low, she expressed herself dissatisfied with her past life and was becoming even more worried about the future. Sadly she no longer had contact with her daughter after a row on the telephone a year or so previously. Apart from the visits from her son's family, her main joy seemed to come from her new cat, almost identical to her old cat, whose death in the year before had been a cause of great distress to her.

Unfortunately, we were not able to visit Rita again. She died four years later at age eighty-nine.

At age eighty-five, **Mary Morrison** had a fall in which she fractured her hip. She needed to stay in hospital for more than a week and thereafter had a month's convalescence. At the time of interview some months later, when she had reached eighty-six years, she was walking with a stick, limited to 'one hundred to four hundred yards' and could not climb stairs unaided. As a result, she was confined to her home. Nevertheless, her mood remained positive, and she felt satisfied with the way she was coping. Her positive self-esteem ascriptions continued to be illustrated with reference to her housework, her son's family and her attendance at church. Her concerns about feeling 'bright and alert' had disappeared, and she presented stoically as someone who "takes life as it comes" and did not worry about her health. Nevertheless, the fall had had some negative consequences on her sense of self. To some ascriptions, she could not give examples. Her sense of confidence had been shaken, her future plans curtailed and her life-world also more restricted.

Mary's fracture of the thigh resulted in a combination of problems when walking as well as weakness in her legs. However, she did return to doing her own shopping as well as housework, and when interviewed three years later at age eighty-nine, she was walking up to a mile with the aid of a stick. Clearly she was still determined to remain active, although she 'could not do all the things she used to'. She was managing to do all her housework, shopping and preparation of meals. Indoors her leisure activities consisted mainly of occasional reading, knitting, looking after her cat and watching TV. Outdoors she continued to go to town 'more than once a week', to visit friends 'two to three times a week' and also attend social clubs and church activities regularly. For her age and particularly considering the effects of her injury four years earlier, she was remarkably active. Her depression score was only slightly raised, and her attitude to her health was unchanged, repeating the same answer as before that she 'did not worry'.

However, her sense of self-esteem had now definitely lowered. Although her cat provided her with motivation making her feel 'useful' and "keeping the flat clean" made her feel capable, she again could not decide whether she got 'little nor much enjoyment out of life' and could not supply an example. She also felt neither 'of much nor of little importance to others' and although she said that she maintained her self-confidence, she could not give an example to illustrate this. She said she had 'few aims in life' apart from

small things I would like to do before anything happens.

A decline in her involvement in life was reflected in other interview material, suggesting that isolation may have contributed to a loss of well-being.

'What would you say are the most important features of your life?'... "I haven't got anything really... I'm on my own and I just do what I've got to do."

One of the reasons for her loss of self-esteem appears to be related to her inability to remain involved in outdoor pursuits.

Not being able to get around to do some of the things I used to.... I used to go to the hospital with the League of Friends... but I can't do it you see.

Life was becoming harder.

It's more difficult and it's lonely. Some of my people have gone... I lost a couple of weeks ago an old friend of mine.

Mary did appreciate the contacts that she still had but they did not seem sufficient.

I've still got relatives and... connections with people.... I'm very fortunate in that respect. I've got people who are still friends.

My son and his wife – they come and visit and take me out sometimes... There's nothing very exciting... You just go on from day to day.

As an older person, she no longer placed a high value on her life.

Nobody could think when you get to my age that it's so valuable. There's nothing that's really – I'm just ordinary.

Subsequently Mary's health deteriorated rapidly, and she died two years later. However, we were able to interview her once more shortly before she died when she was living in a residential care home. According to the head of staff there, Mary had had numerous falls in her ninetieth year and as a result had been admitted to an elderly care hospital for six months as a form of recuperation. Thereafter, it had been decided that it was not possible for her to go back home and that she should move into a residential care home where she had now been living a few months. When first admitted to the home, she had still been mobile, walking with a frame, but she was now confined to a wheelchair. The head of home also said that Mary had been receiving medication because of her 'hyperactivity' and was much 'calmer' as a result. She was suffering from moderate to severe dementia.

When her previous interviewer introduced herself, there appeared to be a glimmer of recognition on Mary's part.

'It's nice to see you again, Mrs...'... "It's nice to see you. It's been a long time."

At the end of the conversation, she also responded appropriately.

'Thank you very much Mrs...'... "Thank you very much. It's been a pleasure."

However, although Mary often gave appropriate responses to enquiries – for example, about the garden of the home – she seemed not to recognize the significance of others, particularly concerning herself – for example, where her room was in the home or what had happened to her cat. The evening before, the head of home told us that Mary had expressed the view, "Oh, I hope I don't go like my mother." This seemed to imply that she recognized her dementing condition.

We were struck by how rapidly dementia could develop, completely altering a person's life. Nevertheless, Mary still retained her former air of gentility and politeness. She seemed to enjoy the company and conversations of others, and according to the head of home had a good appetite. We thought she might live some years more. In fact, she died very shortly after our visit.

Irene Monroe had encountered major changes in her life when we interviewed her again at age eighty-seven after an interval of eight years. Her husband had died soon after the last interview, and Irene had then moved to a warden-assisted sheltered housing apartment. However, her health problems (a combination of angina/arteriosclerosis and arthritis) had become so severe that by age eighty-five she had moved to a residential care home. At the time of the interview, she described herself as having "gone downhill" for about year beforehand and finally having "seized up." She still had a problem walking due to sciatica, which caused "unsteadiness and pain", and she also experienced breathlessness when walking on level ground. This had affected her ability to care for herself, with the care staff carrying out most of the tasks, including help with bathing, although on occasions Irene was doing some shopping on her own. Also her hearing had deteriorated to an extent she said had affected her quality of life.

However, her morale was higher than at the time of the previous interview when she was becoming increasingly stressed by caring for her husband. The depression rating was lower, although she reported occasional difficulty sleeping, collecting her thoughts and starting activities. Her self-esteem had also returned to its initial high level and was illustrated as before by her strong religious faith. Whereas at seventy-nine, she had lost a sense of being important, she now felt that her importance lay in "informing others of Christ" and also felt more capable again, mainly derived from her recently acquired interest in painting. It appeared that she was adjusting herself to a less active life style that accommodated her health problems. She said herself that now she was in a residential home, she was 'worrying less about the help she would need in the future'.

This positive impression was confirmed at our following interview two years later when she was aged eighty-nine years. Earlier in the year, she had taken the decision to move to another residential care home situated in a seaside town twenty miles away. The home was run by the Church Army, and its ethos reflected her own religious allegiance. She enjoyed life there.

Oh yes, very happy, I have some wonderful friends, oh yes, very happy.

She also liked the local church and found the congregation supportive. Her mobility outside the home had increased a little, although the medication she was taking for her sciatica had side effects that concerned her when out walking.

I must say I haven't been to the sea quite as often . . . I don't feel quite so stable when I go to the sea.

Her hearing impairment, even with use of a hearing aid, was still causing her some discomfort.

I do rather annoy people, especially young people . . . Unless people speak direct to me and I'm through speaking I do find that difficult to pick up.

Nevertheless, the picture she gave of her life was a generally positive one. Her self-ascriptions were illustrated as before mainly by reference to her religious faith. Her 'aim in life', for example, was "to make people happy by spreading the faith." Most revealing of her religious attitudes were her written answers on the sentence completion questionnaire she filled in at the time.

'Most important for me' . . . "is to live as my Creator intends: chiefly to walk humbly with Him."
'I believe' . . . "that I am born to glorify God."

She also described how her faith sustained her through periods of sadness.

'When I feel unhappy' . . . "I get to the root of the cause and then ask God to take my thoughts and renew them; which He does."

In comparison with her earlier presentation of self (see Chapter 4), Irene was now feeling more 'capable' and made no reference to the heart trouble as preventing her from participating in activities. She was emphasizing what she could still do, especially her recently acquired interest in painting but also helping in the care home, for example, by "laying tables." A further change was that her family now appeared to be playing a more central part in the way she evaluated her life than in previous years. Altogether her mood was more positive as she illustrated on the sentence completion questionnaire.

'I really feel good'... "when I have had fulfilment in painting."
'I am very proud of'... "my daughter, my grandchildren and my sister."

She also appeared to be deriving satisfaction less from her actions to help others as in the past and more from being less independent and coming to rely on others. For example, she said she derived 'much enjoyment' from "being taken to places, as concerts."

Irene used the opportunities provided by the interview to reflect on her strengths and weaknesses. She continued to be troubled by her deafness, which resulted in her

Talking out of turn and going on talking when shouldn't.

She reiterated this concern in her subsequent written statements.

'My weaknesses are'... "lack of communication when listening for any length of time and speaking out of turn sometimes."

She also considered that she was "confident to speak my mind, but unsure of making decisions." As for the future, her aim was "to live a fuller life and make others happy." Certainly, despite the difficulties she had been through, she had constantly remained hopeful for the future, which she founded on her deep-rooted religious faith. She also saw whatever losses might lie ahead in the same light.

'Later when I'm older'.... "I might experience loss of friends through death... then I am very sad but I try to live with the 'unseen' when sadness is experienced."

When after this interview we attempted to draw together in writing our own conclusions on Irene's sense of self over the years that we had interviewed her, we commented especially on her adaptability in the face of physical decline. Her self-esteem could be maintained and even restored by new interests. In her later seventies, her needlework had kept her feeling capable, and with the deterioration in her eyesight, this had been replaced by a keen interest in painting. Similarly whereas in the earlier period she was still helping to organize church functions, she was now content with the more basic task of laying tables in the care home. Her renewed interest in her family may also have reflected an adaptation to the lessening of her once-large social world.

There were also major continuities in Irene's self-perception. She had always been willing to criticize herself for her failings, particularly a lack of self-confidence, and the feelings of uncertainty this engendered were likely to continue. At the same time her religious faith had shown itself to be robust and a lodestone for the decisions she had made in recent years. There was no reason to think it would not be so for whatever difficulties lay ahead in the coming years. Irene in fact lived to ninety-six years, and we continue our account of her life in her nineties in Chapter 9.

In **Vera Wright's** case, we could only interview up to a certain stage of what could have been a much longer process of becoming yet frailer. Nevertheless, we did obtain substantial information on her response to increasing frailty by the time of the last interview with her at age eighty-six.

When we paused her account in the previous chapter at age eighty-one, she had recently had a hip replacement after a fall. At the time of interview two years later, she appeared to have made a good recovery, had regained most of her previous activities and expressed a high sense of self-esteem, although little hope for the future. Nine months before the interview, she had undergone a second operation for hip replacement and was incurring problems with her eyes due to inflammation and cataracts, which were 'impairing some aspects of her life'. Worsening arthritis in her knee had limited her mobility, and she now no longer travelled to the centre of the city.

But outwardly her life appeared to have changed relatively little. She claimed to be still driving her car – a Triumph Acclaim – and able to walk up to a mile. The car had come to take on a very strong meaning for her, and she was particularly worried that she would not be allowed to continue driving:

If I didn't have the car I'd . . . I would be useless and worthless you know.

Yet the meaning seemed to be principally symbolic because there was no evidence that she had used the car for many months. In fact, it was her son now who collected her pension and helped with shopping. A friend did the gardening.

Vera had a low depression rating and continued to express a stoic philosophy of life, saying that she was not anxious about the help she would need in the future. Indeed, she agreed with the statement that it was 'nice to grow old', which she followed with the comment:

You have to accept it; make the best of it.

Her self-esteem remained high, illustrated with the sense of freedom and control she felt over her daily life, her importance to her son and his family and also her various friends, and most of all by her feelings of confidence and capability.

I still do everything. It's no good sitting down and being miserable – never give up! If I start to do something, I do it. It's better to hope than despair.

The fact that she was still recovering past abilities following her hip operation also gave her positive feelings and aims for the immediate future.

I do things that I haven't done for a long time. I never feel lonely or depressed. [My aims?] Get up and go again. Pick up with things I haven't done for a long time.

The longer future, however, was more uncertain.

I don't know if I've got a future.

We interviewed Vera on two more occasions when she was eighty-three years old. She showed particular interest in the progress of our research project and expressed some pride to be part of it, especially because of her previous university connections. She engaged enthusiastically with our analysis of the basis to her sense of self in the first two of these interviews. In the second, she expressed agreement with our written conclusions and elaborated more on many of the various points that had been made.

She agreed that remaining actively independent on her own gave her a strong sense of purpose, reinforcing a positive sense of identity. Her father, she said, had brought her up to be independent.

My son wanted me to live with them but I'd never agree to that – it would mean giving all the things I love away – they all have meaning for me . . . It's the same with driving – it's important for me – it's a way of getting around . . . There is nothing like independence – it's the best thing.

At the same time, she reaffirmed that her family and long-term friends were an important source of her identity.

Although I've got a small family – my son, his wife and daughter – I appreciate them being there.
Yes – they are very helpful – my daughter-in-law is helpful . . . and my granddaughter. My friends . . . are genuine . . . I've kept up with them . . . I've always kept contact.

Long-term rather than short-term friends 'added satisfaction' to her life. She brought out to show us correspondence from long-standing friends who lived abroad saying:

They're friends I've known for years – I've been all over Europe.

All my friends are old friends. I don't think nowadays people want to bother with old people, so I don't look for new friends.

She also agreed that a key part of her identity was her sense of inner strength and determination, which helped her to surmount difficulties.

My father brought me up (to be independent)... I would never let anybody down and my word is my bond.

It's no good dithering... the thing to do is to make up your mind what you are going to do and finish.

It isn't any good to sit down and think I've got a pain. I mean you get up and about and you never think of pain... Your mental attitude really counts, I think, more than anything.

I persevere with life... I believe in honesty... I learned a lot at... University – they were honest and straightforward. I came back with that attitude and it is important.

It was necessary, she said, to face rather than run away from problems.

It was due to this that I was able to bring up the boys alone.

Never say you can't do it. Have a go and the next time make a better job of it.

Never give up – it's better to hope than despair.

She attributed a lot of her self-belief to Rudolph Steiner's teaching ('a wise person accepts the things that can't be changed' and 'to be wise is to learn from mistakes from oneself'). This had replaced the Christian faith of her childhood and early adulthood and continued to provide a source of strength and identity.

Contributing to society via involvement in politics and helping others was also a significant part of her sense of self. Throughout her life, she said she had striven to contribute to the good of society and the welfare of others. Whereas formerly this had meant being actively involved in politics and as a school governor, she now had to limit her contributions to more practical actions. For example, she still took cakes to her local hospital:

I've always tried to do good where needed... I've helped where I could.

This way of thinking had led her to continue attending a club for older persons at a day centre even though the activities there did not interest her. By joining in, she contributed to the happiness of others.

It's a lot of old people... I shouldn't say that... They play a game with cards and all that sort of thing. I felt I wouldn't do it any more... Then somebody said to me... 'since you've been coming it's made it worthwhile'. So I thought, well, perhaps I'm doing the wrong thing to get out of it.

Despite her age and current health problems, she still identified strongly with being active and thus not 'old'. For this reason, having a car was important to her.

As long as I can get around – I'm still able to drive therefore I can still get around.

Continuing to be active was essential to her sense of self.

It's inactivity that gets me down. I'd be more involved if I could be.

Vera agreed that she adopted a stance of living day to day rather than looking to the past or the future. In particular, she did not dwell on the past.

It no good looking back on things – never look back – it's defeating.

The loss of my son – I couldn't do anything about it – I suppose it was God's will, but he lived a full life.

It was surprising, therefore, that at the third interview some months later, which another of us conducted, Vera did want to reminisce, and in considerable detail. She reflected on the formative experiences that had led her to her present-day attitudes, particularly the end of her marriage and its aftermath, as well as the death in early adulthood of her younger son. She attributed the failure of her marriage to the Second World War. In fact, because of her father's regret of having signed up in the first war, she had advised her husband not to enlist. He had been a journalist, and Vera had travelled with him in their early years together, also helping him correct his writing. But when he returned after war service, he seemed 'morose', and looking through his papers, she found out about an affair he had had during the war with a woman living in the north of England. After some time, Vera allowed her husband to visit his lover as he asked to, and he never returned.

A difficult time followed as her husband tried to gain custody of their children, whom he wanted to send to his mother. The oldest boy, aged five years at the time, was greatly upset and wrote to his father asking him to return, but she received a "nasty" letter back in which her husband accused her of "using their son to bring him back." The bitterness lasted many years, as he never made Vera any payments. It was only when many years later she sued for divorce that the court obliged him to make regular payments. Only recently he had asked whether he could make a final lump sum payment, but she had refused, making it clear to him that he had been the one "to walk out" on the marriage.

Vera had clearly not yet resolved the strong feelings she still felt about the end of her marriage. As a result of it she said her subsequent life had had many hard moments. She expressed considerable anger towards her husband and also to others who had treated her less than generously as she had struggled to make a living for her children and retain a home of her own. Nevertheless, she had been successful in finding jobs and places to live when needed. She had won through her difficulties, and stressed a belief not only in 'Fate' but also in a God to whom she could turn for help.

After these interviews, we questioned whether Vera's attitudes would remain as positive if and when she became more disabled because the most difficult time for her recently had been the period of immobility before and after her hip operations.

From the time of being immobile, it wasn't living at all really, it was just existing.

Now she was facing new types of problems, for example, finding it difficult to identify with older people who were less active than herself but whom she met in the day centres she attended. Vera was also showing signs of her memory problems becoming worse. She was still mentally alert and clear in her thoughts, but memory loss was affecting her daily life, and she complained about encountering particular difficulties with word retrieval.

Nevertheless, Vera was taking steps to compensate for these cognitive failings by writing notes of instruction to herself. Her strong sense of resilience remained. She said she enjoyed life and had no pessimistic thoughts. Again, she took a philosophical stance towards adversity.

You have to accept it; make the best of it.

She had the support of her son and of other close friends and left both her doors open and slightly ajar for them to enter, which showed a strong element of trust. She herself predicted that

When I can serve no useful purpose anymore, I shall pass out quickly.

Vera was interviewed for the last time two years later at age eighty-six years, by which time her GP had described her in writing to us as 'frail and housebound'. She had contacted us earlier in the year to see whether she was still required for interview. Her mobility was further reduced and her isolation increased, mainly as a result of a fall five months earlier, after which she had been hospitalized with a broken kneecap. She was using a Zimmer frame and two sticks as aids for moving around indoors. The experience of walking was accompanied by sensations of stiffness, pain and unsteadiness. Also her social world had diminished with the death of three important friends and the move of her granddaughter – her only grandchild – away from the area. She had finally sold her car and was no longer attending social functions, although she occasionally visited a day centre at a local hospital for some help with rehabilitation.

She regarded herself as still recuperating after her accident and did not appear to have lost any of her determination to improve her situation. She showed no noticeable symptoms of depression and only complained as before about "not enough activity." She was sustained in her relationships by regular visits from her son and one close friend who came every week. She now had a pet bird, and her eyesight was sufficient to allow her to enjoy TV and reading. However, completing household tasks had become more time-consuming and onerous. She was still in charge of her financial affairs, and although having some occupational as well as state pension, described herself as having to "watch every penny." There was no evidence that her memory problems had increased.

She explained more about how her spiritual views had changed in the course of ageing. Religious practice had been important to her in the past. In fact, when working in a nearby cathedral city, she had regularly attended prayers in the cathedral during lunchtime. But she had come to disapprove of the hierarchical side of the major Christian denominations and now equated her own religious beliefs principally with helping others. Nevertheless, she still strongly expressed a belief in God.

God is in His Heaven and will give guidance if there is a wrong turning.

The changes in her self-ascriptions and self-descriptions were perhaps expected, given her present difficulties in movement. She thought she got 'little enjoyment in life'.

I'm fed up because I've always been very active doing a lot.

She still felt capable but only "within the house, not outside", but she still retained aims:

To be able to get out and about and enjoy life a bit more.

Vera was certainly not going "to give up."

I'm [coming to] eighty-seven. I'm surprised I've lived as long as I have, but I never give up.

As a consequence, she did not worry about what the future would hold for her and was not overly concerned regarding the help she might need.

Don't worry as it might never happen. I'll just 'peg out' in the end.

Unfortunately, we were not able to interview Vera again, and we do not know whether her prediction came true. We exchanged Christmas cards for one further year but then no more. However, she avoided any further hospital admissions and lived another five years until her death at age ninety-one.

By age eighty-three years, **Hilda Smith** was becoming of more concern to her family. She had collapsed outside with 'funny turns' on two occasions. The first occurred at a bingo club a year and a half before. As a result, an ambulance was called, and Hilda was in hospital for a week. Another occurred a year later.

I got up... and heard the paper boy come. I got up and felt dizzy and I hung on the door, you know like that, and I went back and got on the bed and then all the walls went. I had to hang on the bed rail, because as much as I hung on there it was getting my head and my eyes were just going like that... and then I was sick.... I stayed in bed two days.

She was taken to stay with one of her daughters for three weeks to recover. Following tests at the hospital, a blocked artery near the brain was diagnosed as the cause of the problem. Pain in her legs and joints were also giving her problems in walking. Her arteries, she said, were "furring up." Moreover, while staying with a son's family over Christmas, she had suffered badly from chest and breathing problems. Her eyesight and hearing had continued to deteriorate as well. As a result, she was not able to read as she had been accustomed to and missed doing so.

However, her self-esteem had been minimally affected by these changes in her health. She remained aware of her central importance to her family, who made "enough fuss" of her. She continued to greatly enjoy the grandchildren and now had twenty-five great-grandchildren! But she admitted that she felt 'useless' because she couldn't "go and mind the babies any more." Despite her difficulties with eyesight, Hilda tried her best to fill in the written sentence-completion task we gave her. Besides her relationship with her family, there were a number of other themes in her answers, firstly an analysis of her personal strengths and weaknesses.

'I am best at'... "listening and hope to give advice."
'My weaknesses are'... "being too soft-hearted."

The past also seemed to be becoming more significant for her, providing both comforting and strengthening memories.

'When I feel lonely'... "I just go back over the years and remember many things that happened."
'My life up to now'... "quite happy, but after plenty of hard work."

She continued to hope for better health and to need less care.

'In the next few years'... "I would like to keep fairly healthy and not be a nuisance to anyone."
'It's hard for me'... "to let people do so much as I am very independent."

She also repeated a concern about dying that had appeared also in her recent interview.

"I really would like to live a few more years... I've dreaded dying."

By the time of our next visit when Hilda was eighty-five years of age, her eyesight had deteriorated to such an extent that she was unable to read the print on the questionnaire we wanted to leave with her and so could not complete it. She had just returned from staying for fifteen weeks with her daughter while her own flat was being renovated by the council. This had certainly improved her living circumstances. The family now took responsibility for housework and some of the shopping and cooking. Although Hilda was able to walk without support, she was using a white stick to signal that she could not see and normally walked less than a mile during the course of a week. Her walking in fact was affected by a combination of difficulties, in particular physical weakness and shortness of breath, which affected her even when doing sedentary tasks such as washing and dressing. She had also been diagnosed with severe angina. She said that she now stayed in most of the time and felt much less active than she used to be.

Despite these problems, Hilda was not experiencing any marked symptoms of depression, and her self-esteem ascriptions had remained largely positive, illustrated as before with a number of references to her family.

Family – they all look after me well. They are good to me.

Not only did her family visit regularly, they also organized visits to one or another family member. Hilda also had a strong sense that she was still "doing things for the family." In addition, she was able to watch television but no longer able to read. Instead, she listened to 'talking books'. She also seemed to have taken to spending quite a lot of time knitting 'squares' for Oxfam.

Perhaps the most striking aspect of Hilda's self-description, particularly given her declining health, was her repeated wish to live long.

'I have a clear aim in life' ... *"To live to one hundred."*

'I look to the future with confidence' ... *"I wouldn't like to die young but don't want to be a nuisance to others. I'm too independent."*

The theme of continued independence was also reflected in other ascriptions.

'I am still capable of doing quite a lot' ... *"Indoors I do bits and pieces and rest in between. Nothing big."*

'I have confidence in myself' ... *"If I make up my mind to do a thing I do it and bother about the consequences after."*

Three years later at age eighty-eight, Hilda's lifestyle had continued largely unchanged. Her family was still supportive towards her, one of her daughters doing the housework and another taking her shopping in a car once a week, an occasion when she also visited old friends and neighbours. Within the past few weeks, the family had provided her with an Alarmline, which connected her with an emergency control service. They were clearly pleased to help her cope as independently as possible but had concerns about possible accidents. In fact, there was one area of disagreement with her family. Hilda considered that she was able to see to her personal needs independently, but her daughter felt that she needed watching when she was bathing. Hilda herself did not agree and felt such supervision would be an affront to her dignity. Apparently she had applied to have an adapted bathroom when the flat was refurbished three years previously, but the council completed the work with a standard bathroom before the application was processed. Shortly after the interview, a shower and other disabled facilities were fitted, and this arrangement allowed Hilda to continue to bathe alone and in relative safety.

Although she was still able to manage the stairs up to her flat, she had developed a technique of going down that she had used successfully over the years. Because of her poor sight and tendency to giddiness, she continued to use a white stick to aid her walking. She was walking less now, only a few hundred yards in a week, limited by her troubles with dizziness and with shortness of breath walking up a hill. To compensate for lack of exercise, she had recently invested in a machine that allowed her to exercise her legs and feet whilst sitting in an armchair. But other heath difficulties were increasing. Partially as a result of the diuretics she was taking, she had continence problems, sometimes first thing in the morning. Her sight was continuing to deteriorate, although she was still able to see images on the TV and knit squares for Oxfam. There was a considerable amount of medication that she was now taking, including for problems with diverticulitis and hiatus hernia as well as with thyroid functioning.

Hilda was continuing to avoid serious depressive symptoms and to maintain a healthy self-esteem, illustrated by reference to her family, various activities and mental capacities.

'I get much enjoyment out of life' ... *"Knitting for Oxfam and the children. My life is in my grandchildren and great grandchildren."*

'I am still capable of doing quite a lot' ... *"I do things in between rests – hoovering and bits and pieces."*

'I am as bright and alert as ever' ... *"I've got my brains about me."*

However, some more negative self-ascriptions were also present.

'I feel useless' ... *"I want to do things but I can't. If I collapse, it makes work for others."*

'I am rather unsure of myself' ... *"At times. I'd like to do things and then think I'd better not."*

Nevertheless, she was still looking forward.

'I have a clear aim in my life' ... *"To live longer."*

But was not able to provide an example for:

'I look to the future with confidence'...

It was clear that the family was central to Hilda's identity, as also her continuing determination to live independently. Her relationship with her family was a warm one. She had an important position as the family elder to whom all her offspring felt a responsibility and great affection. She was an outspoken person who did not hesitate to speak her mind. Indeed, she felt that sometimes she 'put her foot in it' when she voiced her opinion, and she knew that this upset at least one of her sons-in-law. Nevertheless, her grandchildren and great-grandchildren did not hesitate to go to her for refuge, and she greatly valued this role.

Her family seemed to respect Hilda's wish to live independently and enabled her as far as they could to have a good quality of life within her own home. In turn, she appreciated all their efforts, although she did sometimes feel that they were too protective. In fact, she did not always tell them if she was feeling unwell because she did not want to worry them. The family also brought her worries too. She was concerned about the health of two of her children, one son who was waiting for heart bypass surgery, and one daughter who was confined to a wheelchair with rheumatoid arthritis. But there were many family joys as well. Hilda was currently awaiting her thirty-first great-grandchild.

Three years later, at age ninety-one years, Hilda presented a remarkably similar picture of herself, still living independently with the help of her family, alert and well oriented, and with a high self-esteem. At the time of the interview, shortly before Christmas, her daughter was in the flat helping with the housework. The bonds with her family appeared as close as ever and expressing themselves in new ways with the growing younger generation. Her first *great*-great-grandchild had been born three months before. One of her grandsons had printed a telephone list for her in very large letters and also a list of all her Christmas TV programmes. One of her sons-in-law was seeking to a find a new bulb for her magnifying torch. Her flat was neat and tidy with lots of Christmas cards and presents, including flowers from the family. This was to be the first Christmas since her husband died that she would spend alone. It was her choice because she did not want to take her grandson's room. The grandson himself was upset that she would not be there and was intending to visit her during the day.

Hilda's health had remained relatively stable. She had to be careful when walking because of the tendency for her head to spin (vertebrobasilar insufficiency), and she was still taking medication for diverticulitis and thyroid. She had been in hospital in the last year after an angina attack and also attended a dermatological clinic for an irritant skin condition. She was still able to do much of the housework and care for herself, and continued her other activities as before, listening to talking books (and talking papers) by day and the radio at night when she could not sleep, as well as knitting squares for blankets for Oxfam. Her self-esteem ascriptions reflected the balance she had achieved between closeness to her family and personal independence.

'I am of importance to others'... *"If they want anything they know where to come!"*

'I have confidence in myself'... *"If I've got to do anything, I'll do it – and get told off for doing it!"*

One of her daughter's concerns was that her mother's poor eyesight made her vulnerable as she was unable to read the ID of visitors. There had been an incident two or three years before with a bogus water official calling. Nothing had been stolen, but as a consequence, a password arrangement for visitors had been arranged with the council.

Hilda expressed herself as content with her present life, finding it 'nice to grow old' and quite prepared and wishing to live longer. She also agreed that she was satisfied with her past life.

I'd like it over again. Would only change a few mistakes.

In fact, she took the opportunity of this interview to reminisce more than on previous occasions. She remembered the days when her husband was out at work and she supported the family. Even though she had several young children, she used to take in washing (two pence a sheet, a penny a pillowcase, washed, boiled and ironed) and cleaned a couple of houses (five shillings for the two). She spoke about the research project itself and how she had been happy to help with this and also other projects in geriatric medicine. Her association with clinical research was important to her.

I'd rather they try all these things out on me rather than some poor animal, which can't say if it's in pain.

Hilda lived another five years to age ninety-six. We were sorry to miss the opportunity to visit her again in those years.

Becoming frailer in the middle to later eighties

The three remaining women could not be described as becoming frail before their middle eighties. Two of them also lived well into their nineties and thus their later lives are also continued in Chapter 9. Here we note how they adapted to the initial stages of living with the frailties related to ageing.

Although **Evelyn Norris** had encountered more severe cardiovascular problems in her mid-eighties, she showed few or no signs of depression when interviewed again at eighty-six years and said that she continued to enjoy life and did not worry more about the future. She was happy to rely on assistance from family, both for shopping and gardening. She also appreciated the fact that at the time of the interview, her grandson had come to live with her.

Her comments on her sense of self and meaning were amplified at this time by her responses to the life history interview and also by further written comments, which she sent to us afterwards. Taken together with her illustrations for self-ascriptions, they demonstrated the centrality of family for her life, and also the enjoyment provided by friends.

'I feel important to others'... *"They [family] rely on me for my opinions."*

'What has been most meaningful about your life so far'... *"My family... I especially care about my two grandsons."*

'I feel capable'... *"I do everything in the house – cook for my grandson who lives with me."*

'I get much enjoyment out of life'... *"Everything – cards, meeting friends, mixing with others."*

'In your present day life, what are the features you value most?'... *"The love of my children... and the love of people. I think that's the most important thing."*

'What is it in your life that gives you hope?'... *"Family, friends, and my faith."*

At the same time, Evelyn was feeling her growing weakness:

'I feel unsure of myself'... *"I can't make decisions as I used to."*

She also stated that she no longer 'looks forward to the future with confidence' but then added, "I've everything to look forward to really" and referred again to her family.

When we next interviewed her two years later, aged eighty-eight years, she was now sharing her accommodation with her grandson and his new wife. Evelyn was living in a self-contained unit on the ground floor. This was clearly of great benefit to her because it provided the security and extra support to enable her to still live independently in her own home. She had had a stroke a year before, and her health had noticeably declined. At the interview, she still had some speech impediment and was experiencing unsteadiness when walking as a result of deterioration in her sense of balance. She was now using a stick when outside, which enabled her to walk 'up to a mile'. In addition her sight was impaired because of cataracts, and the arthritis in her hands was worse. She was visiting her GP every couple of months and was on medication to thin her blood after the last major stroke.

Despite the increased health problems, Evelyn still showed few signs of depression. Nevertheless, her attitude towards her health had changed markedly for the worse:

I don't feel as I used to.

She had also come to feel that 'there is always something the matter with me' and no longer 'found it nice to grow old'. The latest stroke had clearly left her feeling uncertain and much weaker than in previous years. However, the presence of her grandson and his wife in her home was helping to allay fears regarding support; she said she was in fact worrying less about the help she would need in the future than before. Her daughter was continuing to help her with the housework and take her shopping in the car, while her son-in-law and grandson were doing all the gardening.

Evelyn's self-esteem remained high. Her family appeared as the major factor contributing to her feeling of well-being. She felt 'useful' as she was 'able to help everybody' and gained enjoyment through seeing all the family. Seeing her friends too not only gave her satisfaction but also aims in life.

I look forward to seeing my friends and having them to tea.

Although regretting that she 'could do the things she used to do', she did not feel that she had lost in confidence and kept a positive outlook on life.

I'm alright – the doctor thinks I've got a good sense of humour.

She also showed a stronger commitment to her religious faith than she had indicated to us when she was in her seventies.

I always have the service on ... I think you've got to have faith.

In a subsequent interview some months later, we asked Evelyn's opinion on the conclusions that we had reached on the sources of her sense of identity. She agreed with our major points. Her family was central to her identity. It was particularly boosted at present by the fact that her grandson and his wife now occupied part of her home.

We get on well together. He's ever so good to me.

At the same time, it was important for her to remain independent of her family.

I've got my rooms and they've got their rooms, I think it's better. I've got my own territory – I've my friends in – it's better to be separate.

They've got their own room, and I stay in my room. I could go in there if I wanted to, but I don't do that ... I like my television, you know, and they have their friends.

Her relationships with her own friends were important as well.

They come every week. ... I've known them years. ... One up the road and one in the people's home at X ... she comes on Tuesdays.

Evelyn also agreed that her faith was a strong source of strength and identity.

I do have faith ... I pray for my family to keep well. ... I used to be always at church ... that's how I was brought up.

Also important was her positive outlook on life.

I think it helps too... You've got to have a laugh haven't you.

She also stressed her routine of everyday activities.

I enjoy cooking... but I have to take my time if I'm left alone... the stroke has done something to me... I just got to take time.

I find it beneficial, when I wake up I have my bath when someone's here... I have a routine.

She also confirmed that her deteriorating health detracted from a positive sense of identity.

I used to ride a bike and used to walk, you know, but I can't do it – I can't do nothing now.

I go shopping in my daughter's car and lean on the trolley... but I couldn't go alone.

A further diminishing factor that Evelyn brought into the conversation herself was the loss of loved ones, particularly her sister as well as her husband. However, her immediate family compensated for this loss in many ways.

I'm very, very devoted to my family because they are so good to me. I've got a wonderful daughter. All my family are good.

Evelyn was interviewed by another of us when she had reached eighty-nine years. She spoke a lot about her husband, what a good man he had been, and about their life in wartime, being bombed out of their house and returning after the war. She also spoke about the parish church, how for most of their married lives they had gone regularly, and enjoyed particularly the Easter and Harvest Festival liturgies. Her daughter had been christened, confirmed and married there. She also told about her recent history of strokes, how she was given aspirin to begin with but after a year and because of the internal bleeding it caused, she had been transferred to warfarin, which she cheerfully referred to as 'rat poison'. She spoke about how fortunate she was to have a good family. Her grandson and his wife on the top floor were expecting their first baby within a day or so. It would be Evelyn's first great-grandchild. She was obviously very happy about this. She was lucky also with her friends who visited regularly.

How was it that she was such a cheerful person? It was just the way she was, she said. She was lucky to be so! She said good-bye warmly on leaving, using two hands. On considering her life as she had experienced it, we were impressed by its perceived continuity despite the setbacks caused by the war. A year later, Evelyn incurred another and this time more major stroke. She died soon after at age ninety years.

At age eighty-five years, ***Ethel Willis's*** GP decided to have her admitted to the hospital elderly care unit, as she was generally feeling unwell with a long-standing throat infection. There she developed a chest infection and later started vomiting blood. This was a haemorrhage caused by a polyp in the stomach, which led to emergency surgery. She was discharged to a convalescence hospital but almost immediately on arrival, she had a heart attack and so was returned to the general hospital. She expressed surprise that she had survived this ordeal:

I thought, isn't it awful, what I'm putting my kids through you know. But like I said to you just now, I thought it would be a nice easy way out. I'm not frightened to die. I mean that when I say it. Yet all the people you've ever loved have done it and you've got to do it, but I hope I do it with dignity... And I don't want to sit around waiting for it. I'm fully active, and going to a rest home would frighten me. I'd be the worst patient they ever had!

Despite these recent problems, by the time she was interviewed a year later at age eighty-six, her depressive symptoms had diminished further, and her self-esteem had strengthened (see Chapter 6). For the first time, she replied positively that she did get much enjoyment out of life, citing reading and doing crosswords as examples. There was also a strong theme of maintaining independence in the way she spoke about herself. She stressed that she "looked after herself completely", "kept the house clean" and had "regained the confidence to go out alone." Independence was also a theme in many of her written self-ascriptions, and loss of the ability to look after herself the main fear she referenced.

She also replied more positively about her importance to her children, who "cared very much" for her, and expressed herself more happy and satisfied with her life than at previous interviews when negative attitudes to ageing and loneliness had been more evident.

Her more contented and family-oriented view of life was also evident in her written self-ascriptions:

'Maybe I can'... "be remembered as a good mother."
'The goal that I would like to accomplish in my life'... "love and affection in the years left to me."

However, her hospital experiences had made her more concerned about the process of dying:

'I like to dream about'... "a dignified death."
'If possible I would'... "die suddenly while still having my present state of mind."

When we next interviewed Ethel three years later, she was approaching her ninetieth birthday and remained independent in her day-to-day life. She continued to look after herself. Her mobility was decreasing, but she was still able to climb the stairs on occasions, with some assistance from her daughter. She had suffered another stroke the year before, but the impact appeared to have been mild. Her speech was normal. Deterioration in her sight, however, was causing her trouble, and her depression score had risen. Besides sleep and appetite problems, she indicated that she had difficulties in starting activities and also occasionally in collecting her thoughts. She said she was also generally weary of life.

Her self-esteem had declined. For the first time, positive responses were in the minority. She felt unsure of herself ("especially when I go out"), no longer felt useful, had no aims in her life and little hope for the future, and did not get much enjoyment out of life – although she added, "I enjoy the company of my children." Doing housework still made her feel capable, and the attention of her children gave her a sense of importance. She also still felt 'bright and alert' – "I've still got my marbles." Ethel's answers to the self-completion questionnaire confirmed how her sense of meaning in her life came both from her family's support and her continuing ability to look after herself.

'What is it about your life that makes you feel most alive?' ... *"My son and daughter. They are my only means of getting out of the house."*

'What is it in your life that gives you hope?' ... *"Not to lose my independence; to stand for myself."*

We wrote at the time that the foundation of Ethel's life was now quite fragile. Her morale seemed low.

'What kinds of things do you enjoy doing?' ... *"Very little. With failing eyesight my sewing and knitting have almost come to a standstill."*

But Ethel was in fact to show considerably more resilience and live well into her nineties. We take up her story again in Chapter 9.

When we interviewed **Elsie Darby** at eighty-six after a gap of eight years, we found her to be living in a residential care home. This was the result of a series of negative events that had occurred over the previous year. Although we are not sure of the precise sequence, it appears that her third husband's behaviour had become unacceptable to her, causing her considerable stress. Her doctor and a lawyer had taken action on her behalf to obtain a divorce. In the same year, she had also suffered a heart attack, preceded by a bout of pneumonia. These two factors together had led to her leaving her previous sheltered housing scheme and moving into a care home. Elsie complained of a number of health problems: pain and unsteadiness in her legs, needing to stop for breath even when walking on level ground, both hearing and sight problems and feelings of depression.

Although an understandable decision in the circumstances, the move had had some unfortunate consequences for Elsie. She had been used to leading an active life, and some of her activities had been curtailed. This included not only household activities as cooking, shopping and gardening, but also, as a result of the home's location, her ability to visit relatives and friends on her own. Nevertheless, she was clearly relieved to be released from the ties of an unhappy relationship. She described herself as still being active and busy. She had maintained her various hobbies and interests, knitting, reading, watching TV and also playing the electric organ she possessed. Her family was still closely involved with her. She was taken out regularly in her son's car and other relatives visited her weekly.

Despite the fact that the majority of Elsie's external activities and social relationships had greatly diminished, she had maintained a high level of self-esteem. She seemed to be compensating for her losses by deriving satisfaction from interests performed in her immediate surroundings as well as relying more on her inner sense of regained security. Her knitting and toy making for charities made her 'feel useful'. Her enjoyments in life were illustrated by references to playing the organ as well as knitting. She was 'feeling confident' "to carry on as she was doing" and 'bright and alert' because she "had not forgotten how to go about things." She was 'looking forward to the future' as she had "no worries at all now." Her one reference to her children was when she said that her family gave her a sense of 'feeling important'.

When we interviewed Elsie more than two years later at age eighty-nine, her health seemed to be causing her more problems. The vision in both eyes was weak, with the result that her sight tended to be dissociated. The sight in her left eye was more affected, which she described as "like looking through lace curtains" and resulted in frequent headaches. Arthritis in the hands was restricting her activities, including playing the organ and knitting. She was taking paracetamol to relieve the pain. She had a less positive attitude to health, agreeing with the statement 'there is always something the matter with me' and she had become 'more worried about the help she would need in the future'.

Despite these and other complaints, she agreed with the statement that 'these are the best years of my life', which she explained in terms of "having more freedom." Her self-esteem had remained strong and was illustrated in ways both similar and new to the previous interview. She had begun to extend her activities, getting happiness from "going to church, playing bingo and outings." In describing her importance to others, she no longer mentioned her family but instead referred "to the home" as she was making toys to collect money for it. She was aiming "to win the pools" and was looking forward "to living a long time'. On this occasion, Elsie also completed the handwritten questionnaire for us, which provided more indication of the way that she understood her life.

'When I think about myself' . . . "I often wished my life had been happier as it was hard going when I was younger."

'I am proud of' . . . "Living to the age I am."

'Later when I'm older' . . . "I'll just carry on hoping for better times!"

'I am best at' . . . "Knitting."

She was to explain to us in later interviews much more about her difficult younger life and why she valued the freedoms old age had brought her. She remained determined to make the most of her later years.

To our astonishment, when we contacted Elsie again three years later, she had recently left the care home and returned to living in sheltered housing. Now aged ninety-one years, her health was considerably improved, and she was far more active than she had been at the time of the two previous interviews. We continue the story of her life living independently again in Chapter 9.

Concluding comments

Our attempts to follow our participants through the process of becoming frailer were restricted by the limited access to some of them as their situation deteriorated but principally by the limitations of the resources at our disposal for conducting such an ambitious undertaking (we return to this issue in Chapter 10). Nevertheless, we obtained much interesting diachronic material on the experience of becoming ever frailer with advancing age. As will have become clear, all our female participants were seen to have become frail by their mid-eighties. Rather than attempting a detailed comparison among the twelve cases that have been presented, we draw attention here to some interesting paired comparisons between particular cases. We can perhaps do this most usefully by posing questions of them. For example, what does a comparison of Olive Reid's and Vera Wright's cases suggest about the nature of the concept of resilience? Why did Mavis Dawes demonstrate a higher level of well-being in her later eighties than might have been expected, whereas Mary Morrison, whose life had also been harder than most, declined so rapidly? What were the similarities and differences between Nellie Moreton's and Hilda Smith's activities and interests as they grew frailer? In each of these comparisons, we consider how maintenance of perceived self and meaning contributes to adjustment to increasing frailty.

Olive and Vera provide strongly contrasting cases. Olive had lost both her home and independence at a relatively early stage of ageing, and added to this, she suffered from the distance from her family in Canada. From then on, she appeared to have fought a continuous battle against depression, which did not end until her death eleven years later. It was a brave but relatively unsupported struggle apart from the brief periods in which she was hospitalized for clinical treatment after entering states of severe depression.

Vera, on the other hand, appeared to have developed a strong motivation to be independent and to retain a home of her own, partly a result of her early life, but mainly of difficult experiences after her marriage collapsed during the war. She succeeded in these aims until her later eighties despite various health incidents that increasingly incapacitated her. She also avoided any noticeable sign of depression. In fact, she appeared a good example of the resilient personality to which much current research interest is directed (see Chapter 2). Although she displayed a lot of anger towards those who had misused her during her life, she had not been overwhelmed by feelings of resentment and continued to have broadly charitable attitudes towards others. But her life experiences had led her to come to rely largely on herself. At the same time, she was trusting enough to leave both her inner and outer doors unlocked so that her son could enter at any time – a quite unusual situation in modern British society. This in itself seemed to us to be the sign of a strong personality.

This is not to disparage Olive's failure to avoid depression. She worked hard to find activities that would engage her as her situation became more limited. Her personal meaning system was fundamentally rooted in family life, and despite the efforts both she and her daughter made to overcome their geographical distance, this gap in her life was difficult if not impossible to fill. More could have been done to help her remain engaged with the world outside of a residential care home, but like many people of her generation, she suffered from expectations of family life in old age that were not going to be realized.

Mary had lost her husband during the war and had to work hard to bring up her son unsupported. Mavis had also struggled, bringing up two sons while supporting a husband with chronic mental illness. Both had been active and coped well throughout their lives despite their difficulties. They had other similarities. Both, for example, could call on the resources of their faith to sustain them. Both succumbed to physical disability in their eighties after incurring falls, with serious consequences for their mobility. But for Mary, this led to a drastic fall in self-esteem, and neither family visits nor religious beliefs seemed to be able to support her, whereas Mavis, despite her ongoing worries about one son and her poor health, found life to be still full of meaning. Of course, it could be that Mary's will to live had been lost after she was admitted to a residential care home after another fall. She also came to suffer from dementia. But loss of meaning was already evident in her life before she entered the home and became demented. It is not possible to conclude which factors determined which.

Nellie and Hilda, by contrast, continued to have much in common as they grew older. They both lived active and rewarding lives through their eighties despite their various health problems. Both were well supported by their families and continued to play an important advisory role within them, but both also realized that there had to be limits to the influence they wielded. Both also supported outside charities in their continuing handicraft work. But one major difference between them was that Nellie was also strongly committed to the ethos of the sheltered housing scheme in which she lived and played a major role in its social life. This was a consequence of the very different life that she had lived from childhood onwards, having to make her own way in the outside world, making a career for herself, as well as defending vulnerable members of her family, without the protection and support of older relatives. She had also earlier in life acquired resilience in the face of chronic health problems. This had given her the confidence to continue to take responsibility for others less competent than herself even in the face of her own growing frailty.

8   Men becoming frailer

Every one of the twelve women whose pathways through frailty we described in the last chapter was living alone at the point when frailty became an important element in their life. By contrast, one-half (six of twelve) of the sample of men whom we interviewed at this stage of life were still living with their wives. If this were a large and representative sample, it would illustrate a huge difference in gendered experience of ageing. In fact, we do know that the difference in men's and women's likelihood of widowhood in the United Kingdom has been and remains substantial (Bennett, 1997). Reviews also suggest men fare worse after their spouses' deaths. We did not collect enough evidence to justify this conclusion, but the different nature of male reactions to growing frailty could be illustrated from our case accounts. As with the women, we consider the men in order according to the age at which physical frailty first intruded noticeably on their lives.

Becoming frailer before eighty years of age

As we saw in Chapter 4, **Fred Hobson** had a major heart condition when he entered our study at age sixty-seven years. This was already preventing him doing the heavy work around the house, like decorating, which he had been previously used to doing. His health continued to deteriorate, and he suffered a succession of three heart attacks over the following ten years. When he was interviewed at age seventy-seven, shortly after his wife died (see Chapter 5), he was experiencing a combination of problems when walking, feeling both unsteady and breathless. Some months later, aged seventy-eight years, he also suffered a stroke that resulted in him being in hospital for a period of three weeks.

He was interviewed again at age eighty years. By this time, he considered that he had overcome the problems relating to the stroke, including difficulties with speech and paralysis in his side and left hand. He attributed his success to his own efforts:

I knew it'd have to be me who did it, nobody controlled it.

As noted in Chapter 5, his son's and daughter's families also gave him extensive support with household and gardening tasks, and he was also receiving some additional help from social services. Relatives and friends visited on a daily basis. His lack of depression was remarkable considering his recent bereavement as well as his chronic health problems. His attitude to ageing was also more positive than negative. As noted in Chapter 5, his self-esteem was relatively high and focused on his family and continued ability to undertake most activities of daily living. He illustrated how he had been able to adjust to his failing health by deriving satisfaction mainly from his activities within his home surroundings. For example, instead of gaining enjoyment from going to watch football, he now "got happiness from amusing things on TV and the radio."

When interviewed three years later at age eighty-three years, Fred's heart condition had deteriorated further after another heart attack two years earlier. He was almost completely incapacitated and had to have extensive help from a nurse and social services to remain at home. He was able only to walk a few paces inside his home with the help of a stick. In addition to a nurse and a home care worker visiting on a daily basis, he reported a great deal of support from his family: his daughter and his daughter-in-law were helping with housework and shopping. He had also been given a hernia diagnosis but was unable to have this surgically corrected because of his heart condition. His sight was impaired, and he had considerable problems walking because he felt breathless even when sitting down. Although his depression rating was slightly raised (he was experiencing reduced appetite and sleep problems), his general morale and attitude to life remained positive. He was still enjoying watching TV, reading a daily newspaper and looking after indoor plants with the help of the care worker. He also liked singing hymns by himself.

Fred's self-esteem score was lowered. He said he now felt 'useless' because he "couldn't do anything for anybody", and his ratings of 'capability' and 'enjoyment' were also reduced. Nevertheless, he still felt 'important' to his family and 'confident' because he "still knew a lot." In his written responses, he indicated that it was important for him "to stay in charge of his mental abilities." He was also still 'looking to the future with confidence'. These hopes were based in belief in an enduring reality beyond death.

There must be a future somewhere: it is no good being depressed.

This point of view was also reinforced in his subsequent written answers.

'What do you believe in?' . . . "There must be a life hereafter. We can't be the beginning and end of everything. There must be something greater than us."

All in all, Fred's strong morale in the face of his continuing deterioration was impressive. We noted after this interview that in the way he spoke about himself, he presented an integrated view of his past, present and future. He had reminisced more than before about his earlier life as a military nurse. He also wrote to us that "his belief in himself as a nurse" had been the 'most meaningful' part of his life. Of course he could not say that his present life had the same meaning or value because he was "not doing anything for anybody", but at the same time he was pleased that he was able to keep active in various ways. He pointed out to us himself that he was continuing to contribute to life by participating in our research project. His concerns for his family were also a major occupation for him. He wanted to know both "what they're doing and how they're doing." He realized full well that he was fast approaching death, but this was not a negative thought to him. He wrote to us that his hope was "to go to heaven." In the various ways in which he spoke and wrote to us, he conveyed a sense of his life as being part of a much larger whole which would continue beyond death.

Fred died one year later.

Although *Cyril Steel* was still fit and active when he first entered our study at age seventy-six years, a year later, he had stopped his outdoors activities (especially helping to maintain his club's bowling green) because of his failing eyesight, and appeared very depressed, despite a comfortable financial situation and his wife's support. As we wrote in Chapter 4, it seemed a pity that he did not receive more medical help at this stage of his life, both for cataracts and depression, before he incurred a disabling stroke three years later at age eighty. Two years after the stroke, he and his wife moved from their house to an apartment to make life a little less difficult for themselves.

When we next interviewed him, Cyril was aged eighty-six years, and his health had further deteriorated. He was almost completely immobile and housebound and in addition suffered from incontinence, for which he wore pads. For all his activities of daily living, apart from feeding himself, he required help, and this was provided entirely by his wife. He experienced both 'unsteadiness' and 'breathlessness' if he tried to walk. Neither he nor his wife received any kind of continuing professional help, neither home help nor any form of day care. He had eventually received treatment for his cataracts at age eighty-two and again at eighty-five but was still complaining about his eyesight. His hearing was also impaired.

Cyril's life was limited, restricted to watching TV and reading newspapers. He received few visits and those mainly from relatives. But sadly, they seemed to provide him with little interest, for he commented, "Relatives never meant much to me." His depression rating remained high, and his sense of self-esteem extremely low. Clearly his disabilities had destroyed his self-image as an active and competent person. His aim he said was "only to die." The one area of self-respect he had retained related to his mental faculties. Even when first depressed at age seventy-eight, he had regarded himself as 'bright and alert', stating that "I'm usually on the ball if any little problem arises", and now at eighty-six he felt he same:

My brain is still active.

But at our next interview three years later, Cyril's mental faculties appeared also to have deteriorated. Whatever the reason, probably further damage to the brain combined with a lack of professional intervention, he had difficulties concentrating and sustaining thoughts. This affected his ability both to read and to hold a conversation, and his answers to interview questions appeared disjointed and unreliable. However, it is also possible to interpret the change in his answers either in terms of an enhancement of positive thinking, perhaps facilitated by his mental decline, or a certain detachment from life that allowed him to cope better with his current situation. For example, he was able to say that he felt 'useful' and to provide as illustration "I eat my dinner and . . . I like soup, I like soup too." The desire to die had disappeared. When asked about his aims in life, he responded, "Well jogging along, that's all." He no longer said that he felt negative about old age: "It passes me by." With a seeming element of resignation, he added:

I can't say 'I'll pop in and do that, I'd like to do that'. Can't do it now.

Humour also seemed to be playing a new role in his life:

I never know which is my wife nowadays. . . . I don't know if that's good, but still . . .

In fact, much of the anxiety about his future was being experienced by his wife, as his sole carer. When asked whether he was worried about the help they would need in the future, Cyril replied:

Oh, she worries like anything . . . I never worry.

A further example of the changed situation was when his wife mentioned a pain he experienced in the previous year. On being reminded that the GP visited, Cyril said simply: "He saw to me . . . I forgot all about that." It was his wife who said that she found it 'difficult to be careful of [his] health' and who worried more regarding the 'help they will need'.

The service response continued to seem inadequate. He was eventually offered some day care at a hospital twice a week for a period of six weeks but was not offered it again. They lived in a second-floor apartment, and it was too difficult for his wife to take him out in a wheelchair; thus, Cyril had become permanently housebound. The impression was that he was regarded as too incapacitated to be accepted for social services provision and that attendance at a day hospital was not regarded as appropriate because rehabilitation was not possible. The sole responsibility for her husband was weighing heavily on his wife, and her own mental health was affected.

Cyril lived a further two years, dying at age ninety-one. He has spent well over ten years disabled and with a low quality of life.

Becoming frailer in the early eighties

Harold Rank's severe grief reaction to his wife's dementia during his seventies was described in Chapter 5. He was unfortunate during the same period to become increasingly disabled with hip problems and a trapped nerve, and experiencing a lot of pain. As a result, at age eighty-two, two and a half years after his wife died, he was deeply depressed, disappointed with his children's response to the situation and feeling he was "probably better off dead." His self-esteem had collapsed from a positive impression of himself as confident, caring and capable to almost the opposite view. He was dreading the prospect of needing more care and perhaps having to leave the home that had meant so much to him. Our prediction for the future was mixed. His despair seemed so chronic and profound that it was hard to imagine an improvement. Yet Harold was clearly a man of determination – he had successfully faced many challenges in his life – if only he could find a way of re-engaging with his previous sense of self-efficacy. He also needed to accept more help from others, which was especially difficult for him to do. But we noted the positive relationship he had developed with his new home help.

At our next interview three years later, his situation showed a definite improvement. He was able to dress, feed, wash and bathe himself without help (which he had not been able to do three years before), was walking with the aid of a stick and was even doing a lot of cooking and shopping for himself. He was being supported with these tasks by three members of his family (his son, daughter and daughter-in-law) as well as by social services. Although he was able to go outside the house for small distances, he experienced breathlessness, unsteadiness and stiffness when walking. As a result, his interests now were indoors. He liked watching sport on TV, especially boxing. He sometimes went to the pub with his son and also to visit his sister-in-law, who was in a nursing home.

Harold's depression had clearly lessened. (We had felt it necessary three years previously to alert his GP to his depressed state because he did not seem to be in regular contact, but there was no evidence – nor did Harold report – that he had received any treatment in the meantime.) He had a normal appetite and felt he was enjoying life again but was still occasionally feeling 'sad or low' and experiencing 'fluctuating ideas of failure'. Although he said he "couldn't do what he wanted to", he had "got used to it" and accepted the situation. His previous anxiety about the future had abated.

His self-esteem was also improved. Instead of the feelings of isolation he had expressed in the previous interview, he said that he now felt 'of importance to others', believing that he was "very important to his family, his home care worker and his neighbour." His confidence had returned.

I have no fear of talking to others . . . make myself at home anywhere and crack jokes with people.

He felt 'capable of doing quite a lot' as he occupied himself with household chores. He was not sure that he was always 'bright and alert', as he sometimes felt 'foolish' as he had to double-check everything, like the gas was off and the door locked, but he was "all right when somebody's there." His negative ascriptions involved feeling 'useless' because he "couldn't help anyone or do much", and having 'little hope for the future', which he expanded in the following way:

I've got little hope but I don't want to leave my kids. I'm not worried about going to my Maker but it's how you're going to go.

His aims in life were clear:

To live until I'm ninety and [then] to join my two wives.

He confirmed these views in the self-description he sent back to us in the post (three years earlier, we had not felt able to ask him to do this because of his extremely depressed state). They demonstrated especially his renewed attachment to his family.

'What has been most meaningful about your life so far?' . . . "My family – I've been very fortunate to have two good wives – I've got to go on living because I've got children."

'What is it about your life that makes you feel most alive?' . . . "My children and their children."

But he also repeated his pessimism about the future.

'What is it in your life that gives you hope?' . . . "Not much in this generation – I hope the lads have got jobs to do."

Harold was happy to speak at length about his life with us and expanded on the importance to him of contributing to his family. It was interesting that he was now helping care for his wife's sister, who, like his wife had, was now suffering with dementia and in a care home.

It's been important that I've been able to do a lot of things for my children and a lot of things for my sister-in-law. It gives a lot of pleasure.

He was conscious that it was important for him to be as self-sufficient as possible to maintain his independence.

I don't ask my children to give me anything. I'm in his world to look after myself.

He had recovered his previous strong image of himself.

I've been a very strong-willed man, I've been a very determined man. It's my body that's altered... my values are the same, dear.

The loss of his wife still bore heavily on him, and he responded sensitively to questioning about living alone.

So you miss that company?... Oh yes,.... I've had two good wives... I've got a lump in my throat... no more questions like that please.

He reiterated his main concern to be able to continue living independently in his own house.

I've never wanted a lot of riches or anything like that. I've always wanted to have my own home.

If I get when I don't want to be independent, that's when I want to 'wrap up'.

Two years later, when he was aged eighty-seven years, Harold was interviewed on three separate occasions. In the meantime, he had been hospitalized twice, once for operation on his prostate, the second because of acute pain in his back and legs. He was encountering increased difficulties with unsteadiness when walking, and had continuing urinary problems. His depression rating was raised: he was sleeping fitfully, waking early and was 'weary of life'. But although looking dispirited he was able to brighten up without difficulty and showed the same interest in other people as two years before. His life had changed little, with a similar pattern of activity outside the house as well as indoors and of help received from others. Also his self-esteem remained moderately high, illustrated in similar ways to the previous occasion. He remained pessimistic about the future, especially for the next generation. Nevertheless, his daily round of activities and the support of his family seemed to be sufficient to maintain his current level of well-being.

On the second occasion, he considered the conclusions we had reached on the sources of his personal identity. He confirmed how essential it was for him to retain his independence and to continue his activities within his own home that he had been living in for thirty-four years.

I want to be here... my kids have asked me for Christmas, but I want to be here.

I'm a very independent man, I will not lose it any, any price... I'm scared to death about my independence being taken away from me.

His concern for and interest in his family was also an essential part of his identity. He enjoyed outings to see his family, but he was especially concerned for his sister-in-law, and he felt that he was contributing to her well-being at present if only by making her more comfortable when he visited. He made the connection with her condition and that of his wife.

My wife was seven years like that. I visited her [his sister-in-law] this morning . . . I'm more concerned about her than about myself . . . She's such a lovely person. I visit her three times a week. It's no trouble. I'm going to do it as long as I can.

Reviewing the past also helped to maintain his identity.

I can remember the first day I went to school . . . my mother was a lovely little woman . . . I remember how I met my first wife.

He was proud of what he had achieved in life. His 'motto' was:

Give me a job, and I'll show you how to do it!

But he still expressed ambivalence about the value of his life as a frail elderly man. His health problems were becoming too burdensome to bear.

It makes me feel what am I doing here . . . I'm being a nuisance again to everyone.
I'd like to go to sleep now and not wake up tomorrow.

On the third occasion, with a new interviewer, Harold presented himself again as a 'strong' person, which he needed to be to confront the problems that came his way. He had a diagnosis of prostate cancer that he tried not to think about but was going to beat if he could. He was prepared for a second operation as he was developing problems with urinary retention again. He also stressed how he hated the idea of dependency. He would not go willingly into a residential home, although he realized he might be forced to one day. Every week he continued to visit his sister-in-law in a home and felt sorry for her in that situation. He was determined the same was not going to happen to him.

This was the occasion, to which we referred in Chapter 5, when Harold reviewed his life in depth, speaking in detail about the losses of both his wives and how they affected him. He also described his life growing up in Southampton on the banks of the River Itchen, where for a time he had worked as a ferryman, before developing his trade as a painter and decorator. World War I had been a hard time for his parents. Food was running out of the shops and you had to find out from hearsay where food could be got. He had seen how his mother and father had coped. His father had been strong – he had been in the Boer War with Churchill – but his mother even stronger in the way she ran the household.

He spoke about his education and his belief in the value of discipline, including corporal punishment, which he thought had kept him 'on the right path'. Crime and bad behaviour had increased because of the lack of discipline. He also spoke about the value of Sunday School in his local parish church and his Confirmation there. He had recently written to the vicar and asked for his cremated remains to be placed in the churchyard. It was important, he said, to be taught religion when one was young. Even if you did not take it up straight away, it was always something you could go back to. He stressed how he prayed now every evening and that this was something that he had started after his second wife died. He felt the benefits of prayer and believed in it strongly. He admitted that this was not something he normally spoke about. He imagined his sons would laugh!

Two years later, Harold was interviewed on two occasions once before and once after the ninetieth birthday celebration that his family prepared for him. He was finding it much harder to walk outside on his own, so his son was taking him to visit his sister-in-law. His son had thought of buying a mobility scooter, but his daughter-in-law had objected. He was also falling more within the home now but had found a way of getting up by turning round on his knees and then pulling himself up against a stool or other piece of furniture. He had gone beyond letting external events worry him, and it had to be that way. Even if the IRA [Irish Republican Army] were to set off a bomb outside, he said, he wouldn't take any notice!

He was now more appreciative of the help he was receiving and would have liked more of it. The home carer was coming five days a week, for two hours on two days and three hours on the other days, but he said he could do with more. He had trouble getting himself into bed. He could not have imagined being looked after so intimately by women other than his wives, but he had come to accept this. What was important was not to leave his home except in an emergency, and he had told this to his family. He had been in hospital for another two operations on his prostate. The last time, the doctors had wanted to remove his testicles, but he had refused – he still wanted to look like a man. Just before the first interview, his home carer had called an ambulance to take him to casualty because of the extreme pain in his hip. The condition of his back seemed to be at the source of the trouble.

Again he referred to his religious beliefs, that he had been baptized and confirmed in the parish church and that his ashes would rest there too. He was watching more religious services on the TV than he used to. Yes, he could be described as a Christian. He certainly believed in the power of prayer. God had looked after him and also those whom he had prayed for. He spoke a lot about his family, his relationships with his wives and children, at both interviews. By the time of the second interview, his sister-in-law had died, and Harold had been grieving this further loss.

Despite all his difficulties Harold remained in good spirits, with a low depression rating and moderately high self-esteem, illustrated mainly by his abilities and his own activities at home. He was "not frightened" of doing any job, but he was having quite a few falls. He wished he could do more. He mentioned his friends especially a 'lady friend' whom he saw once a week. He said he felt more distant from his family than before, which seemed sad. They "had their own lives", and it was becoming a "different world we live in." But he was very satisfied with the life he had led.

Through hard work, my children never wanted for anything.

Harold's case demonstrates very clearly how it is possible for an older person to accommodate to loss and emerge from a severe and chronic depressive state at an advanced age. Perhaps the most important factor was that his wish to remain independent and living in his own home was respected, and he was proud of his achievement in sustaining these goals over a long period of time. He died a year later aged ninety-one years.

Ted Jackson was described in Chapter 4 as perhaps the best example of a 'family man' in our sample. After a difficult early life and a failed first marriage, he had found happiness in a second marriage and their combined large family of seven children. We take up his story again when he was diagnosed with rheumatoid arthritis at age eighty-one after he realized he was having difficulties both with transferring from bed and with sitting up.

He was interviewed two years after this diagnosis, by which time he was living a more constrained life. He needed an aid for walking and a stair-lift for getting up and down stairs. He was only able to do a limited amount of housework, some of the cooking and lighter gardening tasks, all of which activities he had enjoyed and had engaged in willingly. The family was helping with the housework and shopping. Ted was also now permanently sleeping in a separate room so as not to disturb his wife with his constant fidgeting. Treatment with steroids for his rheumatoid arthritis had helped him a great deal, he said; he had been even more disabled before treatment. His other major problem was with breathing, which troubled him even when washing or dressing. He was also continuing to experience problems with a tremor, although not enough to impair him, and he had a successful operation for treatment of haemorrhoids, which appeared to have eased his previous problems with constipation.

Since the previous interview, Ted had suffered two sad bereavements: one of his daughters had died during an operation and also a great-grandson with cancer at two years of age. His depression score was raised, which he himself attributed to worry about his wife, and his self-esteem was considerably reduced – he was doubting his abilities, his confidence and what the future might hold – but his identity was still firmly centred on his wife and family. He expressed himself again most clearly in his written responses on the 'life strengths' inventory he later sent back to us.

'What is it about your life that makes you feel most alive?' ... "Wife – five daughters – two sons, fifteen grandchildren, twenty six great-grandchildren."

'What do you believe in?' ... "God, self-preservation, to be able to do the best for my family."

'What is important to you in your life today?' ... "Family – living."

'Who or what do you especially care about?' ... "The health and well-being of my wife. She is my life."

'What has been most meaningful about your life so far?' ... "Wife and family and living long enough to enjoy their company and knowing that you are wanted and appreciated."

He was also finding what enjoyment he could in indoor pursuits.

'What kinds of things do you enjoy doing?' ... "TV – nature [programmes] and horseracing or a good film. Crosswords, Scrabble. Travelling was good – now not possible."

Ted's ill health prevented us visiting him during the next interview period two years later, but we visited him five years after when he was eighty-seven years and then again at eighty-eight years three months before he died. At the time of the first visit, he and his wife had recently celebrated fifty years of marriage. She was suffering badly from diverticulitis but had decided against surgery because the risks were too great. Ted was very concerned about her and also in continuous discomfort himself because of the arthritis in the lower part of his body. He had had another spinal operation on his discs a year earlier. Nevertheless, he was cheerful, showed few or no symptoms of depression, and he and his wife were clearly very happy, much happier in fact than might have been expected given their health problems. The house was clean and bright. Ted said that he still enjoyed going down to the greenhouse to potter around and think back on "old times." He also liked to take his wife breakfast in bed, which made him feel 'useful' (but 'useless' when others told him not to do so much!).

They described the "rota" of care their family had organized. One or other of their children came to the house every day to help with the housework and generally to keep an eye on things. Their grandson took Ted by car to collect his pension. The local welfare services had also carried out some adaptations in the past year, including fitting a shower in the bathroom. Ted's self-esteem was again illustrated mainly in family terms. He was able to say both that he had been 'very lucky in life' and that old age itself was a 'happy time' for him. His aim was to live longer so as not to leave his wife on her own. He was confident and happy for his family's future although not "as far as the country is concerned."

It was in these last two interviews that Ted spoke to us in detail about his early life, his childhood in Lincolnshire, his army career, the shock of his first wife leaving him (although it had been for the good in the end), and his involvement in preparations for D-day. He had enjoyed his army career, the parades and conviviality (which he has missed in his later work in the Post Office). He spoke also about religion, that he had been brought up in a strongly Methodist area of the country where John and Charles Wesley themselves had been. As a child, he had gone to church every Sunday morning. Although he did not go to church now, he believed in God, and Jesus as his Saviour, but had some doubts, especially difficulties with some of the stories in the Bible. He always listened to Sunday morning religious broadcasts (he particularly liked listening to Thora Hird's programme).

One of his daughters wrote to us for Christmas that she was "greatly saddened to have to tell you that my much loved stepfather had died unexpectedly" earlier in the year, and that her mother sent us good wishes for Christmas and for the new millennium.

We also described **Dennis Wilcox** as a 'family man' in Chapter 4. Although he and his wife continued to bicker between themselves, also during our interviews, their lives were clearly bound closely together and devoted to their children. Both had suffered from major health problems in their sixties and seventies, and by the time Dennis was interviewed at age eighty-one years, both could be considered frail. He was continuing to suffer from pain and weakness in his legs and felt considerably disabled by problems with his joints. He had eventually received a diagnosis (as a result of doctor's report when he applied for a passport) of 'sub-acute combined degeneration of the spinal cord', which explained the pain in the muscles and joints of his knees when he walked. He said that it was now difficult for them to get about, and they tended to stay in most of the time. They had been unfortunate to suffer another family bereavement. One of their grandchildren – the daughter of their deceased daughter – had died from toxic shock syndrome at age twenty-eight.

Although not depressed, Dennis's self-esteem was diminished, but illustrated again by reference to his wife and family and the small jobs he could still carry out. These were also the subject of the written responses he sent back to us,

'Who is most important to you in your life today'? . . . *"My wife."*

'Who or what do your especially care about?' . . . *"My family."*

'What has been most meaningful in your life so far?' . . . *"My children's education and academic achievements."*

'What kind of things do you enjoy doing?' . . . *"Gardening, repairing mechanical items like clocks etc."*

He expressed himself to be "agnostic in respect of religion" and his hopes based on "the great advances in medical science."

When interviewed again three years later at age eighty-three, the health of both Dennis and his wife had deteriorated further. She had been diagnosed with Crohn's disease, which she found particularly socially limiting, and this was having a significant effect on the quality of her life. Still they managed to cope with daily life, Dennis taking showers rather than attempting baths and coming down the stairs backwards. They continued to do the shopping between them, catching the free bus, which left from opposite their home, to the supermarket. Dennis remained concerned about the future and needing more help. His depression score was somewhat raised. He said he had difficulties in collecting his thoughts and also in starting activities. He commented that he felt that he was developing memory problems and lacked the motivation to do things.

Dennis's self-esteem remained relatively low. In fact, his wife had to prompt him in answering questions throughout the interview also on self-esteem. The positive elements revolved around his care for and his importance to his wife and family, for example, cutting his daughter's grass. He relativized his problems.

I'm still alive, I'm not suffering. When you see others worse off than you are it makes you realize how lucky you are [a reference to the recent Dunblane terrorist attack].

He subsequently wrote to us that the most meaningful aspect of his life had been "my children's education and academic achievements." Their unmarried daughter lived quite close to them and thus was able to keep an eye on them, but at the same time clearly had some personal difficulties with her parents. She openly admitted that her father irritated her. Dennis and his wife had always been generous towards their children, having recently given them gifts of money rather than risk their investments being used up in care home fees in the future.

Our conclusion was that Dennis was now just living from day to day, enjoying the company of his wife. He was clearly concerned about his own ability to cope without her. But his own identity remained firmly rooted in their contribution to their children's achievements. He continued to underplay his own career, despite being invited at eighty-three years by the AA to appear on their anniversary video as one of the oldest surviving AA patrolmen. We were not able to interview Dennis again. As he had feared, his wife did predecease him three years later, and he declined an interview in the period afterwards. Subsequently he was moved to a residential care home with 'memory problems' and then to a nursing home where he died aged eighty-nine years.

We interviewed **Ralph Hodgkin** at age eighty-four, one year after his disastrous fall from a ladder outside his house in which he suffered multiple injuries. Previously a fit and active man, he had become a disabled person, his movements greatly limited. He still needed help from his wife with dressing, could only walk 'one hundred to four hundred yards' and needed the help of a stick to do so. In addition, he experienced breathlessness and pain as a result of his injuries when walking. However, he felt he that his recovery was "progressing." A determined man like Harold Rank, he also thought that he had coped well.

I remained optimistic. I didn't give way to anything.

He had a low depression rating, feeling 'no sadness', sleeping as usual, with a normal appetite and no difficulty starting or concentrating on things. He continued to be interested in the world around him and said that he "enjoyed life." He even "felt healthy – in spite of my injuries."

However, Ralph's previously high self-esteem had been affected by his health problems – he currently felt 'useless' – but he was determined to recover. His aim was "to get well, back in circulation and be active" and was looking forward to his and his wife's "golden wedding" anniversary. Indeed, one of the most important factors to his well-being appeared to be the increased concern and care of his wife after the accident. She had made him feel of central importance in her life he said. Moreover, he had kept up his indoor interests. When asked about what was meaningful about his present life, he responded:

My home, the stock exchange, sport [on TV] and crosswords – they're part of my life.

He had also adopted a specific attitude to ageing that helped him cope, living for the immediate rather than the distant future.

It's best not to think about getting old . . . just live from day to day . . . get the best out of every minute you are living.

His goal he said was "to live until I'm ninety."

In fact, Ralph lived another ten years after his accident until age ninety-three years. He made a good recovery, became able again to dress unaided and also to drive his car again for another four years, although he still had reduced mobility. He began to experience more unsteadiness, dizziness and shortness of breath related, he said, to "weakness in the leg", but also probably due to his long-standing heart condition. In some other ways, his health improved, particularly his hearing and sight, as a result of wearing a hearing aid and a cataract operation.

By the time of the next interview three years later, when he was eighty-seven, he had recovered his sense of usefulness.

I still do what I used to do – give advice and do many jobs and so on.

His sense of his own capability and confidence remained strong with a broader range of examples than four years earlier.

I feel capable because I can do any job in the house, gardening and mending things. I have confidence as I drive and do income tax returns.

His aims – shared with his wife – related to involvement with his home.

To see things looking nice around the house.

Ralph's involvement in activities at home seemed to have increased as his external activities had declined. He appeared to be less involved with others, meeting friends at the pub 'less than once a week', visiting his son 'less than once a month' and attending social clubs 'less than once a week'. He occupied himself with a great variety of interests and hobbies around the house, including reading, collecting and carrying on repair work, especially of clocks, in his workshop.

Two years later he was even more confined, describing himself as 'housebound'. He was no longer able to drive and experienced unsteadiness, dizziness and shortness of breath. Nevertheless, he continued to show no signs of depression, and his self-esteem remained high.

He went to his club by taxi once a week, and enjoyed visits from his son and grandchild every few months. He appeared to have grown closer to his son, having enjoyed a stay with the family for the Christmas holidays. Although acknowledging the problems ageing brought, he said that his own old age was a happy time through having "a marvellous wife." He remained very much the head of the household but 'bowed' to his wife in important decisions.

I miss the car immensely. Although my eyesight is better than a lot of people that are driving. I wouldn't mind a little mini but my wife won't hear of it.

In his spoken and written responses to us at age eighty-seven, Ralph provided much evidence on the centrality to him of his long-term relationship with his wife. At eighty-seven, he commented:

We are so happy together... if it wasn't for her, I wouldn't live. If she died tomorrow, I wouldn't be long.

At eighty-nine, he wrote that the most meaningful aspect of his life had been his "60 years marriage to my dear wife." He also extolled the value of a happy married life such as they had experienced.

I think we live like you're supposed to live – as one. If you do that in your marriage, you'll last a long time.

In a further interview the same year, he agreed strongly with our assessment that his relationship with his wife was central to his identity, which he linked to his own upbringing.

It is indeed. My mother taught me that marriage is for life.

Keeping up his hobbies, he noted, was also important for his identity.

I am interested in completing my family tree and do that in my office – I'm related to David Livingstone. I also collect cigarette cards and photographs – photography – anything like that – crossword puzzles . . . and I sit up and watch boxing till 12 o'clock.

After this interview, we commented on Ralph's ability to adjust to changed circumstances. For example, he had been able to come to terms with both drastic and gradual changes in his own health over the previous six years.

Yes, I miss it [health] but I don't grieve... The fact that I've lived as long as I have, and I enjoyed good health, I think, that takes the place of anything that comes after it.

But the one negative element in his life was his refusal to adapt to changing standards in British life. He was against immigration and wished that the death penalty could be restored. The deterioration in morality and social standards disturbed him.

I was annoyed when a fellow appeared on TV with his knee out of his trousers. You wouldn't do that when I was a boy.

He had also taken an accepting view to his own future death and conveyed it to his wife as well.

I'm not going to be here much longer so I don't think about it [the future]. It's inevitable that we die.

I've said to the wife if anything happens to me, you do what you feel you want to do because you won't be able to bring me back.

But in the second interview, he repeated his wish, expressed to us five years before, that he wanted to live at least to age ninety.

Ralph was interviewed again shortly after his ninetieth birthday by another interviewer. Both he and his wife presented themselves proudly. They also spoke a lot about their son. It was on this occasion that he reminisced in detail about his early life and his decision to set up his own business independently of his father (see Chapter 4). He talked a lot about his mother as well, how religious she had been and how knowledgeable about religious doctrine, which was appropriate in a descendant of David Livingstone. She had sent Ralph to sing in the church choir as a boy. He remembered in particular how she had told him the story of the Tower of Babel to his questioning of the existence of different languages. He also continued to complain about declining standards in present-day Britain – he was particularly annoyed with the behaviour of banks, how they treated both clients and investors.

Ralph was also interviewed on a further two occasions when he was ninety-two years old, the last just before his ninety-third birthday. His health was continuing to decline. His walking was extremely limited, because of shortness of breath, and he was using both a Zimmer frame to walk around the house and a lift to get up the stairs. He related the pain he felt to his earlier accident. His declining eyesight and hearing made it difficult for him to read and to hear the TV. Nevertheless, he remained calm, with a good appetite and no sign of depression. Old age, he said, remained 'a happy time' as he enjoyed the company of his wife. He also looked forward especially to the regular visits from his son and grandchild. He and his wife received help from a paid cleaner and gardener.

His self-ascriptions were less positive. He was no longer able to describe himself as 'useful', 'confident', 'capable' or 'alert'. He no longer looked to the future as he felt that he was getting 'weaker and weaker'. But these were more objective facts about his life and did not appear to distress him. His self-esteem was maintained by the sense of importance he felt within his family and the enjoyments he still had in life, being with his family, watching sport on TV and occasionally still tinkering in his workshop with repairs and tidying his papers. He was also satisfied with the life he had had. He repeated the story of how he had set up a successful business. His personal religious beliefs remained important to him. More distressing for him than his personal circumstances were the images of the outside world he saw on the media and the lack of moral standards they conveyed.

His son later wrote to us that his father had died of congestive heart failure at age ninety-three years six months after the last interview.

When we interviewed **Leonard Johns** again at age eighty-five years, the stressful situation with his neighbours (described in Chapter 4) was easing, and his depressive symptoms diminished. His self-esteem had also recovered. All of his responses were positive once more, although the examples remained tentative, demonstrating a new preoccupation with the internal functioning of the home. There was no mention at all of his previous physical activities or committee work, which seemed to reflect the effect of his heart condition and of his recent depression. For instance, in explanation of 'I feel useful', he said, "I try to help in the house and finances", and for 'I am still capable of doing quite a lot' he answered "housework, when I'm allowed." Similarly, other ascriptions led to the conclusion that Leonard now just wished for a 'quiet life', a term he stressed himself. For example, for the statement, 'I get much enjoyment out of life', he added, "we have few worries", and for 'I have a clear aim in my life', he answered, "to plod on with no upsets." However, his wife and children clearly still held a firm place in his life as he cited them as illustrations for why he still felt 'I am of importance to others'.

Leonard's modest view of himself and the recent disturbance to their 'quiet life' was reflected in the answers he sent back to us on the self-completion questionnaire:

'I am best at' . . . *"living a quiet life and looking back over a happy childhood and adulthood."*
'When I compare myself to others' . . . *"I am probably considered to be very ordinary."*
'Most important to me is' . . . *"being healthy and living a quiet life."*
'My life up to now had been' . . . *"very ordinary."*

'I plan to'... *"live quietly for a few more years, and the period of stress has been a massive threat to this."*

At the next interview point three years later, when he was aged eighty-eight years, Leonard was beginning to look much frailer. Certainly his breathlessness was marked. His wife continued to seem fit and active and kept a close eye on her husband. She remained during the interview, chipping in comments from time to time. The maisonette looked immaculate, and they were both clearly a lot more at ease because their troublesome neighbours had moved away and been replaced by an older gentleman with whom they seemed to get on well. He was even helping to relieve them of some of their gardening duties. The "six years of awful neighbours" were now behind them, and they had settled down to the type of life that they had both hoped for when they chose their present home.

Leonard was now significantly weaker, with increased breathlessness, but still managed to walk with a stick and carry out light shopping, although he had to stop for breath at regular intervals. Most of his interests were now sedentary ones, reading, listening to the radio and watching television. It was disappointing that a number of depressive symptoms, including low mood, difficulties in starting activities and fluctuating ideas of failure, had become more evident again, despite the removal of the stressful situation with the neighbours. Leonard's self-esteem had also declined again, including significantly on his sense of usefulness. It was interesting that having been an accountant he rated his ability to attend to his finances as being the most important thing he wanted to stay in charge of. However, his sense of significance to his family remained intact and was reflected in the answers he gave on the self-completion questionnaire. He referred to his wife and family on all questions that explored those aspects of his life he most treasured and valued. The proximity of his daughter and her family was clearly a strongly supportive factor in both his and his wife's lives. They were proud of their daughter's status as the head teacher of a local school and the fact that their grandson's education was going well.

We interviewed Leonard again three times at age ninety, the last time shortly before his ninety-first birthday. There had been celebrations both to mark his ninetieth and also the couple's golden wedding anniversary. There had also been a surprise change of diagnosis for Leonard's health condition. His previous GP had retired, and the tests ordered by his new doctor showed that he had not been suffering from heart problems but from emphysema (cryptogenic fibrosing alveolitis). As a result, his medical treatment had been changed, from which he said he had benefitted, although he was by now becoming breathless very easily and found the hot weather during the summer to be a big problem. He felt no annoyance about the change of diagnosis, rather, as he said, taking the news "in my stride." He continued to enjoy walking but with a stick and sometimes a tripod for assistance. He had also acquired a wheelchair. He said he could cope well enough with his health situation so long as he could dictate the pace at which he was required to do things. He and his wife displayed realistic attitudes about the likelihood of death in the near future.

However, his depression score remained raised and his self-esteem score low, although he himself denied that he was depressed. Indeed, he seemed content, as he said again, to "plod along", making the most of his comfortable home life in the midst of his family. They had developed the habit of going to church on Sundays with their daughter and then back to her house for Sunday lunch. Their son also had come to stay (with their daughter) for ten days over Christmas, and they were hopeful that he would marry the new friend he had found.

Leonard considered the conclusions we had reached on his case generally fair and accurate. He and his wife were comforted to see acknowledged the negative effect on them of living six years with noisy neighbours. Leonard agreed that he was of nervous disposition, that it was essential for him to feel in charge of affairs and that the family was the most important part of his life. However, he and his wife were concerned to correct any impression that they were financially well off. Their apparently comfortable situation was only as a result of careful financial management. Leonard had changed his job in mid-career, and his pension situation was not particularly generous. His wife's pension from the NHS was the major contribution to their income. They had not been able to afford to buy another car when Leonard gave up his last one because of poor eyesight, and they had had to give up holidays and other extras.

In the last meeting with a new interviewer, Leonard expanded on the complex history of his working life (see Chapter 4), their struggle to get the right health treatment for their son when he was young, and the stress and anxiety caused by their previous neighbours. They were proud of their comfortable features of their home, which they wanted to show. Leonard certainly did not appear depressed. Perhaps he had been a little demoralized all his life? He died two years later at age ninety-three years, shortly before he was due to be interviewed again.

Becoming frailer beyond eighty-five years

Ernest Davies also lived together with his wife until his death at age eighty-eight in a marriage that had lasted sixty-six years. They were supported in their last years principally by their daughters-in-law. As we noted in Chapter 4, at eighty-three years, Ernest was still keeping up his busy outdoor life on his garden and allotments despite increasing health problems, including a mild stroke and suspected diabetes. His self-esteem was high, and he said he was determined to keep his allotments going because it "gave him something to go out of the house", but he also said that he was "starting to feel his age."

By the next interview, three years later, however, he seemed no longer to be going to his allotment, although he was still doing a lot of gardening. There did not seem to be any major change in his physical health, but there had clearly been a change in his cognitive abilities. At eighty-six, he had experienced some loss of memory capacity and was finding it difficult to concentrate and maintain thought, which reduced his ability to sustain a conversation. Nevertheless, he showed no obvious signs of depression, and his self-esteem remained high, illustrated by his continued work around the house, painting and decorating, and also by a strongly asserted belief in himself, coupled with no small touch of humour.

I am fit and well. I'm eighty-six but I've got a bit more to come yet.

I can look after myself even if my wife died tomorrow.

My wife says I'm daft sometimes, but I'm not.

However, he gave credit to his wife as well as his family, including, importantly, his grandchildren, in the self-completed questions he sent back to us. They constituted the most important and meaningful parts of his life. His social life was now focused around the family visits. But he was obviously missing former male companionship in the neighbourhood that presumably he used to enjoy on his outings to his allotment and around.

I've no male to talk to – only widows.

Two years later Ernest's health had deteriorated both physically and mentally. At our interview, he was helped by his daughter-in-law as he found it difficult to answer questions coherently. He had been diagnosed with Alzheimer's disease, which had been steadily progressing over the past two years, and his speech was also impaired. He had recently been in hospital for a prostate operation and to remove stones from his bladder. He had problems walking, due to unsteadiness and weakness, and was also taking medication for diabetes. He had passed on his allotment to one of his sons.

Although he and his wife were trying their best to support one another, they were both now clearly quite frail and at risk. She had fallen down the stairs in the middle of the night six months earlier, and they had been disturbed by a burglar a week before the interview. A man had entered their home at about midday and stolen cash. Providing help was becoming too much for their daughters-in-law. One was now disabled herself (as was her husband, Ernest's and his wife's son), and the other lived at some distance and was travelling more than fifty miles to take them on a weekly shopping trip (something Ernest regretted – "there was a time when they used to nip up"). They were therefore receiving assistance with cleaning and were also attending day care once a week, where Ernest was helped to take a bath. But it appeared that they needed even more support than they were getting.

A 'philosophical' attitude now dominated Ernest's responses to the questions about his self-esteem, spiced with humour – usually at the expense of his wife.

'Useful?'... "I take life as it is – up and down. I help if I can... What do you think I keep my wife for?"

'Enjoyment?'... "Why not? Nobody can have everything – it's a secret the things I enjoy. Life's what you make it... you make it yourself."

'Confident?'... "It depends what I'm doing. I'm ninety now. I can look after myself and my wife. It's all that's necessary now."

'Bright and alert?'... "Yes... you've got to kid yourself a bit. Life is not bad at all."

Understandably, he was coping with the impending reality of deterioration by implying that it was necessary to adopt a sense of illusion. One had to 'kid oneself' and then 'life would not be bad at all.'

He spoke about the allotment that he had passed over to his son, his memories of working the land since he was young and the continuing importance of his garden to him, gesticulating as he spoke about his back garden.

The whole length there, you see, that's loganberries. Now, down on this side runner beans... this side runner beans... up there runner beans.

He was worried about the real possibility that he might have to leave his home ("I don't want to go away"), and he also remained concerned about having sufficient finance for the future. He alternated between laughing and being serious.

If I can get rid of her [his wife] I can still feed myself, but you must have money.

But really his main concern was for his wife as he observed her increasing frailty:

She... she's breaking up... [he begins to cry]... it worries me.

Their situation was clearly precarious. Ernest died a few weeks later at age eighty-eight.

When we interviewed **John Otterbourne** again at age ninety-one years, he had become noticeably physically frailer since fracturing his pelvis two years earlier. However, his depression rating both at this interview and two years later remained low, and he expressed himself very satisfied with his health, which he attributed to his faith and not drinking or smoking. He was now receiving home help once a week, and his daughter did both his shopping and cooking, but he continued to perform tasks such as housework, gardening and preparing simple meals. He was continuing to play the piano and also carry out some carpentry. By age ninety-three, his walking had decreased to one hundred to four hundred yards a week, mainly because of, he thought, the thinning of the skin under his feet, which impeded his movement. His hearing was also sufficiently impaired to make listening to the radio and TV difficult. But he was pleased that his family, friends and the staff at the day hospital he attended had adapted themselves to the problem.

They know me and they know how to speak . . . and that helps a lot.

However, he was now seeing less of his friends and neighbours, and his main source of support was his immediate family.

John's self-esteem remained very high. Many of his illustrations to ascriptions, for example, to 'feeling useful', 'being capable' and 'getting enjoyment out of life', related to his continuing interest in carpentry.

I do jobs here, carpentry jobs – that thing in the bathroom, there were a lot of shelves and I said we'll take that down and turn that into a little thing for the towel and I made it.

He had also been invited to do a carpentry job for the day hospital he was attending. He also referred to other activities as sources of self-esteem such as playing the piano, gardening, typing and attending to the mail. Some of these tasks had been central features of his past life, and he seemed content continuing to be so involved in them, perhaps to the exclusion of social relationships outside of his family. Some suggestion of this emerged from his answers to the self-completion questionnaire he sent back to us at ninety-three years of age.

'Others think I am' . . . "A queer fellow – 'a square' and one of the 'quiet kind.'"
'It's hard for me' . . . "To adapt to modern ideas."

His previous reference to the importance of friends in his life had been replaced by family, particularly the youngest generation, for example, "putting down a little money . . . something for the children when they are nine or ten."

As on previous occasions, he attributed great importance to his religious beliefs in providing sustenance to himself as he grew older. His 'hope for the future' was derived from "life hereafter" and 'his confidence in himself' was "in the Lord." Such faith was also evident in his more considered written answers.

'The goal that I would like to accomplish in my life' . . . "is to go at the end of my earthly pilgrimage to be with the Lord where sickness, sorrow and death are gone forever."

He seemed to have accepted that his health was deteriorating, and there was an element of humour in his attitude to the situation.

'I am afraid that I' . . . "'have had it' – sight, hearing going and rheumatism not going!!"

Worries about the future had stopped.

No I don't worry about it at all. I can truly say that the Lord looks after me, you see. I have tried to obey his instructions . . . and there is no want for those who fear him, and I've got everything I need.

Perhaps surprisingly there was little mention of his daughter in John's answers. Yet she, and also her husband, were his unacknowledged supporters, caring for both his physical and emotional needs and therefore vital to the continuation of his sources of self-esteem. It was probably due to such close daily contact that he had with them that they were omitted from his responses. After years of living together, it was taken for granted that they were part of his life. John died two years later before we could interview him again.

There were an additional three men in our sample (Stuart Murray, Charles Kitchen and Bill Blackburn) who did not become properly frail until they reached their nineties. They were widowed already at the beginning of our study, and their lives in their eighties were therefore already described in Chapter 6. We were unable to interview Stuart Murray after he became frail, but we continue with accounts of Charles Kitchen and Bill Blackburn in their middle nineties in the next chapter.

Concluding comments

Most of our men had also become physically frail by age eighty-five years, but a number of them, particularly Cyril Steel, Ralph Hodgkin and Leonard Johns, benefitted from having their wife as their principal carer. In Cyril's case, the demands on his wife were considerable and over a long period of time with apparently little or no support from either health or social services. It is unlikely that would have been so if the situation had been reversed and Cyril had needed to care for his wife.

As with the cases of women, we draw here some comparisons between our observations on these men as they became frailer. We consider first Harold Rank and Fred Hobson, both of whom were already disabled by their seventies and lost their wives much earlier than they might have expected. Harold's adaptation to his new situation, although ultimately successful, was a long and hard process, whereas Fred showed a remarkable degree of serenity throughout the difficulties he faced. How can this difference be explained? Three at least of our married men, Ted Jackson, Dennis Wilcox and Ernest Davies, were living towards the end of their lives in situations of mutual dependence with their wives. Both spouses had become seriously frail. Each was greatly concerned about the health of the other, but only Ted seemed to be actively planning for a future in which one of them would be left alone. Why was this so? Finally, we comment on the role of humour in old age, particularly in situations of physical and mental frailty.

If one considers his self-esteem ascriptions in isolation, Harold Rank's journey through old age consisted of two distinct halves. From a peak sense of self-efficacy at the end of seventy years, Harold's sense of self declined to reach a nadir of expressed distress at age eighty such that we, his interviewers, doubted whether he would survive much longer. Yet, despite continuing troublesome health problems, the following ten years saw a gradual accommodation on his part to his more dependent situation and renewed appreciation of life. Perhaps it was the strong sense of himself as an independent and capable man, evident when we first interviewed him, that was his major handicap in growing old. He had been a person who had solved problems all his life, and he was frustrated to be unable to cope with the new situations he faced, both his wife's dementia and his own declining mobility. It took him a long time to accept his new situation. At the same time he did succeed in preserving a large measure of independence and this was largely down to his recovering a strong sense of himself. Harold's case also seems an interesting example of the transition to a more disengaged stance towards the end of life, encapsulated best in one of his final comments that he would not be bothered even if a bomb exploded in the street outside.

On the evidence we collected, it is more difficult to explain why Fred Hobson displayed so much less distress in the process of growing frailer. It could be that the contrast with his previous life was less strong than in Harold's case and the onset of disability more gradual. Perhaps his background as a mental health nurse and social worker meant that he had more insight into his own psychological reactions and thus more control over them – although that is certainly not always the case with health professionals. But certainly his strong identification with his previous profession as a nurse was a major part of his personality, which he retained into old age, and this along with his close involvement with his family and his religious faith (both of which resources Harold also shared) remained a major source of psychological support.

Ted Jackson's forethought for his wife and family was impressive throughout our study, and their appreciation of him was evident in the testimony we received about Ted after his death. Other situations of mutual frailty between husband and wife were less securely founded. That of Ernest Davies and his wife was of particular concern to us. The combination of physical and mental frailty meant they were particularly at risk, not only of injury but also burglary. The support they received from their two daughters-in-law was insufficient not because of any lack of will on the latters' part but because of the second generation's problems with disability and distance from Ernest and his wife. It is difficult to see how their needs could be satisfactorily met. Ernest and his wife did not want to enter residential care together. In fact, it was Ernest's sudden death that resolved the situation as the worries and stress became too much for him.

Increasing dementia was also a factor in Dennis Wilcox's difficulties in the last period of his life. For some years, he had been concerned about how he would survive his wife's death. His own health had long been fragile, but as he entered his eighties, his wife's health situation became even more serious. They had a supportive family of whom they were proud, but the children were limited in the help they could give their parents (unlike the support Dennis and his wife had given her own mother). Unfortunately, we were not able to interview Dennis in the years between his wife's and his own death, but his own chronic ill health and increasing memory problems led to successive moves into residential care and finally into a nursing home.

It is worth making a final point about the use of humour many of the men displayed as they grew older, including Harold Rank and John Otterbourne. Some of the most memorable examples came from men in the most difficult of situations. Ernest Davies joked about his wife at the same time as being deeply concerned about her, and Cyril Steel towards the end of life seemed to have transcended his earlier depressed mood by distancing himself from the worries of his everyday situation. Both men were in states of moderately advanced dementia but, as Ernest said, could still see that it was necessary 'to kid oneself a bit'.

9   Towards one hundred years

Living beyond ninety years is not always seen so positively, and a number of our cases described in the last two chapters have illustrated how fragile life can be as one enters the tenth decade. At least twenty-five of our sample of forty cases reached age ninety years. Many of them were by then in poor health, ten of them dying within two years. Nevertheless, there were others who continued to flourish beyond ninety years and even beyond ninety-five years. The latter could be said of at least eleven of our cases, more than one-quarter of the whole sample. In this chapter, we describe the lives of the six persons, three women and three men, in the sample whom we were able to interview up to and in some cases beyond their middle nineties. Did awareness of their exceptional longevity influence the way that they perceived meaning in their lives?

The oldest women

One of the most remarkable stories in our sample of forty cases was that of *Elsie Darby*, whom we first mentioned in Chapter 4. In Chapter 7, we described her life in a residential care home where she came to live at age eighty-six after a difficult period in which she was in a stressful relationship with her third husband, whom she subsequently divorced, and also suffered a heart attack. Yet Elsie succeeded in leaving residential care five years later at age ninety-one and returning to sheltered housing, where she lived a further six years. How did she manage it? She herself later said that she had been spurred to leave the home by a visitor who had said to her that she was 'taking someone's place'! Elsie had the good fortune that all her furniture had been kept in store at no cost by friends of the family. Therefore, it was relatively easy for her to set up home again.

We interviewed Elsie only a few months after she had moved back to sheltered housing. When agreeing to be interviewed, she wrote to us of her pleasure at having her own home once more.

It is really like heaven being able to do my own housework again and cooking once more.

The interview revealed that there had been many other changes in Elsie's life. Not only was she doing her own housework and cooking, she was also shopping and tending a small garden at the back of her home. Her social mobility had also increased. She was attending a social club two or three times a week, playing darts and going on day trips. She had remained absorbed in making things for charity, which she worked at every day. She even said that she would welcome being involved in more activities.

Her health appeared improved. The one limiting problem she complained of concerned her hearing, which she said impaired some aspects of her life because it made her 'uncomfortable when in conversation'. Other than that, she still experienced some weakness in her legs, which prevented her 'doing all the things she used to'. Yet her accounts of her daily life indicated that she was walking more than a mile every week. She reported that she had been treated for depression earlier in the year before she left the residential care home, but our interview indicated that she was in high spirits and showed no symptoms of depression apart perhaps from fitful sleep and occasional feelings of edginess. She was also receiving treatment for anaemia. Elsie herself said that she felt 'very healthy' and restated her view that these were 'the best years of her life'.

Her self-esteem remained strong, but the sources she referred to were derived now more from actual participation in activities and social events rather than from opinions about her abilities. She 'felt useful' because of her work "helping children's societies, making things such as scrapbooks and toys", 'got enjoyment' out of "going to a social and having a dance." Her sense of 'importance to others' was now more strongly linked to her family, specifically her son and daughter. She 'felt capable' due to "cooking, housework and shopping" and 'gained in confidence' due to "going out and shopping." Her 'aims in life' and 'confidence in the future' were now linked to travelling beyond her present environment.

I would love to visit some of the children's homes which take my toys.

I'd like to go to Canada to see my daughter, but I need the fare.

Her attribution of 'brightness and alertness' was still illustrated by reference to her inner characteristics – namely, her ability to persevere despite difficulties.

I don't let worries get me down.

Her various sources of self-esteem were also reflected in the written answers on the self-completion questionnaire she later sent back to us.

'What is it about your life that makes you feel most alive?' . . . "Being able to do things for myself and being active with it! Planting garden and making soft toys."

'What do you believe in?'... "That there is a God above and He knows one does try and be helpful to others."

'Who is important to you in your life today?'... "My family, also grandchildren and great grandchildren."

'What is it in life that gives you hope?'... "To be able to please myself and not have to keep to rules!"

The direct question about meaning elicited from Elsie an expression of her deep-rooted concern and care for others.

'What has been the most meaningful about your life so far?'... "Being able to help people and seeing faces happier for them."

After this interview, we decided to compose a draft 'theory' of Elsie's sense of identity. A key starting point was further information she had provided about her early life during the interview. Her mother had died when she was very young, after which she and her sister had spent unhappy years being passed around from one 'mother' to another while their father was often absent. She began reviewing her life spontaneously to us.

My past life wasn't very happy.... We didn't have a mother, a proper mother and a proper father when he was away.... The children use to gang up on us, my sister and I. That wasn't very happy.... There was so much up and down and upheaval.

We never knew what it was to have a cooked meal... we were so hungry... And I took a handful of dog biscuits to eat and fill us up because we were really hungry.

An important factor contributing to her bewilderment as a child was her inability to understand and cope with the death of her real mother.

I was so small to say goodbye to my mother, to say goodnight to her. I didn't know that she was dying then. That's remained in my memory....

If I'd have been older when my mother died, I could have understood, I should have known how to cope... I didn't know how to.... I had to just let other people do what they had to do!

Elsie made an explicit comparison with her present situation.

Now that I am older I know what to look for and know what to expect.

In contrast to a childhood in which she could not exert control, was unable to understand the situation and, therefore, could not cope, her life in old age was "so much happier." This was because it contained an element of certainty that enabled Elsie to remain independent through her own self-control. Independence and control had become central values to her, which she expressed through her ability to carry out various activities, including when she had been in a residential home, also contributing to children's welfare through her making of soft toys. 'Contributing' especially was a central element in her sense of a good life.

That used to give me a kick to give, rather than somebody giving to me.

Giving to others supplied purpose and meaning to Elsie's life, which in turn was linked to her belief and faith in God who "knows one does try and be helpful to others." She had had to resort to a more inner sense of herself when she lost her home and been moved to residential care but had found ways even there of continuing to work for children. Now that she was independent again, she could give full expression to her wish to do things for others.

It could be, we thought, that the positive features of her present life had provided her with the security to look back on and accept the shadows of her youth, to relate her whole life in one single narrative and so achieve a more integrated sense of identity. One new striking feature in Elsie's presentation of self was her expressed interest in her own family. In previous years, her family had not featured strongly as a source of her identity, but at the time of this interview her "family, also grandchildren and great-grandchildren" appeared to have become a more central feature in her life, even the most important.

Two years later, we interviewed Elsie again at age ninety-four. The main change she herself reported was the recent death of her third husband, whom she had divorced eleven years earlier. But there had also been some deterioration in her health, as she spoke of a mild stroke she had incurred earlier in the year as well as pain in her back, hip and legs, which she put down to sciatica and had reduced her walking to 'less than one hundred yards' a week; this also prevented her from doing any gardening. She needed now to stop for breath when walking at her own pace on level ground. She was receiving assistance with cleaning her apartment once a week from a Social Services home help.

Elsie's depression rating had increased, which she attributed to the stroke, but otherwise she continued to express positive attitudes, interest in her surroundings and other people as well as optimism about the future. Her self-esteem also remained high. She felt 'useful' making toys for charity, enjoyed greatly her attendance at the various social clubs she still attended and playing the organ and felt 'capable' because of the various activities in which she engaged. Her family remained important to her, as she did to them. In fact, she derived her sense of 'brightness and alertness' from being a confidant to them.

My family always ask for advice if they have a problem.

Yet she also valued her sense of independence. Illustrating why she looked to the future with confidence, she indicated her self-reliance.

When you're alive you've got to make life happy – to depend on yourself. You can't always depend on other people.

At a subsequent interview with another of us a few weeks later, Elsie wanted to introduce herself again, together with her life story. Especially striking were her memories of her mother's early death and the lasting visual images that accompanied them. She spoke emotionally of having being placed in a house across the road from where she lived, and "peeping through the curtains" seeing a coffin being brought into her parents' house. 'Why was a big box being brought into her mother's house?' Her older brother had noticed blood dripping on to the pavement, and had later told her that their father had been "bad." He had been with another woman she knew as "Auntie Min" before their mother had died.

From then on Elsie's life had been rootless, moved around from one foster family to another. She and her siblings would ask each other, "Who is going to be our next mother?" Elsie said that she was telling us these things because it helped explain why she chose to marry first a widowed man already with children of his own. She had felt sorry for them. The marriage had not been perfect, but still he had given her three children of her own in addition to the two stepsons. She had been happiest with her second husband, but he had not lived long. She had then married her third husband, a friend of her second, but he had caused her a lot of 'trouble wanting to do things she did not like'. Her health had deteriorated, and her doctor and a lawyer had taken action on her behalf to request a divorce. But it was the early experience of abandonment that she stressed had been the key motivating factor through her life. This also explained, she said, her present values, why, for example, she spent so much time making toys and also scrapbooks, some going to the local centre for children with learning disabilities.

Elsie also spoke at this interview about her time in residential care and how continuing to play the organ and to knit had been so important. The ability to make her own music was still a great comfort to her at present. She wanted to take the opportunity of this visit to express her worries about her health, particularly her recent stroke, but also her concerns about the neglect of the environment around where she lived, the uneven paving stones and the fast traffic in the road. She had written to her councillors about both problems. As was the case with many people in our study, Elsie was concerned the world was becoming worse. People did not have time for another as they used to. In these attitudes, she was pessimistic, thinking that things had deteriorated too far to become as they had been. The war she thought had had a decisive influence. She spoke as well about her large, extended family, including five children, fifteen grandchildren and fourteen great-grandchildren. A stepdaughter had recently come to visit her from Australia, together with her two sons.

Our last interview with Elsie took place three years later when she was aged ninety-seven years, a few months before she died. Her lifestyle, activities and positive attitudes had remained remarkably unimpaired despite some recent health problems. Earlier in the year, she had been in hospital with a chest infection and in addition had been told that a valve was not working in her heart. She was also currently experiencing difficulties with her legs, some pain when walking and shortness of breath. But apart from sleep disturbance, she did not show any other symptoms suggestive of depression, although she herself said that she occasionally felt depressed. She was continuing her active social life, attending six clubs in the vicinity, as well as continuing to 'knit dolls and play the organ'. She continued to feel that these were 'the best years' of her life. Her self-ascriptions remained entirely positive, illustrated as before by reference to her household and outdoor activities, especially attending her 'many clubs' and the attention of her family and friends. Although she was 'happy in her own home', she said she was most 'alive when she was with others'.

When three years earlier, we had presented our own 'theory' of her identity to Elsie, she agreed with our major points, firstly her need for independence.

I was called Mrs Independent in the home. I've always had to look after myself.

She also agreed that her identity was reinforced by contributing to others.

My happiness is taken from giving rather than receiving. I've always been that way.

Her connection with every member of her family was important, including her daughter in Canada.

That's where I get all the lace from. She sent it for Christmas.

But also important were her contacts with the people she met in the local clubs. She had actively sought out these clubs by "asking around."

I like going to the clubs. We are all friendly. At the '90 Club, we have a chat, a cup of tea, they bring us back, it's friendly. Not only that, you meet more people and more friends.

The clubs also provided a routine, which she needed.

Mondays we go to Silver Threads; Tuesday the Community Club; Wednesday Bingo; Thursday Bingo in the evening . . . so I have a regular routine. It's all mapped out . . . At the weekends I'm visited either by relatives or friends.

Her neighbour opposite provided key support.

She's only seventy-five. We belong to most of the same clubs and go together. If I'm worried about Council things or any letters, I've only got to just knock on her door.

Seemingly underpinning all the other sources of identity was her belief in God, which she said had remained constant throughout her life.

I don't think [my faith] will ever leave me.

She also acknowledged the difficult elements in her life, firstly living alone. Indeed, she was prepared to get married again 'if she found the right man'. She also acknowledged the advantages of living in a residential care home.

There was so much activity in the home, something going on all the time. I'm quiet here and I have to adjust . . . I play the organ and I'm as right as rain!

Health problems, especially if prolonged, also lowered her sense of well-being, primarily because they kept her in.

I've been a bit depressed because it [a cold] has lasted so long. I haven't been able to go out at all since the holidays.

Worry about her family also made her sad, especially if they had health problems.

I'm easier now because my son is willing for my daughter to live with them. She is coming [from Canada] next year.

Despite the bouts of loneliness and depression, Elsie was fortunate to live such a happy and relatively healthy life in her nineties. Her unhappiness in early life had made her appreciate what life had to offer all the more and she was able to do so right until the end.

When we last described **Ethel Willis's** life in Chapter 7, she was nearly ninety years old, but the impact of a stroke the previous year, coupled with her deteriorating eyesight, had limited her life and led to an increase in depressive symptoms. Her morale was low, and we doubted whether she would regain it. However, when interviewed two years later, despite further health problems and the persistence of depression, she was very much in control of her life. She was still living alone in the downstairs part of her house. She normally liked to go upstairs to take a bath, but because of her current illness, she had been unable to go upstairs for the past two weeks.

Earlier in the year, she had been admitted to hospital where she had been diagnosed as having gallstones. Because of her age, she had been told that surgery would not be appropriate. Ethel had also been unwell for about two weeks before the interview, starting with cystitis and followed by back pain, which she assumed emanated from her kidneys. In addition, she was suffering from constipation, which was being monitored by the district nurse. The nurse, as well as Ethel's daughter, were present at the beginning of the interview and were trying to persuade Ethel to eat more as well as to take the laxative she had been prescribed. This was all rather difficult for her as she had had a small appetite since surgery on her stomach a few years earlier. This, together with her problems with sleeping, accounted for her raised depression score.

Under normal circumstances, she was still undertaking a lot of the activities needed to look after herself, preparing her own meals, doing her shopping with transport assistance from her daughter, and doing some of the housework. She was receiving home help from social services for one hour a week as well as support from her neighbours, who called frequently to see whether she needed anything. One of the neighbours was also there when the interview began.

Ethel's attitudes to her situation remained rather negative. She did not 'feel very healthy' and did not consider old age to be 'a happy time' for her. She said she was quite ready to "pop off." However, her sense of self showed signs of strengthening. She had regained confidence in herself. Doing housework gave her a sense of 'still being capable'. The "caring people around me" gave her a sense of importance, and she most certainly considered herself 'bright and alert'. In fact, she considered herself a "good advert for my age." Although she now said that she 'felt useless', she attributed this to her current state of ill health and expected to improve.

I hope to feel useful again when I'm feeling better.

She expressed a continued sense of involvement with life around, concerned with the health problems of her son and daughter and keeping in touch with current affairs. She was pleased to have the opportunity to debate particular issues. The *Sun* newspaper 'hit the right level for her', although she joked that her son said he was too embarrassed to fetch it for her!

She remained determined not to move into a residential care home or sheltered accommodation. As well as having concerns about the costs, she shared popular conceptions about what life was like in a home:

You just sit there and look at each other all the time.

She also had no wish to move in with her daughter, having assessed the fact that they simply could not get on together in the same house. She said that "it just wouldn't work." She was well aware of how dependent she was on the goodwill of family and neighbours but still wanted "to die in harness", in control of her own remaining life. She could manage on the state pension with some additional income support that she now received. She was not afraid of death. She said it would be no worse for her than it was for her husband and all the other family members she had seen die.

It must be OK up there because they don't come back!

At a follow-up visit some weeks later, Ethel was in much better health. Already that morning she had cleared out a blocked drain, swept the garden path and washed some curtains! She was happy to confirm the twin bases of her identity: her determination to remain independent so long as she could and her deep concern for both her son and her daughter.

Another of us went to visit Ethel the following month. She was lively and eager to speak. Much of the time she reminisced, including almost every period of her life. She had been the last of seven children, with an older father of fifty years and a mother of forty. Her father had a smallholding out in the countryside where he kept animals, including pigs. There was always a leg of pork for Christmas. It was "lovely"; she "could taste it now." She had started working, fifty-five hours a week for thirty-two shillings and sixpence, as a tailoress for a Jewish family in the centre of town before the armistice in 1918. She spoke about her marriage in 1925, the births of her son and daughter, and an ectopic pregnancy in the late 1930s, which was still difficult for her to speak about. Her husband had earned three pounds a week as a ship's carpenter. In the early years of their marriage, he had been away on ships around the world for much of the time, but a trade union official had helped him obtain a job in the docks after their son was born in 1935.

Perhaps as a consequence of her husband's frequent absence, Ethel became active outside as well as inside the home. She had always done a lot of sewing. But thinking back on the situation, she was surprised how her husband tolerated her outdoors work. She became secretary of her local ward's Conservative Party Association and was also active in a number of other organizations, so that she was out many evenings a week.

She also spoke a lot about how religious life had changed. When she was young, she had attended church services three times a day on a Sunday, mornings, afternoons and evenings. After she married, she did not go anymore. She still felt some shame about this. What would God think, that we only pray when we are in trouble? An issue for her was that she had always been a sceptical person, questioning the stories in the Bible, such as the account of Creation in Genesis. But at the same time, she marvelled at how perfect the world was and could not accept Darwin's theory of evolution as the whole answer. She argued about these things with her son, who was well read in biology.

She spoke a lot about her son and daughter, her gratitude to the health service, the state of the Conservative Party and politics in general, and her support for the Saints (the Southampton Football Club) who had had a successful season but just lost their manager. She showed particular concern for older people with dementia and thought it tragic for all those who were affected. She was pleased to have avoided that so far. All in all, she seemed a well-adjusted person, although with an element of sadness related especially to her regrets over a world that had passed. Retaining her independence was important to her, but she was interested to hear descriptions of residential care homes that encouraged activity and tried to preserve individuality.

We interviewed Ethel for the last time two years later when she was approaching ninety-five years. She had had no further major health problems. A first appointment had to be cancelled because of the interviewer's illness. But Ethel made no problems about this. She said that she had set to and washed her bedroom curtains instead! She remained cheerful and active, almost sprightly for her age. During the interview, she sat in her chair with her feet tucked up under her. When she got to her feet, however, she seemed rather unsteady. Her feet swelled up a lot, and she agreed that she ought to sit with them up on a stool to aid her circulation. Still determined to continue living at home, she appeared to be coping well. She complained good-naturedly about her home help, saying that she was not thorough enough and so Ethel had to "do" in all the corners and under the bed. Her eyesight was still good enough to read, and she particularly enjoyed biographies.

She was close to her two children and her neighbours. Her daughter's health was her major preoccupation. She was accepting of her own death, seeing it as a natural progression. She seemed to have resolved whatever doubts she may have had about religion, saying that she had lost her religious beliefs after her husband died. She had started questioning things she had previously accepted and concluded that religion was pointless. Her self-esteem ascriptions and the illustrations she gave remained similar to the previous time. She still felt capable because of the housework she did, enjoyed people around her and felt important to her family and neighbours. 'Useful', however, she could not feel, particularly after the busy life that she had had. But more significantly she now said that she found it "nice to grow old", that she had "been very lucky in my life" and that old age was "a happy time for me."

Ethel died one year later in hospital at age ninety-six years.

At our previous interview with **Irene Monroe** in her ninetieth year, she had appeared to have come to terms with her more limited life style. Sustained by her faith and her newfound interest in painting, she was happy to be living in a Church Army residential care home. When interviewed three years later at age ninety-two, she was recuperating from a severe bout of influenza. She said this had left her feeling depressed, which was reflected in a raised depression score. Irene reported a number of other health problems, deafness sufficient to impair her quality of life, shortness of breath, stiffness when walking and a general weakness in her arms and legs in part attributable to being knocked down by a car a year before, for which she had been hospitalized. She said that she was 'worrying more' regarding the help she would need in the future and that her failure to be as independent as she wished was making her "cross." She was also feeling 'unsure of herself'.

I haven't felt well. I have horrible feelings, and it is not me at all.

Nevertheless, she was continuing to be busy within the residential home, doing some housework, shopping, cooking and gardening, including watering all the plants within the home, as well as 'walking up to a mile' and 'going to town once a week'. She was still enjoying painting as well as collecting stamps and picture postcards. She was visiting friends and family less outside the home but was compensating for this by socializing more within it. Her sense of self-esteem had remained high, despite some feeling of insecurity and loss of alertness. This was evident both in her responses to choosing between positive and negative ascriptions about herself and also in the answers she sent back to us on the self-completion questionnaire. As before, the illustrations related to activities in the home, her friends and family, but above all to her religious faith.

'What kinds of things do you enjoy doing?' ... "Talking to my friends who interest me; needlework; reading; watching specific TV programmes."

'What is important to you in your life today?' ... "My nearest relatives – my sister, daughter, grandchildren and certain friends."

'What is it about your life that makes you feel most alive?' ... "When I experience the joy of being a Christian."

Many of her activities in the home were in fact church related. She helped prepare the chapel room for Holy Communion and took seriously her self-appointed task of reading the Bible systematically and sharing her faith with other residents.

It was at this interview point that we explored our participants' sense of identity by asking them how they would describe their life story. Irene's answers were forthright and clearly expressed.

'Are there any terms that you could describe your life with?' ... "My root causes are my faith."

'What have been the major contributions you have made to life?' ... "It is difficult. I would say my faith. ... I have been able to share my faith with others ... it has made me very, very happy."

'What have been some of the main features of your life?' ... "Falling in love with my husband and having twin girls unexpected."

Most striking to us was how Irene was now drawing on past experiences as a source of satisfaction, specifically her previous relationship with her husband, a subject that had been rarely referred to in previous interviews. She described how she was "very proud" of her husband's past achievements as an archivist, and when asked to describe the event that was 'most meaningful' to her life, she answered: "I should say my marriage is the biggest thing because my husband got the MBE [Most Excellent Order of the British Empire] and went to Buckingham Palace."

We interviewed Irene on three occasions two years later, one year before she died, as she reached and passed ninety-five years. Her health had deteriorated greatly in the intervening period, her mobility reduced to walking 'less than

100 yards a week' as she experienced pain, breathlessness and unsteadiness in her legs. She was unable now to take a bath without help, could no longer climb stairs and had been upset by a fall two months earlier. She also reported having had a mild stroke six months before the interview and to having felt depressed on occasions because of "being alone so much" in her room. This was again reflected in the depression rating taken at the time. However, she was able to visit her sister every fortnight, being taken to her sister's home and back by taxi, and although she was not able to attend the local church anymore, she still took responsibility for preparing the chapel in the home for Holy Communion.

Irene's self-esteem remained high and was illustrated by her activities within the home, forming new friendships among the other residents and continuing to be able to read. Companionship made her feel 'bright and alert', although she added that she sometimes felt 'foolish' when she "thought wrong things." She enjoyed her fortnightly visits to her sister and took pride in her granddaughter gaining a university degree. But as at previous interviews, her religious faith provided the majority of positive examples. It was the source of her confidence.

I thank God I have courage because God is in my heart.

Her faith gave her the assurance that she would "never be alone." Her aims were expressed in both general terms – "to love mercy and walk humbly with my God" – and more practically – "to read the Bible every day."

She compensated for her nonattendance at church by watching religious services on television.

I enjoy the TV services at half-past nine on Sunday morning and Songs of Praise.

She also continued to share her faith with others through having established meetings of a religious group, named 'Open Doors', at the home within the past three years. This provided her with a new source of achievement and interest. It helped her to feel integrated within a circle of friends who had the same interests and beliefs.

Last night I gave myself over to prayer, the wonderful prayers of all these people. I've never heard prayers like them.

In these last interviews, Irene was happy to engage with us in an evaluation of the origins and sources of her identity.

I love to look back on life as I have been very, very fortunate.

She reflected on her early achievements as "a children's nurse, a district nurse and doing chiropody" but also on the new skills she was able to learn later in life.

I learned to drive when I was seventy – then drove for six years. I'm surprised at what I've been able to do.

She also identified with her husband's achievements. She described how she had recently given her granddaughter her husband's MBE and added: "I hope that she is worthy of it."

As expected, her religious faith emerged again as her primary source of strength and identity.

God is my all in all.

Her relationships with family and friends also continued to reinforce her positive sense of identity and gave her a sense of satisfaction.

My daughter rings me twice a week and's coming for my birthday next.

The organist comes and the vicar came when I had a small stroke ... I like people to talk to me about what they do.

She also enjoyed making new acquaintances.

There's a person came yesterday that gave me great joy. He gave a wonderful prayer and his relatives said, 'Oh I am pleased he's at your table'.

Nevertheless, her declining health had reduced her sense of satisfaction in life, particularly because it had produced an increase in isolation. Her previous life had revolved around contacts with others, and she appeared to need the stimulation of their contributions. She disagreed that it was 'nice to grow old' and found it 'difficult to be careful of her health' because 'there was always something the matter'. However, her ability to adjust and adapt to changing circumstances, as well as her strong inner faith, seemed to sustain her despite the difficulties with her health. She also expressed an increasing acceptance of death.

I feel I could say that – I can say 'Lord now let they servant [depart in peace].'

In the second interview, Irene engaged fully in commenting on the 'theory' we had developed on her underlying sources of identity. Particularly interesting were her responses to conclusions that she had not considered before. She agreed that the ability to adjust and adapt is important in later life and had helped her maintain her identity.

You sometimes don't realize until you look back and then you see how you've changed.

However, she disagreed that increasing health problems in themselves had reduced her self-esteem. These she had simply accepted.

I still feel contented as I just know who to pray to for advice.

She did agree though that her reduced outdoor activities reduced her sense of well-being. Indeed, since the previous interview, she had attended a church service outside the home more than once and was determined to keep on going. She was considering which was the most feasible for her.

I do miss [outdoor activities]. I've got to make up my mind whether I'll stay on at Saint .... I went there because of the organist as he gives me a lift.... I go to another church once a month in Saint.... second Sunday in the month. Again I'm given a lift by the church warden. But it's going to close down.... I always go when I can – I have to go to Church.

Irene confirmed the centrality of faith in her life and particularly that the new Open Doors meetings were extending her identity further afield: "reaching out all over the world."

Last night [the meeting] was wonderful – we met in the chapel and prayed for the suffering, the suffering of little children. There were ten of us.

She also agreed that her duties in the home, activities that she had carrying out for eight years since arriving there, also added to a positive sense of identity. Reading the lives of others also helped, providing "inspiration." Also thinking back on her past achievements contributed to the joy she experienced.

I thank God for what I have done – being a nurse – which I enjoyed. I had wonderful patients in the London Hospital.

Last, but certainly no less important, her family and friends constituted an essential part of her life. Memories of her husband indeed seemed to have an increased presence in her life.

I've still got his letters, and I sometimes read them. I read them the other day. There was a wonderful letter written about him by the Church.... I want to be buried with him and have the service in the same church, Saint..., in Southampton.

In the final interview, Irene wanted to tell the new visitor more about her career as a Christian missionary in Asia (she showed a painting she had done of mountains in Sri Lanka), her association with the evangelical ministry of Holy Trinity Brompton in London and the healing mission of Dorothy Kerrin. She asked about the origins of our study and expressed her appreciation of having being part of it. Irene died a year later, aged ninety-six years.

The oldest men

Bill Blackburn was the only member of our sample of cases whom we interviewed beyond age one hundred years. He had not been expected to live so long. When we last described his situation in Chapter 6, he had been admitted at age ninety-two to an elderly care ward because of increasing weakness, but he had subsequently fallen there and fractured both his shoulder and pelvis. When we interviewed him a few months later, he was practically housebound. His situation was drastically changed, as he acknowledged himself.

When I was ninety, I could walk and dance and drink and stand up and walk miles . . . it's only since I broke my pelvis that I have been wrecked more or less.

He was no longer able to use stairs and therefore was living on the ground floor of his house. He was reliant on a combination of helpers including Meals On Wheels, home help and neighbours. Since his fall and broken pelvis, Bill had used two sticks to help mobility, but because of the combination of weakness, dizziness and disability, he experienced great difficulty walking. He got extremely short of breath just washing and dressing. He was also diabetic and had problems with urinary retention. His financial situation continued to be tight. He agreed that he had to "watch every penny."

Despite these difficulties, Bill was still aiming to continue his social activities as before. A neighbour was taking him by car to his local pub for a few drinks. Remarkably, he had avoided severe depression. Indeed, most of his symptoms on the Wakefield Self-Report Questionnaire – tiredness, sleep problems, anxiety going out of the house on his own and difficulty doing the things he used to – could be explained by his recent experiences with becoming disabled. On the Montgomery-Åsberg Depression Rating Scale (MADRS), his depression score was lower and had decreased further when he was interviewed three years later at age ninety-five. By then he had moved home. His old house where he had lived for more than sixty years had been condemned on environmental health grounds, and he had accepted the offer of a ground floor flat on a large council estate. This was a long way from his old haunts and his old friends. Nevertheless, he seemed to be adapting to the new circumstances. This was helped by the fact that he had retained his old home help, and his friend 'the lollipop man' (who guarded street crossings for children walking to and from school) still visited. It was also noteworthy how regularly he was writing letters to friends.

Bill's resilience was demonstrated above all in his self-ascriptions and illustrations. After the collapse in his health, there was a hint that his self-esteem might start declining through a realization that he might be becoming a burden on others, but three years later, he had become surer of himself again. This was exemplified in the change of his self-ascription from 'feeling useless' to 'feeling useful'. At age ninety-two, he had said he had felt useless "when I'm a burden on someone", but at ninety-five, he felt useful because "I have the will to cope for myself." He explained further in describing why he thought himself 'still capable of doing quite a lot':

I sometimes ignore people who want to help. I want to try to cope on my own.

His general sociability gave him a sense of importance: "I'm liked and like most people." As in the past, the one weakness he admitted – which led to him regarding himself as 'foolish' – was his naivety.

I'm easy-going. I take everything I'm told as the truth and then realize I'm being taken for a ride.

In saying this, Bill demonstrated himself to be wise, possessing the ability to be realistic about his weaknesses.

It was after this interview when he was aged ninety-five years that we attempted to draw up a 'theory' of Bill's identity. It seemed to us that throughout his life, he had managed to make the best of what he had. Despite having no children, he had had a happy marriage. Since the death of his wife, he had adjusted well, making many friends through an active social life, even though his lifestyle may not have been in the best interest of his financial situation or his long-term health. It was this adaptability and outgoing nature that enabled Bill to cope with his increasing disability and the trauma of the changes that had taken place over the past few years, including the pelvic injury and the relocation. Indeed, it may be that his physical surroundings had never been particularly important to him but his interpersonal relationships much more so. The increasing emphasis on correspondence meant that despite physical isolation, he could continue to keep in touch with others.

The answers that he sent back to the sentence completion stems at this time gave evidence of this.

'I am best at' ... *"liking people and making friends."*

'I plan to' ... *"keep my normal habit, keep in touch with friends and have a wee drop."*

'Most important to me is' ... *"wake up in the morning and go and see friends and write letters."*

The importance of an independent spirit was also demonstrated.

'Others think I am' ... *"I don't think what other people think, I have a mind of my own."*

It has been through this independent spirit that Bill had preserved his self-esteem through a lifestyle which may have appeared inadequate or even mildly deviant. He had evolved his own concepts of living space, finance and health maintenance, which allowed him to maintain his morale through circumstances that might have defeated others.

Three years later, now in his ninety-ninth year, Bill was still living relatively independently. Although there had been no further dramatic health event, he was now more reliant on others, needing help with dressing, shaving and bathing. He was also experiencing a combination of pain in his joints and unsteadiness in his limbs, which made walking difficult. Social services had recognized his greater needs, and while keeping on his council flat, he had been offered the opportunity to stay in a social services residential home (referred to as 'part 3' accommodation) for respite care every few weeks. At the time of the interview Bill had been staying in the home for several weeks and was due to return to his own home in about a week.

He was still talkative, although his speech impairment made it difficult for him to be understood. A further hindrance was that he salivated excessively and so tended to dribble and spray when talking. He also was affected by some degree of hearing loss and complained that they 'spoke too quickly for him on the radio these days'. His sight had deteriorated as well, and he was now more or less blind. Sadly, this meant that he was no longer able to correspond in writing as he had liked to do before. His depression score was raised, but he noted perceptively that he was not so much depressed as lonely.

Despite the difficulties, Bill took the opportunity to talk more about his past life that he had ever done before with us. He spoke about how much he loved his wife and also how he had lost contact with his father. It seems that his mother died when he was quite young. One day, after her death, he found his father in bed with the barmaid from the local pub, and as a result he lost respect for his father. Later his father married the barmaid, and as a result they lost contact altogether. Although Bill's lifestyle had been associated with drinking and gambling, he appeared to have had high moral standards where conduct with women was concerned.

Bill spoke almost continuously for two hours, which demonstrated both his need and ability for communication. However, in the end, he tired himself out talking and so could not come to the end of the formal interview. Later in the interview, it also became less and less clear whether he was talking about the present or the past. Nevertheless, the information collected indicated that he had a continuing positive sense of self-esteem.

'I get much enjoyment out of life' . . . *"my thoughts, seeing people, personal contact."*

'I am still capable of doing quite a lot' . . . *"as long as the home help puts things back in the right place* [so he could find them again with his poor eyesight]."

'I have a clear aim in my life' . . . *"I have faith in people."*

'I have confidence in myself' . . . *"I am sure of myself . . . I give facts."*

He said that he did not feel useful or useless and gave an explanation for this, indicating his acceptance of dependency.

I am more or less useless. I can't cope unless I have help, but I can get by with help.

Bill was clearly suffering from the fact that he was becoming more and more isolated, mainly because of his increasing sensory defects. He appreciated the companionship and stimulation provided by his periodic stays in residential care, and it was interesting how he took the opportunity of the interview to talk more generally about himself and his life. It was sad to hear though that he was critical of his home and did not like his flat or the neighbourhood in which he had been placed. He claimed that he had been the victim of various petty thefts over the past six months, which inevitably had made him feel more vulnerable living there. He was still visiting his old social club from time to time, taking a taxi to travel there and back. His aim he said was to arrive at one hundred years of age.

When we interviewed Bill two years later, he had reached this goal. In the intervening period, he had become a permanent resident of the residential home he had been attending for respite care. He seemed quite content in these surroundings despite his increasing dependence on others. He was fond of and respected his carers.

Since I've been blind, I've been coming to this unit four weeks at a time, perhaps three or four times a year, and then I decided that I couldn't cope any longer, so I told them I would like to be a permanent resident. They accepted me, and then they've been very kind to me ever since. The nurses are kind to me, and they wash all my clothes, keep me clean, shave me and that, put me to bed, get me up and give me breakfast. I do everything myself, wash myself down every morning.

As he would have been unable to hear the questions properly and would have tired himself well before the end, the full interview was not attempted. The self-esteem section was attempted with limited success. Instead, Bill was encouraged to talk about himself.

He was by now very deaf and quite blind. His speech, however, was still coherent, although it took some effort to understand it. He obviously still enjoyed communicating. He could walk for short distances using two sticks and with the assistance of a caregiver.

They help me to go to the restroom but otherwise I, as soon as I stand, if they didn't get hold of my arm I would fall down.

Despite the help he was receiving, he was continuing to experience falls and therefore had frequent injuries. At the time of the interview, he had a dressing on one of his hands and was still experiencing pain in his wrist as a result of his most recent tumble. It appears that he fell over in his bedroom, injuring his arm and shoulder. He was told that he had broken his arm, but he disputed that diagnosis, claiming that it was just dislocated. He had also damaged the ligaments in his throat during the fall and had since had to have all his food cut up for him to eat. The damage to his throat had also inhibited his ability to enjoy alcohol.

I can't drink much now because of the ligaments of my throat, whisky's a bit on the strong side. So I have a drop in moderation but you got to watch yourself because whisky on its own now, it could catch my throat you see.

He rarely left the home. Indeed, at the time of the interview, he had not been outside for several months. He attributed this principally to problems with his bowels (constipation) and the need to be near a toilet in case the medicine he was taking had its intended effect.

Bill continued to make positive self-ascriptions as before, although there was somewhat less coherence in his answers. The MADRS scale was not attempted, so there was no measure of depression. The main indication of his general morale was that he emphasized he did feel lonely despite the fact that he had people around him most of the time. Nevertheless, he was "not down."

I get me lonely days cause there's thirty-six women and there's only five men. I sit at a table with two women... they're getting on in years, and they speak very quietly. I get really lonely in the sitting rooms, nobody talks all day long. It's very lonely, but I'm not down, I think a lot...

He referred also in his self-esteem illustrations to his ability to "visualize" his life in the past.

I think a lot. I don't think of the present or the future. My mind goes back to me sisters and me brothers.

This seemed to be Bill's way of dealing with the reduction in his interpersonal relationships as a result of sensory deprivation. He was continuing to adapt.

The most significant event in his life recently had been his one-hundredth-birthday celebration.

I had practically twenty birthday cards and my niece in..., she sent me a cheque... my next-door neighbour for thirty odd years, she sent me a cheque for thirty quid, the Home Secretary sent me a birthday card and the leader of the Social Services sent me a bottle of whisky and a birthday card so I'm very lucky. Oh and the Queen sent me a what do you call them...

Some of his old friends and neighbours did visit him, in particular his long-term neighbour who visited Mondays, Wednesdays and Fridays. He had been made Bill's next of kin and given responsibility for handling all his affairs.

Another of us visited Bill later the same year. Although asleep at first, he was pleased to talk and straightened himself as if getting ready to answer questions, with a dignified appearance despite his frailty. He described how he came to live in the care home but then went on to reminisce about his life. He spoke especially about his mother – "a lovely woman" – who had been "so kind" to her children. She had been the major influence on him despite her dying when he was only ten years old. His father "went to pot" after she died, taking to drink. He also spoke with great love of his wife – "a beautiful Scottish girl" – only four feet, ten inches high. Her womb had been too small to bear children. Their GP had told him to "forget it." They had had cats and chickens, a two-week holiday every year in Blackpool, Plymouth and the like – he was proud of this fact – and a very happy marriage. His wife had died suddenly at age seventy of a 'blood clot on the brain'. He spoke of his old neighbourhood in Southampton, he stressed how he "loved people . . . liked people." When told how much we appreciated the help he had given to our project, he repeated what he had said at the beginning that although he could not see, he could hear. He wanted to hold hands, "God bless" he said, and repeated it twice more.

We visited the home later the next year, some months after Bill had died aged one hundred and one years. The staff member we spoke to emphasized what a "*very* popular" resident he had been. It had been a little sad though, she said, that in his last year he had changed somewhat. He had wanted to stay in bed more, no longer asking for his tot of whisky nor eager to go to his old social club. Perhaps he had set up too high expectations of himself through his remarkable sociability in the preceding years.

Charles Kitchen was also last considered in Chapter 6. When interviewed again at age ninety-two years, he was still in remarkably good health, his only problems being some hearing impairment and a degree of anaemia that was being treated by monthly iron injections. His reaction to the latter demonstrated the importance of golf to his well-being.

[The doctor] advised me to have these injections, but I was feeling tired, you know, before that . . . I was pleased I can tell you because I was playing golf . . . it got a bit arduous, especially particularly this last hill, but I can do it better now than what I did before.

Charles was demonstrating a continued ability to live an active, independent life, coping with the pressures of driving in his nineties as well as a willingness to face up to developments in technology, installing a satellite TV aerial to take advantage of enhanced news and sports coverage. His self-esteem ascriptions remained entirely positive, illustrated by his various activities and interests as well as the help he gave to his sports partners.

By the time of the next interview when he had reached ninety-five years, Charles had experienced another significant bereavement, the death of his brother. He expressed a stoic acceptance but also a determination to carry on as before.

[Death] is one of the surest things in life that's going to happen to you, however it comes . . . [but I wish to] live my life as in the past doing a good turn wherever possible.

His self-esteem remained stable, illustrated in much the same way as three years before.

I do lots of chores including heavy gardening jobs.

I'm in reasonably good health and I enjoy all the things I do – house, sports and going to the markets [He especially enjoyed the Southampton–Le Havre twinning 'Le Weekend' market].

I give lifts to other people in the car.

It was on this occasion that he completed a revealing written self-description, which he sent to us in the post. This indicated a general satisfaction with his quality of life as he approached one hundred years, some concerns for the future, but also an interest in the younger generation and in continuing to provide help to others.

'I feel really good' ... *"when I have a good round of golf and wake in the morning feeling fine."*

'I am afraid that' ... *"I may have to give up some of the manual efforts to keep the bungalow in repair."*

'In the next few years' ... *"I want to see my younger grandchildren achieve the same status as their parents."*

'Maybe I can' ... *"maintain my present mode of life longer than general expectations."*

'I plan to' ... *"teach all my offspring a good way of life."*

'I intend to' ... *"live my life as in the past doing a good turn whenever possible."*

'I believe that' ... *"I can achieve a century of life."*

Clearly a great deal of Charles's self-esteem and perceived meaning in life was closely associated with his continued ability to maintain his good health. His current strategy had served him well and he hoped it would continue to do so. But we also considered that his self-esteem would be vulnerable if his health were to decline in ways that disabled him given that he expressed so much pride in his abilities. He also seemed to imply that he saw himself as a role model of ageing for others.

Three years later when next interviewed, Charles was in his ninety-ninth year. Fortunately, there was little significant change in his situation. He was still living independently in his own home. The house was clean and tidy, as was the garden where he was still growing his own vegetables. He seemed fit and well, although he believed that he tired more easily now. He had reluctantly given up playing bowls as all his companions no longer played, although he said he would start again if he found suitable partners. In its place he said he was interested in joining the new bingo club that was opening up in the city. He was attracted by the promised social facilities as much as by the prospect of bingo. He was still driving his own car. In fact, he had bought a new bright red one in the previous year. Apart from the monthly injection to control his pernicious anaemia, he was in receipt of no other medical treatment. The only changes he noticed in himself were some unsteadiness in walking and a loss of strength in his limbs. He had some hearing loss but not enough to inconvenience him. His sight remained excellent. He still made a point of reading the newspapers every day and attended all the home Hampshire Cricket Club matches in the summer. This was also the season when he played golf regularly. He also played from time to time in the winter.

At the time of the interview, Charles had suffered a disturbed night, having been woken up by police who told him that his garage had been broken into. His golf clubs had been stolen. His son was currently dealing with the damage to the garage. Charles seemed not to be unduly upset by this event and wanted the interview to proceed. He expressed appreciation for a copy of a video interview we had made with him after the previous meeting. He said he was delighted to see and hear himself for the first time in his life.

His self-esteem ascriptions showed some subtle changes. For the first time, he could not say that he 'got much enjoyment out of life'. The loss of his bowls activity was something he particularly regretted. All his other self-ascriptions remained positive, but there was a declining emphasis on physical ability in his illustrations, and a greater stress on his inner qualities. For example, describing his 'brightness and alertness', he said, "I watch other people, especially golfers, and can see their faults." His comment that as soon as he lost confidence in his ability, he would stop driving suggested that he was aware that time might be approaching. Charles also sent back further written comments on this occasion that confirmed the view of himself he had presented before as an active and helpful man.

'What kinds of things do you enjoy doing?' ... *"Golf, bowls, driving my car, talking to friends."*

'What kinds of things do you like working at?' ... *"Carpentry where necessary, decorating, cooking and keeping the place ship shape."*

'Who or what do you especially care about?' ... *"I care about anyone who needs help, where I am capable of giving help."*

Hi family also featured strongly in his responses, although somewhat impersonally. Most important were the underlying principles he believed in.

'What has been most meaningful about your life so far?' ... *"My family. I taught them to be helpful to other people and law abiding."*

'What do you believe in?' ... *"The Ten Commandments."*

Charles was a self-contained individual, and very fortunate indeed to have kept his good health so long. He appeared at last to be gently preparing himself for a time when he would be less physically active. He was also beginning to speak more about his past life, particularly when he was in the navy, but although he spoke about 'putting things down in his memoirs', there was no indication he had started this process of systematic life review. He was still busy leading a well-ordered, independent existence. He died suddenly the following year just short of one hundred years.

George Rowan, like Charles, lived through his tenth decade of life without becoming noticeably frail. We last described his situation in Chapter 5 at age ninety-two after the death of his wife, to whom he had been devoted. Initially he had been devastated, and we had predicted wrongly that he would not recover his previous level of morale. Yet already at an interview a year later, he was recounting with pleasure the romantic story of their lives, and although still greatly missing his wife, expressed above all emotions of thankfulness for her, including that he had been able to be with her when she died.

We interviewed George again three years later when he was aged ninety-six years. He presented cheerfully. Although admitting that he still missed his wife very much and was often tearful, he had made an effort to be in contact with others as much as possible and was enjoying life. At the same time, he was doing his best also to prepare himself for his own death. He said that closeness to death had also made him feel closer to God on a personal level. Religion he said meant more to him than when he was younger, although he did not speak with the minister of his church.

He had established several social contacts, including with neighbours down the street and also "over the garden wall." He was attending a men's club at the local parish church and also going on organized outings. He had also become quite adventurous with trips abroad, the last one being to Egypt and Jordan, and the previous years to Australia and to Barbados. He had thoroughly enjoyed himself on each occasion. Everyone had been so considerate and friendly, especially the women! He considered himself to be 'comfortably well off' and that was "thanks to a thrifty wife."

His house looked much the same as before. He employed a cleaner and a gardener but still did much of the intermediate work himself. He prepared his own food made up mostly of easy-to-prepare meals. His hearing had deteriorated, and clearly he had difficulties in following conversation despite the use of aids. But overall he amazed us by his high level of morale. Although he had given up driving because of the slowness of his reactions, he was active outside the home, going to the centre of the city two or three times a week, looking, he said, for "any excuse" to do so. Like Charles, though, he was becoming aware of a changing sensation in his legs, a kind of numbness, and his muscles were losing strength. He was having more difficulty opening jars, for example.

His self-esteem was high again, and his illustrations conveyed a considerable joie de vivre.

Everything I do I enjoy. I want more of it, especially contact with human beings.
Considering my time of life, I amaze myself with what I do.

I go out as I feel inclined and contact people as I wish. I take up opportunities as they offer themselves. I want more but don't know how to engineer them.

I'm ready to enter into anything or go anywhere as it comes along.

Although he could not say that his old age was as he wanted it – especially now without his wife – he was very satisfied with the life that he had had together with her.

Another of us interviewed George three years later when he was aged ninety-nine years. His health was still very good for his age, although he was now much less active and unable to climb the hill leading to his parish church anymore. He referred appreciatively to the regular visits he received from members of the Salvation Army. Prayer and his Christian faith, he said, remained important to him. Sadly, his own church had not responded to his absence from the services. He did not complain about this but at the end of the interview spontaneously asked us to put him in contact with the Anglican minister.

Later in the year, just before sending him a birthday card for his one hundred years, we spoke with middle-aged friends who over the years had become his principal caregivers. They confirmed that George was still in very good health, although his memory could be poor at times. They were particularly concerned that he was too readily welcoming inside his home any visitors who knocked at his door. They had also had to be more understanding of him lately because he had hurt their feelings by asking them not to come to the birthday celebration, which they themselves had wanted to hold for him. Apparently distant relatives from Scotland had found out about his century and had wanted to come to visit him for this special occasion. George had been pleased about this but felt that he could only cope with small numbers of people at a time. Nevertheless they understood that he had limited energy now and had to decide on what were his priorities. He had not seemed to realize that this refusal was hurtful to them.

George died one year later, aged one hundred and one years.

Concluding comments

All six of our cases whom we interviewed in their middle to later nineties retained a high quality of life in these years. We recorded at most only small decline in their self-esteem and sense of meaning in life during our interviews with them. All presented in a strongly individual light, and their personalities perhaps became even clearer and sharper with age.

Of course, they were a select group, survivors of a twenty-five-year longitudinal study, but as we have already argued, it is important to examine paradigmatic cases that can reveal more about the possibilities of very late life. Perhaps what impressed most was the tenacity with which they each pursued their goals throughout their nineties: Elsie Darby and Bill Blackburn, their needs for regular contact with other people; Ethel Willis, her ability to continue living in her own home despite her disabilities; Charles Kitchen and George Rowan, their varied outdoor and social activities; and Irene Monroe, her religious evangelical vocation. That they generally succeeded in their aims probably accounted in part at least for their longevity.

The support services they received in their nineties generally met their major needs. Four had supportive families who understood them and provided whatever additional needs they had for care and company. The two without families were most objectively at risk of loneliness, yet they both lived the longest, beyond one hundred years. In Bill Blackburn's case, it was only at the very end of his life that there was a clear mismatch between his need for social contact and the provision that was possible within a care environment. This was principally due to Bill's sensory failings. The more intense contact with carers that he required was, and probably is, not realistic in most residential settings. George Rowan was also becoming more of a worry at the end of his life. His only regular support came from friends. No formal monitoring appeared to have been set up for him. But this itself was a consequence of his remarkable good health right up to age one hundred years.

10   The future of later life: personal and policy perspectives on ageing and meaning

Our forty case studies of persons growing old in the last quarter of the twentieth century indicate something of the variety of different trajectories possible in later life. However, these accounts may be already too distant in life experience and expectations to constitute comparable models for ageing in Britain in the twenty-first century. The physical realities of biological ageing including its variability across individuals may remain similar for the foreseeable future, but the social, psychological and spiritual resources at older persons' disposal in coping with physical and mental decline are already noticeably changed. It is these resources that largely determine how we experience the later period of ageing, whether as a welcome new stage of life with positive characteristics of its own despite the increasing limitations or as a potentially long trial to be resisted, endured or terminated as soon as possible.

Research in social gerontology has expanded considerably in the ten years and more since we completed interviews with the remaining participants of our longitudinal study. Within the United Kingdom, results have been published of two major government-funded research programmes on ageing, the first of which examined factors related to quality of life in later life including issues of identity and meaning (Walker, 2005). However, recent North American studies have paid more explicit attention to the subject of existential meaning (e.g. Krause, 2009; Hill and Turiano, 2014). These have highlighted the significant role played by perception of meaning and purpose in life in a person's continued flourishing and survival throughout adulthood and into old age. They indicate the importance of correctly identifying and sustaining sources of meaning in a person's life.

In this final chapter, we present our own thoughts on what we have learned from studying individual older people's lives and in particular how self and meaning are maintained in the process of growing older. We note those aspects of ageing that have made the most impression on us as investigators. We also consider the implications of our observations for future policy, taking particular note of the strong relationships within families evident in so many of our cases. We examine as well how the results of our case analyses correspond to current thinking within the psychological literature on development and adaptation to ageing.

But first of all, we want to draw conclusions from our experience of conducting individual case analyses over some twenty-five years. We begin with an admission of the limitations of our project, but also reassert our claim for the importance of individual case analysis – where it can be done well. Despite the emphasis by researchers on variation in experience of age, there appears to be little growth of interest in the study of the individual person growing old, apart from within nursing studies. We do not see the study of the person as an alternative to quantitative analysis of data collected on large samples but as a necessary adjunct to such study. Case analysis has remained an underdeveloped discipline within the social sciences as a whole, and especially within psychology, where it is often considered an activity more relevant to the humanities. But understanding at the level of the individual case is as essential to psychology as explanation in terms of general principles. Moreover, developing skills in conceptualizing and drawing conclusions about the person is also relevant to the many applied disciplines that draw on psychology such as clinical psychology and social work, as well as to clinical medicine.

Self and meaning at the level of the individual case

Although we felt justified in including in this book every one of the forty case studies that we began writing, not all of them reached the standards that we originally aspired to. Our initial target was to study older persons' perceptions of self and meaning in relation to the changing events of their lives until their deaths by means of regular interview and observation. But limitations of time and funding meant that we could not visit people more than once every two years on average, and we were not able to follow a few of the younger cases in their last years (one participant lived thirty-five years from the beginning of our initial survey). In a few cases, we could not continue our investigations because of relocation or refusal on the part of the participant. Incompleteness of the data set is an inevitable limitation in any longitudinal study.

Another key element in any social research project is the validity of the conclusions drawn. The most common form of validating assessments is comparison with an independent standard. In the case of this research, we aimed for two sources of validation, first involving an additional investigator and second providing the opportunity to the people under investigation to comment on our conclusions about them. The second of these forms of validation was an important feature of our original plans for case study investigation. This is not to say that the subjects of case study always deserve the last word about themselves, but their own perspectives need to be included, not least we believe for ethical reasons. We succeeded only partially in both of these aims. In some the failure was unavoidable because of the premature death of the participant, but in others the failure was a direct result of lack of resources. We would recommend that future studies of this kind pay particular attention to the adequacy of funding for a sufficient number of repeat interviews and over the necessarily long period of time required. Compared with large-scale surveys, case study analysis of a small number of persons is not an expensive method of research but nor is it a cheap option. It needs to be properly budgeted for.

Nevertheless, despite these limitations, we are proud of our achievement in conducting a significant number of longitudinal case studies, which has enabled us to present a detailed picture of the last years of these persons' lives in a form that they would probably have accepted themselves. It is therefore worthwhile here to briefly summarize the conclusions of some of the most considered and finished examples among these cases. We have used the two criteria of completeness of data and its adequate validation in making this selection. Thus we have had to exclude such distinct cases as those of Emily Shields, whom we failed to follow up in her nineties, and Stuart Murray, who unfortunately would not agree to be interviewed after he became physically frail in his middle nineties, as well as some of the more tragic cases of relatively early disablement as Doris Iveson and Cyril Steel. There follows a final paragraph on each of twelve cases with whom issues of self and meaning were thoroughly discussed in the last years of their life and a personal theory of identity formulated. In these summaries, we focus in particular on our conclusions about the internal and external resources that these participants were able to bring to their particular experience of ageing.

Margaret Baker was one of the most intriguing cases in our sample. She consistently expressed a very low self-esteem over the twenty years that we interviewed her, based on her negative opinion of her own abilities and contributions compared with others. This appeared to have its roots in childhood but also in her perceived lack of control over her earlier adult life. She had been obliged to delay marriage until middle age, and her husband had died after only seven years. Although she entered a period of depression in her mid-seventies, by her early eighties, she was much happier. Her physical health remained good, and she especially enjoyed her relationships with friends. Margaret eschewed any sign of self-pity and remained resolute in her focus on the problems of the outside world rather than her own. She died after a short illness at age eighty-eight.

Bill Blackburn was one of the longest lived of all our participants, reaching age one hundred and one years. This was a great surprise to us when we considered his extreme lack of both financial and family resources (he had no children, and his greatly loved wife had died when he was aged seventy-four years), as well as his lifelong liking for gambling and drinking alcohol. He began to encounter major health difficulties in his later eighties. Yet his strong desire for contact with people and his general interest in life seemed to be the principal motivation that drove him forward. He repeatedly said how much he 'loved people'. It was only in a residential care home right at the end of his life that he began to experience loneliness as both his sight and hearing failed, which meant that he could no longer engage with others as he needed to.

Elsie Darby achieved the remarkable feat of successfully leaving residential care for sheltered housing at age ninety-one and living independently until her death at age ninety-seven. In her later interviews with us, she revealed a lot about her motivations both to retain her independence and to continue contributing to children's welfare, the roots of the latter lying in her own unhappy childhood. Like Bill Blackburn, she also needed to be socially active to avoid loneliness. She had to struggle hard against depression at times but clearly knew what her needs were and showed huge determination in achieving her targets of continuing to mix with others and make contributions even when she was living in residential care.

Marjory Evans needed to present herself as both competent and caring, whatever difficulties she faced. This proved to be a grave handicap after her husband died suddenly when she was aged seventy-nine years. She tried to carry on as before and eventually succumbed to a severe depressive illness, for which she had to be hospitalized. Although she recovered well from this and remained physically fit and active, she continued to show a tendency to depression, and her husband's death remained a traumatic memory for her. Nevertheless, her self-esteem was consistently high based on her relationships with her family and with neighbours and keeping her home and herself looking well. She died at age eighty-eight after a short illness.

Ralph Hodgkin had, by his own description, been something of a loner most of his life, apart from a very close partnership with his wife. In addition to his praise for her, his sense of self during his seventies was very much based on his varied activities and interests. A serious accident at age eighty-three and his resulting incapacity lowered his self-esteem, but it had recovered a few years later, still based on his wife's support and the indoor activities he could continue to undertake. His sense of self then remained relatively stable until his death at age ninety-three, with some broadening of its basis to include also his son's family together with a strong assertion of traditional moral and religious values.

Ted Jackson expressed great enjoyment of his life with his wife and the families of their seven children. His first marriage had failed, and so he was especially grateful for his subsequent good fortune in finding a new wife and establishing with her a happy family including all their children. His sense of self was almost entirely identified with his family's welfare. Both he and his wife developed chronic and limiting health problems in their eighties, Ted with rheumatoid arthritis. They also suffered family bereavements including the death of one daughter. But Ted retained his highly satisfied view of his life, and his identity remained firmly focused on his wife and family until his death at age eighty-eight. Their children reciprocated the love shown to them with a well-organized rota of care.

Leonard Johns and his wife were unfortunate in that their well-planned late-life relocation plans resulted in some years of severe neighbour stress in Leonard's early eighties. This, combined with health and worries about his son, led him into a severe bout of depression. However, he recovered well with the support of his wife and family. His nervous disposition had probably made him somewhat more vulnerable to stress, and his self-esteem generally lowered with ageing. But his readiness to rely on his wife together with his focus of interest on his family's welfare meant that he could in his own words satisfactorily 'plod along' with his 'quiet life' until his death at age ninety-three.

Irene Monroe and her husband had lived a life very much focused on religious ministry and welfare work. Its continuity was threatened in her later seventies and early eighties by both her husband's and her own ill health. Yet after his death when she was aged seventy-eight years, she was fortunate to be able to find a place in a religious charity–based home that allowed her to continue to pursue her profoundly felt vocation for many more years and to keep at bay the depressed feelings to which she was prone. Her morale remained high in her nineties, despite a continuing element of self-criticism, and she expressed herself content with both her own life and that of her husband before her death at age ninety-six.

Evelyn Norris had survived being bombed out of two houses in World War II and been widowed relatively early at age sixty-two. Thereafter her life was focused on her daughter's family as well as her sister, who lived next door. A series of strokes beginning at age eighty gradually took their toll on her physical abilities, but she avoided any significant sign of depression. Her family remained supportive, her grandson coming to live with her, first on his own and then together with his new wife. Evelyn's self-esteem remained high throughout her eighties, illustrated by her strong interest in her family, as well as by contact with her friends and her religious faith, until her death at age ninety. She had no explanation for her remarkable cheerfulness, it was just the way she was, she said, grateful for the help and contact she received.

Alfred Parker expressed a consistently positive view of his life over the twenty-three years we interviewed him, despite his wife's and his own health problems. He had lived a life committed to welfare work for disabled people. His religious faith had also long been central to his sense of self and became more evident in his self-descriptions as he aged. He gave many illustrations to show how it allowed him to remain serene through the decline and death of his first wife when he was aged eighty-three years and his second wife seven years later. His second marriage revitalized him at a time when he had begun to think his life was over. He died at age ninety-one shortly after moving to sheltered accommodation to be close to his son.

Harold Rank expressed an extremely high sense of self-efficacy when he was first interviewed at age seventy, based largely on his past and present role within his family. In the succeeding years, he suffered two major blows, the onset of his wife's dementia followed some years later by her entry into residential care, and a chronic painful and disabling condition affecting his hip, back and legs. By his early eighties and following his wife's death, Harold's self-esteem had plummeted, and he had become very depressed. But over the succeeding ten years, until his death at age ninety-one, he gradually adapted to his situation, became again happily involved with his family, even helped in the dementia care of his sister-in-law, gradually accepted his own need for care, and found solace both in prayer and reviewing his own past. His main concern in his last years was to retain his independence in his own home in which he succeeded.

Ethel Willis had been widowed at age sixty-two; she expressed feelings of depression and low self-esteem in her mid-seventies as a consequence of her changed lifestyle with the loss of her previous social roles and mounting health problems that seriously affected her mobility. Yet through coping effectively with the challenges she faced of keeping her independence, she appeared to become gradually more contented. She still missed her busy previous life, but succeeded in achieving her two important goals of remaining living at home until her death at age ninety-five while continuing to keep close relationships with both her son and daughter.

These brief summaries of a number of our most complete cases illustrate some of the challenges people can encounter as they grow older. They also demonstrate how persons even of advanced age can overcome the difficulties they encounter and continue to meet their basic psychological needs and find meaning in life. What is necessary is access to sufficient resources within themselves as well as in the world around. We will return to consider some of these fundamental needs and resources in the final sections of this chapter. First, however, we turn from the particulars of the individual case to some general observations on the sample as a whole.

General observations on the experience of ageing

It is important to note that ours was an especially long-lived sample, with most of the participants living beyond ninety years. This was the result of selecting our cases for analysis only after the average age of the sample was over eighty years. Unsurprisingly health emerged as the major factor affecting quality of life and well-being. Chronic conditions affecting the joints or heart (or both) had begun to affect fifteen of the forty members of our sample before age eighty, generally in their later seventies, but the majority did not encounter limiting health problems until their eighties. Two of the men, Charles Kitchen and George Rowan, remained without significant health problems even beyond age ninety and took advantage of their good fortune in continuing to lead very active lives.

Despite a decline in health, quality of subjective well-being generally remained high within the sample. Most members retained or recovered the generally high level of self-esteem with which they entered the study. Nevertheless, severe ill health and disablement did take its toll, as did bereavement. Every member of the sample was or had been married, but there was a large gender difference in age of bereavement of spouse. All but one of the women were widowed by age eighty, whereas half of the men had their wives still living at the time of their death. In assembling the material for this book, we were struck especially by the impact of bereavement of spouse and the consequent need for a long chapter on the subject (Chapter 5). The effects were often profound and long lasting. Identifying protective factors was therefore of particular interest. Besides health and socioeconomic factors, the presence of a strong supportive family and a religious belief seemed the most important resources within this sample. Bereavement in later life is now gaining the recognition it deserves from researchers both in the United Kingdom (e.g. Bennett, 1997; Speck et al., 2005) and in the United States, where it has recently been the subject of a special multidisciplinary issue of the *Journals of Gerontology (Psychological and Social Sciences)* (Lee, 2014).

Significant depressive feelings and thoughts were expressed at some point by most of our participants, and some, such as Elsie Darby, Irene Monroe, Ethel Willis, Marjory Evans, Rita Fletcher and Leonard Johns, had to fight repeated battles against depression. However, these struggles were generally successful, and for the most part our participants in their later eighties and throughout their nineties expressed calm emotions. The poorest quality of life was found among those who incurred severe disability relatively early in the process of ageing, including Cyril Steel, Olive Reid and Doris Iveson. Some participants, however, as Fred Hobson, Ted Jackson and Nellie Moreton, coped especially well with their health difficulties, close family relationships again appearing to be the major supporting factor. There were some remarkable recoveries from low depressive points, especially so in the case of Harold Rank. There were also striking examples of women coping well alone against the odds, such as Helen Procter, Margaret Baker and Vera Wright. Some of the men in particular used humour to defuse negative feelings in the face of growing disability and threat to well-being, especially Ernest Davies and Cyril Steel.

Family relationships were strong in nearly all members of our sample who had spouses and children, and exceptionally strong in some of the female cases –

for example, Hilda Smith and Emma Lawson. Those women without both, such as Doris Iveson, Helen Procter, Margaret Baker and Eva Chester, appeared particularly vulnerable to loneliness and low morale. In contrast, those with children living nearby benefitted hugely from regular contact with them. Some of our participants in their later eighties and nineties, such as Marion Goodall, eventually went to live with their children. In the case of Emma Lawson, this was to be for as long as twelve years from age eighty-seven until her death at ninety-nine. Some children, as in Emily Shields's, Agnes Coombs's and Emma Lawson's cases, or grandchildren, as with Evelyn Norris and Robert Gardiner, came to live with their elderly parent or grandparent. In all cases, close relationships with the extended family appeared to be to the benefit of the older person. It was also notable how appreciation of their families seemed to become of increasing value to our participants as they became older. This was true even of those who before had not referred much to their children as part of their self-descriptions, such as Elsie Darby and Thomas Johnson.

Although physical decline could be gentle in its progress, we were struck by how often serious falls were the origin of a trajectory of physical decline for participants in their eighties, for example, for Bill Blackburn, Mary Morrison, Ralph Hodgkin, Mavis Dawes, Thelma Swinton and Vera Wright. Serious falls were also incurred by Margaret Baker, Agnes Coombs, Helen Procter, John Otterbourne, Eva Chester and Rita Fletcher, thus altogether in well over one-quarter of the sample. In most cases, these accidents were probably avoidable. Alongside cardiorespiratory and arthritic conditions, falling appeared as a major threat to older people's physical health.

Christianity played a significant part in many of our participants' lives. In some cases, particularly with Irene Monroe, Alfred Parker and Stuart Murray, religious convictions appeared as the primary motivator of action and the central focus of self-description. But prayer and belief could also be important in those who were not generally churchgoing persons, as with Marjory Evans and Harold Rank. Both impact and value were attributed to early religious socialization, and religious allegiance sometimes emerged later rather than earlier in the study, as in the cases of Evelyn Norris, Harold Rank and Ralph Hodgkin. In all cases in which religious faith played a role in participants' later lives, it appeared to be a positive one.

A further element in the interviews that increased with time was the presence of reminiscence. This was most likely the result of increased ease of the participant with the interviewers but possibly also reflected the need to life review and sometimes, most clearly in a number of women's cases (Elsie Darby, Rita Fletcher, Mavis Dawes, Vera Wright and Nellie Moreton), come to terms with a difficult past. It was interesting too how consoling memories of own parents, especially of mothers, entered the interviews, more so perhaps with men (Harold Rank, Bill Blackburn and Ralph Hodgkin, for example).

Although it was not a primary purpose of the study to comment on service provision, the benefits of high-quality service were recorded, for example, of adapted and sheltered housing in Mavis Dawes's and Nellie Moreton's cases and residential care in Irene Monroe's case. Home care assistants or 'home helps', as they were then called, also played a major role in supporting persons through difficult periods. This was particularly noticeable in Harold Rank's recovery from depression and low morale as well as Bill Blackburn's adaptation to being relocated away from his former area of the city. However, in the case of most of the men who needed help with their daily living activities, the assistance was provided by their wives or children, or both. Because the stress on wives was not assessed, the pressure on Cyril Steel's wife through eleven years of supporting a severely disabled husband, in which she received little in the way of other assistance, can only be imagined.

Resources for supporting ageing in the future

Much is expected of persons in their later years in coping with challenges that they have not faced before and often with diminished internal and external resources. But perhaps one of the worst aspects of ageing is its unfairness. Although there is a pattern to ageing decline, it is experienced unequally. Ageing does not proceed like the growth of children in recognizable stages that can be related easily to chronological age. Some people age faster, some slower. This inequality in physiological ageing is also paralleled and heightened by the other inequalities to which ageing is subject, especially in physical, financial and social resources.

Thus, some persons encounter only minimal problems with their health until advanced age and enjoy strong financial and social assets. Others struggle with major health problems from a relatively early age, sometimes in isolation and with little support from family, friends and statutory and voluntary agencies. Some physical decline and accumulation of bereavements is to be expected in later life, but the timing can be particularly unkind or gentler in its impact. More control, however, can be exerted on the development of personal resources with which to deal with ageing. These are often the result of lifelong investments, but we live in a culture that has given little attention so far to such investment beyond providing limited financial security. The impact of ageing is often not considered before it is already upon the person. In earlier societies, even though people did not live so long, they knew they had to make provision, and the one in which they invested most was the creation and nurturing of children. Children still remain the major resource people have in their old age, as so many of our case studies illustrated.

The evidence collected for the Mental Health Foundation's recent report on the future mental health needs of the UK baby boomer generation has suggested that those born in the years after World War II are "unlikely to enjoy more disability-free years of good health in their old age" (Mental Health Foundation, 2012, p. 36). The report points out that around one-half of the baby boomers in the Age Well YouGov national survey were concerned about their future health. They are at increasing risk of diabetes, high blood pressure, heart disease and cancers because of lifestyle factors such as diminished activity levels, poor diets, obesity, and alcohol and drug misuse. Income inequality, another factor associated with increased ill health, had also become greater in recent years.

Therefore, although continuing improvements in the possibilities of clinical interventions will likely lead to longer life expectancy, this increase in life may be proportionately more in conditions of poorer rather than good physical health. This in turn implies the likelihood of higher levels of poor mental health among older people. On the positive side, the YouGov survey shows that middle-aged generations, and especially women, are taking the safeguarding of their health more seriously. But all in all, there can be no expectation that ageing is going to be more disease free in the near future. In the twenty-first century, dementia has become the major concern associated with the experience of ageing. It had an impact on a number of our cases, affecting either the participant (Mary Morrison, Ernest Davies, Dennis Wilcox and Susan Turner) or their spouse (Harold Rank and Alfred Parker) and is likely to loom larger as the proportion of very old people in the population rises. But as a result of the increased focus on dementia, it is important not to lose sight of those elderly people who become isolated as a result of physical rather than mental frailty and who, without regular support from family and friends, can suffer from heartbreaking loneliness. We may have lost proportionately more people who entered such conditions from our longitudinal study. Their problems and needs are more likely to become invisible to policy makers.

In considering the future role in ageing of family relationships, it is important to note that our study was almost exclusively of a white British sample with long family roots in Britain or Ireland (Eva Chester was the only participant whose early life took place elsewhere in Europe). Considerations of ageing in Britain in the future have to take account of the rise in the proportion of the population of older people who came to Britain in the post-war years who were initially from former British colonies and more recently from the European Union and elsewhere in the world. These have brought with them somewhat different family values. Thus greater care has to be taken in drawing distinctions between different groups in the population. For example, although generally social isolation and loneliness may become greater problems for future generations of older people in Britain as a result of increased mobility and family breakdown, this may not be so for those immigrant groups that succeed in maintaining traditionally strong family ties.

We were impressed by the care shown by families to their older members in many of our case studies. In most cases, the level of help seemed to be correctly judged in line with the older persons' needs, providing physical shelter and family warmth in the children's homes where this was the parent's wish, but more often supporting the older person to live independently in his or her own home. (Hilda Smith's family was an excellent example.) Family ties were strong and reciprocated in most cases, becoming if anything more valued by the person as he or she grew older and frailer. The welfare and love of the family was the major value in most of our sample, reflected both in our participants' verbal and written self-ascriptions. The difficulties of those in poor health who had no children to rely on were evident in a few of our cases. Rarely did friends provide equivalent levels of love and support. Of course, the importance of friendship relationships may well increase in the future, but if so it will need to be a change of sufficient proportions to compensate for any decline in the caring role provided by the British family. Government policy needs to consider not only whether it can do more than it currently does to foster family support, but if it calculates that its importance will decline, it needs urgently to consider how it can encourage alternative networks of support within and across generations.

One clear gain for the experience of ageing in the twenty-first century is the greater equality and life opportunities offered to women. Some of our female cases had lived lives much more limited than they would have wished (Margaret Baker was a clear example). A number had missed out on educational opportunities and clearly said that they regretted this as they grew older (Emily Shields, Mavis Dawes, Nellie Moreton). The relative lack of personal control over their lives was reflected in the way they reviewed their lives. Those like Vera Wright whose parents had encouraged them to achieve a higher level of education seemed to have benefitted in terms of self-confidence and determination to succeed.

The important role of religious belief in a large minority of our older people's lives was one of the most interesting findings of our study. An earlier analysis had shown a decline in religious allegiance by as many as a quarter of the original Southampton Ageing Project participants, particularly in the course of the 1980s (Coleman, Ivani-Chalian and Robinson, 2004). But approximately one-half of the remaining sample had seemed to have retained their essential Christian formation until late life. It was a live faith and closely involved in the everyday challenges of ageing. However, it was only the large scope of the original Southampton Ageing Project survey questionnaire and its inclusion of a detailed inventory on daily and weekly activities that had permitted questions about religious practice and its importance to participants to be included in the schedule. Most British studies on ageing have continued to neglect the topic of religion despite the clear evidence for the greater religiosity of the pre-war birth cohorts and the likely importance of religious faith to them in coping with the losses associated with ageing.

As the influence of Christianity on British life has declined, so the question of investigating the value of alternative ways of thinking and feeling about life has become more important. For example, do other aspects of human culture, such as theatrical, musical and artistic performance, offer adequate substitutes for the powerful practices, symbols and values of religion (Eagleton, 2014)? Perhaps the key research question for research on ageing is whether nonreligious forms of thinking and feeling about life can provide alternative ways to preserving a sense of meaning amidst the changes of later life (Wilkinson and Coleman, 2010). Sherman (1981) first coined the term 'psychophilosophy' to refer to attitudes to life in the later years that were grounded in serious thinking about the meaning of life and conducive to serenity in the face of decline and death. The need for strengthening the capacity to acquire such inner resources is increasingly evident. There are already cases of older people, reported in the media, asking for assisted suicide not only because of painful chronic illness but because they cannot cope with the rapidity of social and technological change.

Of course, there were among our cases many examples of people who remained resilient and retained positive attitudes to life without a strong religious faith, often as in the case of Helen Procter in the face of considerable difficulties. Some as Vera Wright and Ethel Willis spoke about how they had distanced themselves from Christianity. Emily Shields in particular (see Chapter 5) talked with us in depth about how she had wrestled for a large part of her life with questions about religious belief and the purpose of life. She had eventually come to her own reasoned conclusions with which she felt at peace. She provided a detailed explanation of her rejection of religious faith and her continued inability to see any helpful meaning in it for herself, although she readily acknowledged that it brought solace to many other people. At the same time, she demonstrated a high level of perceived meaning in her life. Most telling was her refusal to allow her local Christian minister to pray with her after her husband died because it would have been inappropriate to her own beliefs. Relatively few of her generation perhaps would have had such strength of conviction, yet this kind of assurance seems to be a most important factor in adjustment to bereavement (Coleman et al., 2007).

Some comment needs to be made on the general issue of personal resilience to stress. Will older people in the future be more or less resilient than present and past generations? There is a general expectation that they will be less resilient not only because of higher rates of physical survival of more frail older people to extreme old age, but also because of the lower exposure to previous life stress in those cohorts growing up in the post–World War II years. There is little evidence yet on this subject, but the previously mentioned report on the likely mental health needs of the baby boomer generation (Mental Health Foundation, 2012) suggests that men born in the 1950s already showed some greater tendency to depression and anxiety when they entered adulthood. This was a time of rapid social change and so perhaps raises concerns about how this generation will adapt to what could well be a harder life in old age with lower pensions and more limited social support in their later years than they might have anticipated. Personal resilience is again closely related to access to resources. Vulnerable personalities can be protected if they live in a network of strong social support, as illustrated in the case of Leonard Johns (see Chapter 8).

Implications for the psychology of ageing

Do our case analyses agree with recent thinking on adjustment to ageing? Or to look at the matter from the point of view of the individual case, does current theory actually help better understand a particular person's response to ageing? We would like to comment briefly on three issues: changing sources of the self in later life; the optimal balance between strategies of resistance and acceptance in adaptation to change; and the continued needs for autonomy, competence and relatedness.

In our accounts of the cases, we have often closely associated a person's self-esteem and sense of meaning in life. Partly this is because to have a sense of meaning is itself an aspect of the self. But our data collection (see Chapter 2) was also influenced by the view that perception of meaning may become a relatively more significant aspect of the self in later life and one under greater threat in modern society. With retirement from work and disengagement from other formal roles, the meaning of daily life has to be discovered from the inside rather than imposed from the outside.

Our cases for the most part demonstrated both a continuing high self-esteem and a retained sense of meaning in life. Where either failed, the reasons were usually clear. Doris Iveson for example lost the meaning of her life with her husband's death and her own declining health. She appeared to have no further sources of self on which she could build a life that would have comparable value to the life she remembered. Some of our participants, such as Margaret Baker and Ethel Willis, seem to have always been rather self-critical. Margaret's case (Chapter 6) is particularly interesting because she expressed chronically low self-esteem throughout the study yet at the same time expressed a strong sense of what Adler described as *Gemeinschaftsgefühl* (social interest; see Chapter 2). She provided a good example of why the study of exceptional cases is valuable. The external focus of her interests seems to contradict the importance commonly attributed to high self-esteem. She was able to age well according to other types of criteria outlined by Carol Ryff (see Chapter 2) without a well-established sense of identity. Her case we think illustrates how a sense of meaning in life can be even more important than high self-esteem in the experience of ageing.

A number of our cases illustrated how 'communal' sources of self-description increased in importance in later years in both men and women, as 'agentic' sources decreased. Perhaps the most striking example was Thomas Johnson, who had worked until age eighty years and apparently needed to maintain his own sense of himself as an active person. Yet in late life, he appeared much more content in his family roles without any evident regret that his 'agentic' self was now limited to his past memories of war service and to keeping his house in good shape. It was unexpected how much pleasure and pride he found in his grandchildren. Also women, such as Irene Monroe and Elsie Darby, who had made major investments outside the home in their earlier adult lives, appeared to value their relationships with their families more as they aged. In many ways, our study demonstrated the importance of family life for older people, from the infectious joy expressed by Ted Jackson to the deep pride of Nellie Moreton. Those without families or more limited contacts with their families had more difficult later lives. George Rowan was perhaps one exception to this generalization, but he was blessed with exceptionally good health in his tenth decade. However, at age one hundred years, he was also looking to establish new family connections with long-distant relatives.

The generally accepted view in the present literature on adaptation to ageing is that at some point in the transition between 'third age' and 'fourth age' living older people may need to disengage from previous goals and lifestyles if they are to avoid depressive states (Brandtstädter, 2006). At the same time, too early a disengagement can lead to negative outcomes, including cognitive decline and premature death. What seems to be required is the ability to strike the right balance between assimilative processes of changing behaviour to continue meeting long-established personal goals and accommodative processes of gradually relinquishing those same goals. Our case studies illustrate how this transition involves subtle processes of change and is dependent on individual circumstances. This view is consistent with the observations from another major longitudinal study of persons over eighty-five years living in California conducted by the medical anthropologists Colleen Johnson and Barbara Barer (Johnson and Barer, 1997). Like the present study, they also illustrated how a very old person's well-being could improve in the last period of life despite an increase in disability. A growing introspection or 'interiority' often accompanied a greater acceptance of dependency. But this 'surrender of control' tended to be selective. Control over areas of life that were key to the person's sense of self tended to remain the longest. An important implication for practice is the need for those offering support to seek an optimal balance between a person's psychosocial and physical health requirements.

Most of our participants demonstrated similar modes of coping as they passed through their seventies to their eighties and even through to their nineties. Examples of presumed late-life adaptations such as increased accommodation and self-transcendence were not prevalent even at advanced ages. Harold Rank (Chapter 8) provided a good example of a person who had struggled hard against the odds to preserve his desired style of life through his seventies and early eighties. He suffered bouts of severe depression as a consequence. It was only at the end of his life that he came to be accepting of personal care at home, and he still found the idea of residential care unthinkable. His eventual adaptation included strong elements of disengagement from the outside world and a closer attention to an internal life of prayer. Nevertheless, it could be argued that his initial resistance was valuable in preserving his identity, especially given his strong need for autonomy.

Elsie Darby's remarkable assertion of independence in her nineties was also adaptive, despite the fact that leaving residential care to live on her own again made her more vulnerable to feelings of loneliness. This was a price she seemed willing to pay for recovering her old style of life. It would only have been too easy to yield to pressures to stay in care when clearly this was not what she needed. But it was only the good fortune of having understanding and supportive relatives that made this reversal possible. Ethel Willis's case illustrated similar points. Episodes of depression were a consequence of her determination to remain living at home, but this did not mean that this was not the right decision for her. Her life had been marked by a considerable degree of autonomy, and it was unacceptable for her to lose this at the very end. Perhaps struggles with depression and loneliness are an inevitable price for maintaining independence in old age.

A degree of autonomy over one's own life is one of the three fundamental human needs identified by Deci and Ryan (see Chapter 2). Virtually all of our cases illustrated its importance. Entering residential care was feared by many and only accepted reluctantly by others. However, struggles to maintain a sense of identity could still take place within a care setting and were illustrated positively by Elsie Darby and Bill Blackburn and most poignantly by Olive Reid (Chapter 7). Others seemed to succumb to decline after entrance. Only perhaps in Irene Monroe's case could entry into residential care be described wholly in positive terms, and this is perhaps because the second home she entered possessed an ethos with which she could identify strongly. Unfortunately, unlike provision elsewhere, relatively few British residential care homes are founded on principles of collective identity for which entrants actively select.

Relatedness is a second principal need and was strongly displayed by many of our participants in their attachment to their families, which often increased in late life. This was expressed in their self-descriptions in various ways, in how their own sense of usefulness was judged, in how they in perceived themselves as valued, but also in their worries about the health and well-being of family members. Bereavement of spouse was an underlying concern, but even more worrying was the prospect of death of children. Marriage breakdown within the family was also a source of noticeable distress. This fear was perhaps less in those with larger numbers of offspring. As persons aged this sense of belonging to an ever-extending family could grow and was perhaps best exemplified in the medallion that Nellie Moreton wore around her neck with a photograph of her first great grandchild.

Nevertheless, a sense of belonging usually needed to be balanced with an adequate sense of autonomy. We were struck by how well this negotiation was handled in our sample of cases. As stressed before, many children responded well to their parents' needs not to be alone. In some cases, as with John Otterbourne and Emma Lawson, the provision of annexes to existing homes worked extremely well, providing a measure of independence together with the possibility of regular company. Children of other participants respected their parents' wish to remain living in their previous homes but still provided regular support and care. The examples of Hilda Smith's and Ethel Willis's cases have already been stressed. To achieve her goal, Ethel moved her living quarters downstairs. Only in a few cases did the situation appear precarious, such as that of Ernest Davies and his wife, who were both growing ever frailer and could only be supported by difficulty with children who had to negotiate both distance and their own disabilities.

The third fundamental need stressed by Deci and Ryan is one they describe as competence. Certainly a sense that one can still perform self-care and home-care activities adequately is important and was illustrated by many of our participants' self-descriptions. However, what seemed to us to be as or even more important was a sense that the person was still contributing, whether to his or her own family or the broader community. This was an important element in many of our participants' sense of identity and one that seemed generally beneficial, although in Marjory Evans's case, her need to present herself consistently in a positive light made her vulnerable to depression. The types of contribution varied from Elsie Darby's and Hilda Smith's determination to benefit disadvantaged children to a desire to help a particular member of the family, as in the provision Stuart Murray had made for his disabled grandchild. For some participants, such as Vera Wright, Hilda Smith and Fred Hobson, even contributing to research projects such as ours had value in itself.

The importance of a sense of contribution is perhaps one of the more underrated aspects of individual identity in later life, and we should explore new ways of enabling older people to continue to feel involved. Religious traditions have long emphasized the value of older people's prayers for the world – well-exemplified in the prayer group that Irene Monroe set up within her residential care home. Technological advances in communication offer new prospects for engagement in the world's concerns also in the last years of life.

Appendix: Participant characteristics

Pseudonym	Birth year	School-leaving age	Principal occupation (Husband's in brackets)	Age at death
Margaret Baker	1911	15	Clerk	88
Bill Blackburn	1895	15	Skilled labourer in naval stores	101
Eva Chester	1912	16	(Power station manager)	93
Agnes Coombs	1912	14	(Stevedore in Southampton docks)	87
Elsie Darby	1901	13	(Steel plater in ship-building company)	97
Ernest Davies	1907	14	Painter and decorator	88
Mavis Dawes	1907	14	(Plumber)	89
Marjory Evans	1910	13	(Supervisor engineering stock control)	88
Rita Fletcher	1913	14	(Ironmonger's pricing office clerk)	89
Robert Gardiner	1909	11	Ship mender plate maker's mate	86
Henry Goodall	1910	16	Gas board official	86
Marion Goodall	1911	14	(Gas board official)	Unknown
Fred Hobson	1910	14	Army psychiatric nurse	84
Ralph Hodgkin	1906	14	Builder with own business	93
Doris Iveson	1908	14	(Office manager at retail department store)	87
Ted Jackson	1910	14	Army regimental sergeant major	88
Leonard Johns	1905	15	Head cashier at retail department store	93
Thomas Johnson	1911	14	Chief petty officer, Navy boiler rooms	89
Charles Kitchen	1895	12	Marine engineer	99
Emma Lawson	1911	14	(Hotel cook)	97
Dora Meadows	1901	14	(Cost accountant)	90
Irene Monroe	1900	14	(Assistant archivist)	96
Nellie Moreton	1911	12	Cook at children's school	91
Mary Morrison	1904	14	Shop assistant	91
Stuart Murray	1904	14	Chief administrative officer Indian Government	96
Evelyn Norris	1907	15	(Tool inspector engineering company)	90
John Otterbourne	1897	15	Clerical worker in town council	95
Alfred Parker	1909	18	Accountant in insurance company	91
Helen Procter	1911	18	Buyer for cosmetics and jewellery firm	82
Harold Rank	1908	14	Painter and decorator in shipping company	91
Olive Reid	1901	16	(Civil servant)	91

(*cont.*)

(*cont.*)

Pseudonym	Birth year	School-leaving age	Principal occupation (Husband's in brackets)	Age at death
George Rowan	1902	18	Cashier in bank	101
Emily Shields	1912	15	(Policeman)	99
Hilda Smith	1907	14	(Transport worker in Southampton docks)	96
Cyril Steel	1901	14	Aircraft engineer	91
Thelma Swinton	1910	14	(Carpenter and joiner)	93
Susan Turner	1908	13	(Joiner and silk finisher)	90
Dennis Wilcox	1912	14	Patrolman for the Automobile Association	89
Ethel Willis	1904	14	(Carpenter at Southampton docks)	96
Vera Wright	1912	18	Trained pharmacist dispenser	91

References

Bakan, D. 1966. *The Duality of Human Existence: Isolation and Communion in Western Man*. Boston: Beacon Press.

Baldock, J. and Hadlow, J. 2002. 'Self-talk versus needs-talk: an exploration of the priorities of housebound older people', *Quality in Ageing* 3: 42–8.

Baltes, P. 1997. 'On the incomplete architecture of human ontogeny: selection, optimization and compensation as foundation of developmental theory', *American Psychologist* 52: 366–80.

Bennett, K.M. 1997. 'Widowhood in elderly women: the medium- and long-term effects on mental and physical health', *Mortality* 2: 137–48.

Brandtstädter, J. 2006. 'Adaptive resources in later life: tenacious goal pursuit and flexible goal adjustment', in M. Csikszentmihalyi and I.S. Csikszentmihalyi (eds.), *A Life Worth Living. Contributions to Positive Psychology*. New York: Oxford University Press, 143–64.

Brink, T.L. 1979. *Geriatric Psychotherapy*. New York: Human Sciences Press.

Bromley, D.B. 1977. *Personality Description in Ordinary Language*. London: Wiley.

Bromley, D.B. 1986. *The Case-study Method in Psychology and Related Disciplines*. Chichester: Wiley.

Bruner, J.S. 1986. *Actual Minds, Possible Worlds*. Cambridge: Harvard University Press.

Busse, E.W. 1985. 'Normal aging: the Duke longitudinal studies', in Bergener, M., Ermini, M. and Staheline, H.B. (eds.), *Thresholds in Aging*. New York: Academic Press, 215–29.

Butler, R. 1975. *Why Survive? Being Old in America*. New York: Harper & Row.

Carp, F.M. 1974. 'Short-term and long-term prediction of adjustment to a new environment', *Journal of Gerontology* 29: 444–53.

Coleman, P.G. 1984. 'Assessing self-esteem and its sources in elderly people', *Ageing and Society* 4: 117–35.

Coleman, P.G. 1997. 'Last scene of all', *Generations Review* 7 (1): 1–5.

Coleman, P.G. 2002. 'Doing case study research in psychology', in A. Jamieson and C.R. Victor (eds.), *Researching Ageing and Later Life*. Buckingham: Open University Press, 135–54.

Coleman, P.G., Aubin, A., Ivani-Chalian, C., Robinson, M. and Briggs, R.S. 1993. 'Predictors of depressive symptoms and low self-esteem in a follow-up study of elderly people over ten years', *International Journal of Geriatric Psychiatry* 8: 343–9.

Coleman, P.G., Ivani-Chalian, C. and Robinson, M. 1993. 'Self-esteem and its sources: stability and change in later life', *Ageing and Society* 13: 171–92.

Coleman, P.G., Ivani-Chalian, C. and Robinson, M. 1998. 'The story continues: persistence of life themes in old age', *Ageing and Society* 18: 389–419.

Coleman, P.G., Ivani-Chalian, C. and Robinson, M. 2004. 'Religious attitudes among British older people: stability and change in a 20 year longitudinal study', *Ageing and Society* 24: 167–88.

Coleman, P.G., McKiernan, F., Mills, M.A. and Speck, P. 2007. 'In sure and uncertain faith: belief and coping with loss of spouse in later life', *Ageing and Society* 27: 869–90.

Coleman, P.G. and O'Hanlon, A. 2004. *Ageing and Development: Theories and Research*. London: Arnold.

Cohen, G. 2005. *The Mature Mind. The Positive Power of the Aging Brain*. New York: Basic Books.

Deci, E.L. and Ryan, R.M. 2000. 'The 'what' and 'why' of goal pursuits: human needs and the self-determination of behaviour', *Psychological Inquiry* 11: 227–68.

Dittmann-Kohli, F. 1990. 'The construction of meaning in old age: possibilities and constraints', *Ageing and Society* 10: 279–94.

Dittmann-Kohli, F. and Westerhof, G.J. 2000. 'The personal meaning system in a life-span perspective', in Reker, G.T. and Chamberlain, K. (eds.), *Exploring Existential Meaning. Optimizing Human Development across the Life Span*. Thousand Oaks: Sage, 107–22.

Eagleton, T. 2014. *Culture and the Death of God*. New Haven, CT: Yale University Press.

Erikson, E. 1968. *Identity, Youth and Crisis*. New York: Norton.

Erikson, E., Erikson, J. and Kivnick, H. 1986. *Vital Involvement in Old Age. The Experience of Old Age in Our Time*. New York: Norton.

Fishman, D.B. 1999. *The Case for Pragmatic Psychology*. New York University Press.

Frankl, V.E. 1964. *Man's Search for Meaning*. London: Hodder & Stoughton.

Freden, L. 1982. *Psychosocial Aspects of Depression: No Way Out?* Chichester: Wiley.

Gearing, B. and Coleman, P.G. 1996. 'Biographical assessment in community care', in Birren, J.E., Kenyon, G.M., Ruth J-E., Schroots, J.J.F. and Svensson, T. (eds.), *Aging and Biography. Explorations in Adult Development*. New York: Springer, 265–82.

Gearing, B. and Dant, T. 1990. 'Doing biographical research', in Peace, S.M. (ed.) *Researching Social Gerontology. Concepts, Methods and Issues*. London: Sage.

Hall, M.R., Briggs, R.S., Coleman, P.G., Everett, F.M., Harris, J., Marcer, D. and Robinson, M.J. 1982. *The Southampton Ageing Project: A Trial of KH3*. University of Southampton.

Hall, M.R., Briggs, R.S., MacLennan, W.J., Marcer, D., Robinson, M.J. and Everett, F.M. 1983. 'The effects of procaine/haematoporphyrin on age-related decline: a double blind trial, *Age & Ageing* 12: 302–8.

Hill, P.L. and Turiano, N.A. 2014. 'Purpose in life as a predictor of mortality across adulthood', *Psychological Science* 40: 1507–16.

Hunt, A. 1978. *The Elderly at Home: A Study of People Aged Sixty-Five and Over Living in the Community in England in 1976*. London: HMSO.

Johnson, C.L. and Barer, B.M. 1997. *Life Beyond 85 Years: The Aura of Survivorship*. New York: Springer.

Johnson, M. 1976. 'That was your life: a biographical approach to later life', in Munnichs, J.M.A. and Van den Heuvel, W.J.A. (eds.), *Dependency or Interdependency in Old Age*. The Hague: Martinus Nijhoff, 147–61.

Kelly, G.A. 1955. *The Psychology of Personal Constructs*. New York: Norton.

Kivnick, H.Q. 1991. *Living with Care, Caring for Life: The Inventory of Life Strengths*. Minneapolis: University of Minnesota.

Krause, N. 2009. 'Meaning in life and mortality', *Journals of Gerontology, Series B: Psychological Sciences and Social Sciences* 64: 517–27.

Lazarus, R.S. and Lazarus, B.N. 2006. *Coping with Aging*. New York: Oxford University Press.

Lee, G. 2014. 'Editorial. Current research on widowhood: devastation and human resilience', *Journals of Gerontology, Series B: Psychological Sciences and Social Sciences* 69: 2–3.

Lieberman, M.A. and Tobin, S.S. 1983. *The Experience of Old Age. Stress, Coping and Survival*. New York: Basic Books.

McAdams, D.P. 1990. 'Unity and purpose in human lives: the emergence of identity as a life story', in Rabin, A.I., Zucker, R.A., Emmons, R.A. and Frank, S. (eds.), *Studying Persons and Lives*. New York: Springer, 148–200.

McAdams, D.P. 1993. *Stories We Live By: Personal Myths and the Making of the Self*. New York: Morrow.

McAdams, D.P. and Ochberg, R.L. 1988. 'Psychobiography and life narratives' [special issue], *Journal of Personality* 56 (1).

Mental Health Foundation. 2012. *Getting on with Life. Baby Boomers, Mental Health and Ageing Well. 2012*. London: Mental Health Foundation.

Montgomery, S.A. and Asberg, M. 1979. 'A new depression scale designed to be sensitive to change', *British Journal of Psychiatry* 134: 382–9.

Pomeroy, V.M., Conroy, M.C. and Coleman, P.G. 1997. 'Setting handicap goals with elderly people: a pilot study of the Life Strengths Interview', *Clinical Rehabilitation* 11: 156–61.

Reker, G.T. and Wong, P.T.P. 1988. 'Aging as an individual process: toward a theory of personal meaning', in Birren, J.E. and Bengtson, V.L. (eds.), *Emergent Theories of Aging*. New York: Springer, 214–46.

Remmerswaal, P.W.M. 1980. *Verplaatsingsproblematiek bij bejaarden. De eerste achtien maanden in een verzorgingstehuis. (Relocating Older People. The First Eighteen Months in a Care Home.)* Report no. 57. Nijmegen: Gerontological Centre.

Runyan, W.M. 1982. *Life Histories and Psychobiography: Explorations in Theory and Method*. New York: Oxford University Press.

Runyan, W.M. 1990. 'Individual lives and the structure of personality psychology', in Rabin, A.I., Zucker, R.A., Emmons, R.A. and Frank, S. (eds.), *Studying Persons and Lives*. New York: Springer, 10–40.

Ryff, C.D. 1995. 'Psychological well-being in adult life', *Current Directions in Psychological Science* 4: 99–104.

Schultz, W.T. (ed.) 2005. *Handbook of Psychobiography*. New York: Oxford University Press.

Schwartz, A.N. 1975. 'An observation on self-esteem as the linchpin of quality of life for the aged', *The Gerontologist* 15: 470–2.

Sherman, E. 1981. *Counseling the Aging: An Integrative Approach.* New York: Free Press.

Snaith, R.P., Ahmed, S.W. and Mehta, S. 1971. 'Assessment of the severity of primary depressive illness', *Psychological Medicine* 1: 143–9.

Speck, P., Bennett, K.M., Coleman, P.G., Mills, M., McKiernan, F., Smith, P.T. and Hughes, G.M. 2005. 'Elderly bereaved spouses: issues of belief, well-being and support', in Walker, A. (ed.) *Growing Older. Understanding Quality of Life in Old Age.* Maidenhead: Open University Press, 146–60.

Thompson, P. 1992. ' 'I don't feel old': subjective ageing and the search for meaning in later life. *Ageing and Society* 12: 23–48.

Walker, A. (ed.) 2005. *Growing Older. Understanding Quality of Life in Old Age.* Maidenhead: Open University Press.

White, R. 1975. *Lives in Progress.* 3rd edition. New York: Holt, Rinehart and Winston

Wilkinson, P.J. and Coleman, P.G. 2010. 'Strong beliefs and coping in old age: a case-based comparison of atheism and religious faith', *Ageing & Society* 30: 337–61.

Wimmers, M.F.H.G., Buijssen, H.P.J. and Mertens, G.H.M. 1989. 'Welbevinden van ouderen na verhuizing. Gegevens van een longitudinal onderzoek (Well-being of older people after relocation. Data from a longitudinal study)', in Munnichs, J. and Uildriks, G. (eds.), *Psychogerontologie (Psychogerontology).* Deventer: Van Loghum Slaterus, 330–9.

Index

243